Miles Apart

Miles Apart

A heartfelt guide to surviving miscarriage,
stillbirth and baby loss

Annabel Bower

Published by Tablo

Publisher and wholesale enquiries: orders@tablo.io

20 21 22 23 LSC 10 9 8 7 6 5 4 3 2 1

Table of Contents

A note about terminology

I have thought long and hard about how to refer to babies who die in utero. I have found it hard to say the words; my baby died. But despite how harsh it sounds, that's the reality of the situation: my baby died.

I think people who have not experienced the death of a baby in utero first-hand, also struggle with saying this. The concept of a baby dying before it has been born or taken its first breath can be hard to rationalise. If you carried the baby, however, it is painfully clear that your baby was alive inside you until their heart stopped beating.

The most common way we refer to babies who die in utero is as 'lost babies'. Baby loss is often used as the overarching title for this topic and encompasses the death of a baby at any stage of pregnancy and in infancy. Other terms used are 'angel baby', 'lost pregnancy', 'interrupted pregnancy', 'born sleeping', 'miscarried fetus', 'unviable embryo', 'retained products of conception', 'genetic termination', 'termination for medical reasons' and 'born still'. Ultimately, they all mean the same thing: a baby who has passed away before, or after birth, and heartbroken parents with empty arms.

Those of us who have lived through this tragedy know, that we did not lose our babies, or simply forget to bring them home from hospital with us, they died. For me, the term I found myself saying the most was 'we lost our baby', especially in the early stages of grief. It took me a long time to say the words, 'Miles died'. I also consider the many parents who have also walked this path to be part of the 'baby loss community', so I decided to use the terms 'lost baby' and 'baby loss' throughout the book.

Saying 'lost babies' or 'baby loss' is not an attempt to shy away from the distressing reality that my baby and so many others have died. It's simply the description that flowed most freely as I was writing. I do also say, 'when Miles died' or 'after Miles died', as this accurately describes different points in time, and I encourage you to substitute whatever words feel most comfortable for you as you read through the pages ahead.

Annabel xx

Introduction

First of all I want you to know that you will survive this. You probably don't believe me, or think that it is possible, but please have faith that one day, you will smile again. The loss of a baby is achingly sad, life changing and shocking. I think most people are completely blindsided, their world abruptly turned upside down by the realisation that their precious baby will not be coming home with them. In the blink of an eye, what is supposed to be a happy, life-giving experience becomes one of utter heartbreak. Perhaps you woke up one morning full of hope, your head and heart full of dreams for the future, a future that involved the exact child you were carrying. You were excited to be off to a scan to see your baby, or your mind was occupied by this special news that you were yet to share with others. By day's end, that excitement had evaporated, your heart was broken and your innocent bubble of happiness had abruptly burst.

We first learned of Miles' condition amidst an ordinary morning's chaos. It never occurred to me that by afternoon, our world would be devastated. During the scan where we first received the bad news about our baby's condition, I thought, *No, not us. This can't be happening.* I thought it had to be a bad dream, a nightmare. Was it something I'd done wrong during the pregnancy, something I'd eaten? Or was it down to my age and doing too much?

When you are in the initial throes of losing a baby or have just been told that your baby has died, these questions are ever-present and unanswerable. When the reality of our situation and its inevitable consequences hit, what followed for me was pure fear and overwhelming doubt as to whether we could survive what lay ahead.

I started to write this book when I was beginning to navigate the heartbreaking death of my baby boy, Miles. He was delivered stillborn almost six months into my pregnancy. Until that point in my life, I had never felt such pain, disbelief or utter despair. When I lost Miles, I had the unwavering support of my husband Josh, as well as friends and family who would have done anything to help, yet I still felt utterly alone and inconsolable. I was living in my own world of pain. No one could help me; nothing could ease the heartache. I couldn't imagine ever finding a way to live with my loss. I searched endlessly for answers, both before and after Miles was delivered. I felt like I had read the entire internet, seeking information and looking for comfort; mostly hunting for stories that would give me some hope of survival.

Over and over again, I couldn't find what I was looking for, or I found something that resonated, only to click past the page and forget where I'd read it. The internet also has a cruel way of reminding you of what you are not. While searching for stories of baby loss, ads for maternity wear appeared and notifications inviting me to see my baby's progress popped up. The algorithms could not register my loss. These reminders sent me crashing down: the internet was proving more foe than friend.

I was searching for a heartfelt guide, not an overly medical piece or a carefully worded article giving generic advice. I found many stories that focused on the days and the actual events surrounding the loss of a baby, but couldn't find many that focused on surviving the grief and heartache in the weeks, months and years afterwards. I needed an honest account from someone who'd been through this shocking experience, something I could return to, like a trusted friend. A warts-and-all book in which it was all laid bare; a story told with absolute honesty and zero filter. I wanted to know that what I was feeling was normal and to hear the experiences of other women who had endured this pain, to read about how they had survived the aftermath and learned to live with their loss. There was very little out there. After a while, I decided that I should write the book I'd wished I had on my bedside table.

I knew that even though I'd never had (and never would have) the chance to get to know my baby outside the womb, this did not alter the significance of my loss. No one other than Josh had had the chance to get to know Miles. This, too, did not make his existence any less of a life. It did not minimise the grief of his death, or make his legacy any less important. The death of a baby in utero is a death different to most others, however it's just as painful and just as devastating. This was why, for me, hearing the experiences of women who had been there before helped me immensely. I want to do the same for others, by ignoring the silence and stigma attached to baby loss and speaking openly of my experience and the enormous love I have for my baby.

The loss of a baby is a deeply traumatic life event, one you should never feel you have to 'get over' or 'be okay' with. You can grieve for as long as you like and miss your baby every single day. Grief is a long, hard road, not one to be rushed or forced. I hope you find some practical, honest support in the pages ahead and at the very least, feel less alone in your pain. I am not a psychologist, writer or grief counsellor. I am the very proud mum of a beautiful little boy called Miles who never got to come home with me. I didn't think I'd ever be able to smile or feel joy again after the day I had to put him down in that hospital cot and walk out the door, leaving him behind. I felt like my heart had been ripped out of my body and my stomach kicked in. But somehow I did learn to feel happy and experience joy again. And I learned that this didn't take anything away from the love I felt for Miles: it was okay to be both happy and sad.

Baby loss is the loss of a baby at any stage of pregnancy, whether it's an embryo, an ectopic pregnancy, an early or late miscarriage, a stillbirth, the loss of one twin in utero, or the loss of an infant. Each is different. Each brings its own sorrow and heartache. Miscarriages often go unannounced and are rarely publicly shared, which means women miss out on the support they so desperately need. We are encouraged not to tell people about a pregnancy until twelve weeks. If the baby is lost before this point, it may remain shrouded in secrecy. There doesn't seem to be an avenue to talk about it openly.

Baby loss is such a taboo subject. Sadly there is a secret society of women who have endured it, often silently. It's hard to talk about, and people avoid talking about it, as they find it too confronting. People who haven't experienced baby loss find it impossible to understand the depth of anguish that is felt by those who have. Perhaps that's why it's not mentioned: people just can't bear to wrap their minds around it. The loss is unbelievably isolating, which made it even harder for me to cope with. I was fortunate in the most bittersweet of ways. I had the support of a very close friend, Anna, who had lost her baby ten years before I lost Miles. I had someone to call, someone to tell me that I wasn't going crazy, that my grief was normal, my recurring thoughts understandable and my feelings valid. I told her things I couldn't tell other people for fear of freaking them out and making them feel uncomfortable.

I hope this book is as comforting to you as my friend was to me. I hope the result of me honestly telling my story is that other parents facing this devastation won't feel like they are alone. I hope it will also help those supporting bereaved loved ones to offer them the best support possible. By reading my inside perspective of what it's like to lose a baby and to navigate the grief that follows, they may better understand the experience, and what does and doesn't help.

I truly hope this book gives an insight into how those enduring baby loss might be feeling, and what it is like to be the person at the centre of the storm. When I was in the first, dreadful stage of my grief, I couldn't articulate how I felt. I was completely numb. I didn't know how to talk about it – and I didn't want to, as that would make it real. Looking back, I can see how my silence would have made it incredibly hard for those around me to know what to do and say. Baby loss is so tragic, so gut-wrenching, that people find it hard to imagine. Outsiders are often at a loss for words, or stumble through and end up saying something offensive. Sometimes they're just trying to be sympathetic. Sometimes they just don't get it and have absolutely no idea where to begin. This is understandable.

Many people are scared of mentioning the name of a lost baby, as they are scared of upsetting the bereaved. They don't realise that you cannot upset someone who has gone through absolute hell by acknowledging their child. In fact, it is quite the opposite. Hearing your baby's name presents an opportunity to talk about them, and your experience of baby loss in general. When you lose a baby, you think of them constantly. You will not be 'reminded' by someone who talks about them or mentions their name. I found it hugely comforting when people spoke of Miles. It showed that they valued his life, his presence in the world. It gave me permission not to hide my grief. I want to share insights like this – thoughts and experiences that are familiar to those who've been through baby loss, but hard to guess at by those on the outside – to educate those supporting bereaved parents, so they are better equipped to offer what is needed.

As a society, we need to normalise how we talk about baby loss at any stage of pregnancy, to lift the stigma and open up the conversations that should follow baby loss. Early pregnancy loss remains hidden in the shadows because it is considered to be relatively common. This seems absurd: statistics do not alter grief or its intensity.

We live in a world obsessed with pregnancy and babies. Women are often asked if they have children before what they do for work or pleasure. Pregnancy is publicly celebrated with social media announcements, gender reveals and baby showers. Conversely, pregnancy loss is kept in the dark: brushed aside or not spoken of. To go from one side of the equation to the other in an incredibly short space of time is traumatic. One minute, people are asking, *how are you feeling?*, *when is the baby due?*, *do you know what you're having?* But when a baby dies, people can be unsure of what to say or do. Sometimes they completely ignore the fact that your baby died, heightening your isolation.

For some women, the baby they lose is their first child, their first experience as a mother. For others, it may be their second, third or even fourth pregnancy. It may not the first time they have lost a baby. It's not possible (or desirable) to compare or measure one situation against another. They are all tragic, they are all devastating and no loss should be considered greater or less than another. Until you have walked in another's shoes, you cannot begin to imagine their experience. Loss is loss, grief is grief, and heartbreak is heartbreak. There is no hierarchy. We are better off channeling our energies towards supporting each other than competing for whose grief is the worst. I can only speak from my own perspective: of losing a baby after having three healthy children. So I have made sure to interview women who have different stories, and researched other experiences.

Each woman's response to loss will be influenced by our individual experiences, as mothers and as people. For me, no number of living children could ever make up for the one that was lost. I think this is a common experience, no matter the number of children we have had, or have lost. When you are pregnant, it's not just the baby inside you that is growing. With each pregnancy, I feel my heart growing bigger too. It's like an extra chamber is opened up, to hold the love for that child. I lost my baby, but that extra chamber remains open, and the love remains too. They are forever a part of me. It's so difficult to find somewhere to direct this love when your arms are empty and your dreams are shattered.

Life after loss can be brutal, so be kind to yourself. It will take time to navigate your way to a new normal and for a long time, you may feel that you don't possess the strength to do this. Early on after losing Miles, I made a decision that somehow I was just going to have to survive. I was completely broken, but I didn't want to stay broken. One life had already been lost. I felt I owed it to Miles to make the most of the life I still had; it was (and is) a wonderful one. I hoped that one day, the pain and sadness would ease, but I knew it was up to me to start finding my way through the darkness. There is no quick fix, no magic potion you can swallow. You just have to start moving forward, one small step at a time, at your own pace.

If I had to explain this to someone in the simplest of ways, perhaps this is how I might begin. It's like you're on a beautiful sailing boat, setting out on the trip of your dreams. It's something you've talked about, wished for and now it's finally happening. Suddenly, without warning, your boat is met by an unexpected storm: the vicious waves and howling winds instantly change its course. There is no way back and your boat can't be turned around, no matter how hard you try. You fight with all you have, you plead with the storm to spare you from what is ahead, you know, in your heart of hearts that it's not going to be good.

You end up shipwrecked, alone, terrified and bewildered. This was not the plan; this is not where you were supposed to be. There is no way of retracing your steps to try to work out how things went so terribly off course. There's no point: it is what it is. You're stuck here now. Other travellers made it to their beautiful islands. In the distance, you can see the bright lights and hear the hum of joyful celebration.

You may be lucky enough to set sail towards your dreams again, but it will be with the knowledge of what it felt like to be blindsided by a storm. That knowledge has changed you forever. For now, you are stuck on the dark island, desperately wondering if you'll ever find a way off it. That is, if you even *want* to leave. It's sad and harrowing, but it's your island. Your connection to something so precious that, you may realise, it's okay if a little part of you stays there forever.

Over time, the storm's intensity will dissolve. Slowly and gradually, your island – the one you never asked to go to in the first place – will come back to life. It, too, is beautiful, and it's yours to stay on, or to visit whenever you like.

If you are reading this book, I can assume you are enduring what will (hopefully) be the worst time of your life, or you're looking for ways to support someone through this harrowing life experience. I have addressed this book to other baby loss parents, who I imagine as my first readers. But I hope it will also be read by their loved ones and supporters, healthcare professionals, and anyone else looking for an inside perspective on baby loss. You can read the book in whichever order works best for you and start with whatever you feel will help you the most right now.

In Part 1, I tell my story – Miles' story. In Part 2, I talk about baby loss and how it is typically dealt with in our society, as well as the various parts of grief that shocked and outraged me, and what ultimately comforted me and helped me put myself back together. This is not an easy story to tell, but like any story of baby loss, it's a story of love mixed with heartache. The story of a mother desperately wishing for a different outcome, but having to find the courage to say goodbye to her much-loved baby, knowing there was no alternative.

Whether you have had to say goodbye to your baby as an embryo, at any stage of pregnancy or as an infant, you have lost a child – and all the dreams and plans attached to them. I don't have all the answers (I wish I did), but when it happened to me, I did have hope. I want anyone reading this to know that you may never completely get over this, but you will survive it. It's hard, it's exhausting and it's lonely. Sadly, others have been there before us and many will follow. If only we could all talk about this topic more openly, I think that would make the journey through baby loss just that little bit easier.

To the little boy who I will always see missing at my kitchen table, who will never get to be part of the beautiful chaos that is my family: we love you and miss you every single day. Not one day goes by that I don't imagine who you would have become.

For Miles: Miles apart, forever in my heart.

Part 1 Our story

Chapter 1 My Family

Life doesn't always go to plan. We hope it will, but there are many things that are completely out of our control, especially when it comes to starting or creating a family. Miles was a planned, much-wanted baby. My husband Josh and I were incredibly excited when we saw those two positive lines on the pregnancy test. I immediately began to imagine our future with a new addition to the family. These days, four children is considered a big family, but it's what we wanted. When Josh told a mate he was off to meet me for the twelve-week scan, his friend replied, "Is Annabel fucking mad? Four kids!?". Maybe I was, but it was what I'd hoped for. My journey through motherhood had not unfolded as I'd hoped in my girlhood dreams – there had been a few challenges along the way – but Josh and I didn't hesitate when we decided to have a "fourth and final baby".

My two older boys, Alfie and Ted, are from my first marriage. Their dad and I had known each other since we were teens. We started dating in our mid-twenties and married when we were both twenty-seven. Alfie arrived one week before our first wedding anniversary and Ted twenty-one months after his brother. Sadly, our marriage broke down after four years. I was devastated that my family was torn apart and terrified of what the future might hold for me as a single mum. This family was far from what I had pictured for myself.

Many of my friends were planning their weddings or having their first babies while my marriage was disintegrating. I hated being the single mother at friends' barbecues, arriving with my bowl of potato salad, never quite at ease, as no one was there to help me keep an eye on the boys or lighten the burden of always having to be on guard. Heading home to an empty house, I missed having someone to share my funny stories about the boys with. It was an exhausting, lonely time. I grieved the end of my marriage and naively thought that if I could survive this, I could survive anything. Little did I know that it was just a warm-up for the future. The pain of my divorce would be insignificant compared to my pain at losing my child.

During the divorce, I put on a brave face and tried to just get on with things. I gritted my teeth through conversations with other mums who said things like, *I know how you feel, I'm practically a single mum myself as my husband works so much*. I couldn't be bothered explaining to them that having limited help with the kids was one small part of being a single parent: it was the financial responsibilities, lack of companionship and permanent mental and physical juggle with zero respite that really wore me down. Doing the lion's share of the parenting was the least of my worries.

I hated feeling pitied. I was sick of worrying that having divorced parents would mess the boys up forever. I just wanted to do my best to get through it. I did consume a fair bit of white wine, though I can't necessarily blame that on divorce. Having two boys close together in age can surely do that to the toughest of mothers! Fast forward several years and – hand on heart – I can say that everything worked out for the best. My ex-husband and I both remarried and we all get along. The kids are happy, well-adjusted and as far as I can tell, unaffected by the divorce (even if at times, it would be handy to blame really naughty behavior on it!).

During the process of separation, I went back to work. Before having children, I worked in events and catering for a big corporate firm. It couldn't be done part-time, so I resigned rather than take paid leave. When Alfie turned one, I was working out what to do with my career – only to find out I was pregnant with Ted. I decided to stay home and go back to work once both boys were older. I had run my own catering company in my early twenties and was keen to get back into it, combining it with motherhood. So when I found myself suddenly single and needing to go back to work, I initially worked for a very good friend who owned her own catering company. Eighteen months later, it was time to go back out on my own again.

The only problem was that I had a tiny kitchen, with the worst oven in Australia. If I was going to make my business viable, I would have to renovate. All I needed was a builder. Enter Josh: a friend of a friend who I *might* have hired to take on the project more for his good looks than his company's good reputation. I had met him socially at a mutual friend's birthday lunch, where I was struck by his kindness. Alfie was with me; his little four-year-old arms were struggling to reach the table. Josh picked up a stool and lifted it over to Alfie, who promptly hopped up and began devouring his burger and chips. I thought it was a very sweet thing to do. Apart from that, I didn't know much about Josh. I spent the rest of the lunch catching up with other friends. That said, he had sparked my interest.

A week or so later, another mutual friend suggested I call Josh to help me with my renovations. It turned out my modest kitchen renovation was much smaller than the kind of builds he normally managed (his usual projects involved stunning architectural renovations, not piddly kitchens). But he had a soft spot for single mothers (he was raised by a rather formidable one), and decided to help me out. Once the plans were approved, he suggested we go out for dinner to celebrate. I rang a friend and asked, "Did your builder take you out for dinner when you signed the contract?"

"No," she answered. "I can't even get mine to return my bloody phone calls."

So it would seem I'd bagged myself an excellent builder *and* a boyfriend, in one fell swoop. The first date turned into a second, soon a third, and before I knew it, he suggested we move in together when my renovations began; not the usual company policy, I can assure you. Josh reasoned that there was no point in us dating for a year before living together, only for him to only realise that living with someone else's children didn't suit him. Better to rip off the bandaid and find out, here and now. He joked that if it all went to shit, mine would be the fastest renovation he'd ever done, so he could get me the hell out of his house and back into my own.

After a whirlwind three months of dating, the boys and I packed up and moved in with Josh. Very unorthodox and much faster than even I would have thought appropriate – but we both just *knew* this was it: we had found the person we wanted to be with. I exhausted myself trying to make it look like my two- and four-year-old boys were angels. Josh says that in these 'glory days', as he now refers to them, it was like eating at Ottolenghi every night. Gourmet dinners flying out of the kitchen, laundry folded and actually put away! I went out of my way to make the 'working mother of small children' thing look effortless. The poor man – the contrast to today is brutal. It turns out this was completely unnecessary. Josh and the boys got along better than I could have ever dreamed: in fact, I think they liked him more than me most of the time. (He's way more fun than I am!) Once my renovation was completed three months later, none of us wanted to move back home and away from Josh. A little family had been formed.

The builder, now my husband, still claims I played him like a drum – set the whole thing up in order to snare him – to which I usually respond, "Darling, who in their right mind would make up a renovation in order to meet a man?" That said, it was pretty effective, so I do recommend it. In fact, countless mutual friends had thought to set us up, so we just beat them to the chase.

We were married after a year and immediately started talking about having a baby together. When we'd been together for about a month, Josh had asked me if I was willing (in a general way, not necessarily with him at that early stage) to have more children. It was hugely important to him to have children of his own, even though he thought of my boys as his own and loved them as if they were. For me, the reply was simple and obvious: "Yes, absolutely!" I'd always wanted four kids, so the idea of having more children (albeit in my second marriage) felt completely natural.

Chapter 2 When four becomes five

We started trying for a baby five months after we were married and were incredibly lucky to fall pregnant immediately. I knew how fortunate we were. I was thirty-five and Josh forty-one. Not old, but not exactly spring chickens. To say I was elated was an understatement. I was off the planet, over the moon. With the boys, I hadn't told anyone until the traditional twelve weeks, but with this pregnancy, I couldn't contain my joy. I started telling people as soon as we saw a heartbeat at nine weeks. By this stage my catering company, which had been reborn from my newly renovated kitchen, was going gangbusters. The catering orders were endless. I was worked off my feet, and had an average of three to five staff in the kitchen most days, to help with prep and events. With work and two energetic little boys, life was pretty hectic. (I'm exhausted just writing that!)

I'd ridden out the bad years and everything was finally coming together. I had a beautiful little family and another baby would be the icing on the cake. When I was pregnant with the boys, I'd never had any desire to find out if I was having a boy or a girl. But with this baby, I decided I'd love to know – just for something different. I had a new obstetrician, as the doctor who delivered the boys had retired. I felt optimistic, but also aware that late in my pregnancy with Ted, my placenta had started to fail in the final weeks and he had stopped growing. So I didn't have rose-coloured glasses, nor the naivety I had blissfully enjoyed during my first pregnancy. I knew things could go wrong.

But perhaps it was our turn for a lucky break, I thought. Josh had been through a painful divorce and had tragically lost his father in a house fire a few months before we met. It was almost as though I imagined that each individual on earth is given a quota for pain and suffering – and, *fingers crossed*, we had already used up a good chunk of ours. Logically, I knew that life doesn't work like that and we didn't deserve any more or less than anyone else, of course. There is no way to safeguard yourself against random misfortune and tragedy. Some people cruise through life encountering few obstacles and very little heartache, others seem to face many harrowing events. It's indiscriminate.

Towards the end of my pregnancy with Ted, I felt his movements slowing and told my obstetrician I was worried. After mentioning it again at my thirty-seven-week appointment, I was sent for a scan.

Ted had indeed stopped growing at least a week before the scan. His size and the condition of the placenta were indicative of intrauterine growth restriction (IUGR), and I was booked into hospital to be induced the next day. I am forever grateful that I listened to my gut and insisted that things weren't right. Had Ted been allowed to go to term, it is highly likely he would have been stillborn. I'm pleased to report that Ted has suffered no ongoing effects: he is one of the most energetic, crazy, funny kids around.

When I fell pregnant again, I was well aware there were risks involved. With my history of IUGR, I was considered a high-risk pregnancy. But none of this could dampen my elation. At about the ten-week mark, I completed an enormous catering job, a sit-down lunch for 150 guests. By the end of the event, I felt like I had completely overdone it. I was heading to Sydney the next day for a rare child-free holiday; Josh was to join me a few days after that. On the flight, I felt lethargic and out of sorts. I just couldn't get comfortable, so I slouched in my seat, fell asleep and woke just before landing, feeling groggy and disoriented. I had booked lunch with girlfriends that day and dinner at my cousin's house the following night and was doubting how I'd make it through either.

Sydney is a glorious destination: as the plane comes in to land you are treated to a magnificent bird's-eye view of the harbour. Sydney's spring weather compared to Adelaide's is practically tropical, so even though I was feeling rotten, it was hard not to get excited about soaking it all in with Josh once he arrived. We planned to eat ourselves silly in Sydney restaurants, sleep in and totally unwind. Ignoring my fatigue, I was optimistic that after a quiet lunch with friends and an early night, I would feel like a million dollars. I told myself I was pregnant, exhausted and nothing more.

I woke up the next day still feeling terrible and again put my fatigue down to early pregnancy and working too much. I thought perhaps because I was finally on holiday, my body was taking a rare opportunity to rest and recover.

A day later, I was feeling even worse. I called the midwife at my obstetrician's rooms. By now I was really worried that the pain I was in was not normal. A searing, persistent burning was increasing on my left side, both front and back. I'd never felt anything like it before. She said it was likely a sore back from working too much, reasoning that the pregnancy hormone relaxin can wreak havoc on our usual capabilities. She suggested rest.

Resting had zero effect, so I visited a local GP, who insisted I go to the local emergency department immediately. In the waiting room of the nearest hospital, I started feeling faint and was close to blacking out. My whole body shook violently and I was delirious with pain. I rang Josh to tell him to come straight to the hospital when his flight landed. I was admitted straight away, a drip inserted for fluids and pain relief. I had to keep reminding everyone taking care of me that I was pregnant, as it was suggested I have morphine injected directly into my stomach. Nothing else was fast or strong enough and I was deteriorating rapidly. I kept refusing, as I was sure it would be harmful to the baby, despite the fact that I was starting to go into shock from a severe kidney infection.

An e-coli bacteria in my bladder, rather than presenting as an UTI, had entered my kidneys and was spreading through my bloodstream. I underwent scans for gallbladder and kidney stones, as they tried to find some reason for my condition. Lying on the bed while the sonographer looked for possible causes, my heart was in my throat. I wanted to ask her to check if the baby was okay, but knew that this was not what the doctors in emergency had requested on the referral from. It was assumed that the baby wouldn't survive. Josh came in, wheeling his suitcases, straight from the airport, as I was being transferred to the gynecological ward. I was still refusing injections of morphine and instead, without really realising what was happening, I was hooked up to some pretty hardcore antibiotics and pain relief medications intravenously. And then I passed out.

I woke up the next morning in tears, assuming I had lost the baby. By some miracle, despite what my body had just endured (a raging temperature, severe blood poisoning – which would have led to organ shutdown if untreated), my little baby was still bobbing about with a very strong heartbeat. I couldn't believe it. The next three days were a blur of heavy pain and heavy medication. When I got back home to Adelaide, my obstetrician said she was very surprised to see me. Most pregnancies that encounter pyelonephritis don't survive. Yet again, I felt like I had dodged a bullet. I was even more nervous than before and felt incredibly lucky to still be pregnant. I was well aware that this was no small miracle.

I cut back on work, cancelled a few upcoming catering events and tried very hard to take it easy. I was mindful of just how ill I'd been and didn't want to risk anything. Soon after Sydney, we had our twelve-week nuchal translucency scan. When results are bad, you often sense it immediately. A subdued presence seems to fill the air and eye contact is broken. Josh and I were ushered into a private room connected to the clinic and told the supervising radiologist would be in to talk to us shortly. The delivery of bad news is often accompanied by a slight tilt of the head, a sympathetic smile and then the news itself, delivered clearly (often without great emotion), with polite pauses along the way that allow you to digest the information being shared.

Our scan and the blood tests showed a 1/60 chance of Down syndrome. Odds at my age were usually high, but not this high. We decided to have the Harmony test, a non-invasive prenatal blood test for common genetic conditions, including Down syndrome, the option below an amniocentesis. We would assess the situation from there. Josh and I had very different views on what we would do if the result came back positive, so shelved the conversation until we knew what we were dealing with. The results came back negative, there was nothing obvious to worry about except a low result on the Papp-A test (which measures levels of pregnancy-associated plasma protein A, one of several proteins produced by the placenta). Low levels are an early indicator of potential growth problems or issues with the placenta later in the pregnancy. I felt by now that any problems with this pregnancy were likely the result of my actions. I had clearly pushed myself far too hard, worked too much. I was convinced it was my fault. At this early stage, there was nothing they could do to monitor growth, so until about twenty-four weeks, when the baby would be viable, it would be a wait-and-see scenario.

For the next twelve weeks or so, we enjoyed a blissfully normal pregnancy. Then at twenty-seven weeks, a scan showed that the baby had stopped growing. We knew this could happen, but did not expect it so early in the pregnancy. We were being prepped to potentially deliver in the next week: at twenty-eight weeks' gestation. I was given steroid shots to strengthen the baby's underdeveloped lungs and counselled about may lie ahead, with a very small premature baby. Then our baby started growing again, much to the surprise of everyone – including our obstetrician. We held on for another seven weeks, having weekly scans to monitor the baby's growth and the movement of blood to the baby via the umbilical cord. At thirty-five weeks, the baby's growth declined at an alarming rate, then pretty much stopped altogether. I was given more steroids and booked into hospital to be induced immediately after they began to work.

Our little baby arrived on Easter Thursday. Josh's first biological child and my first baby girl. She was a tiny two kilograms, very small, as she had stopped growing in-utero for about a month, in total in addition to being born a month early. Our precious little baby was whisked off to the neonatal intensive care unit (NICU) straight after delivery. I was overwhelmingly grateful that she was with us. The scans over the past seven weeks had been stressful: before each one, I was convinced that bad news lay ahead. That the placenta had failed, or that (at the absolute worst) our baby would have no heartbeat. At the start of each scan, I would hold my breath, shut my eyes and say a little prayer that the baby was still alive. I'd only allow myself to relax once I heard the baby's heartbeat through the monitor. Permanently convinced that tragedy would strike at any moment, I was a nerve-wracked mess and wracked with nerves – not the best emotional state for heading into newborn territory.

Bonnie, our beautiful little cherub, spent four weeks in the NICU, graduating from a fully enclosed cot hooked up to a million wires, to an open cot. The last hurdle was the removal of her gastric feeding tube. It was a month like no other. I'd set my alarm for 6am to drive down to the hospital to give Bonnie her first feed, at first through the gastric tube. As time went on and she grew stronger, I simultaneously breastfed her. I'd meet with her doctor, express milk for later feeds, change her and wait for the next feed at 10 or 11am, after which I'd pump more milk to keep my supply up, and do any tiny task I was allowed, which helped me feel like I was mothering my baby. At about 2pm I'd set off to collect the boys from school and kindergarten, take them home, sort out dinner, pack their lunches for the next day and wait for Josh to get home. As soon as he did, I'd go back down to the hospital for 1–2 feeds, before getting home and crawling into bed. Overnight, I'd wake up to express breast milk … and then repeat it all the next day.

Leaving your baby behind in a NICU is incredibly hard. I cried and cried the first night I was discharged from hospital. I remember feeling so angry with people who said things like, *Well at least you get to skip the night feeds and have some sleep.* In reality, I was getting about the same amount of sleep as any newborn mother, without the joy of holding and cuddling my baby in my own home. Another unhelpful comment was, *At least she will be in a good routine from being in hospital.* Which was true, but not a worthy trade-off for the stress of seeing your baby attached to wires in a room full of strangers. It was tough, but as hard as it was, I had a baby to hold, feed and nurture. And I knew she would eventually be coming home with me.

After four exhausting weeks, I ended up having a fairly robust conversation with Bonnie's pediatrician. I wanted to remove the gastric tube and to try to move her to breast and bottle feeds only.

I felt the tube was delaying her progress, as she was always so full when fed through it. She never had had to cry out for a feed or learn what it felt like to be hungry. She was like a *foie gras* goose, always force-fed and full to the brim. Eventually, the paediatrician allowed that if after forty-eight hours of no tube feeds, she gained weight, we were free to go. We scraped in by fifteen grams at the final weigh-in. The NICU nurses said they had never seen anyone pack up and leave as quickly as I did. Having everyone home together was my absolute dream. The NICU is a strange, clinical setting; if it weren't for the incredible nurses who work in this area, I'd say it was an utterly depressing place. The nurses who looked after Bonnie were brilliant women who made a tough time bearable.

After the complications of Bonnie's pregnancy, we didn't make the decision to have another baby lightly. We talked about it a lot and agreed it would be the cherry on top of our happiness. Josh has always felt like the boys are his own and sees them as no less 'his' than Bonnie is, so for him one more child was an indulgence, an added blessing. I wanted another baby for many reasons, one being that I'd always dreamed of having four children. I can't really articulate why. Our household was already very busy and chaotic, but I loved it. Most of all, I absolutely loved seeing the kids together and witnessing their friendships. The boys had gradually increased the time they spent at their dad's from three to five nights a fortnight by the time Bonnie was eighteen months old. This created a huge shift in the dynamic of our household every other week.

The adjustment from being little sister to two crazy, highly entertaining brothers to being an only child was a lot for Bonnie to handle. She missed her brothers and would crawl around the house searching for them. I knew how she felt. I have never gotten used to the boys leaving. Even years later, I still miss them when they're at their dad's. I wanted to give Bonnie one permanent sibling who'd always be there, and would be closer to her in age.

Around the time we gave serious consideration to trying again, I started having severe abdominal pain. A series of scans revealed that what had begun as a small follicular cyst had grown to an alarming size and I would have to have it removed by laparoscopic surgery. My overactive, disaster-oriented imagination went into overdrive. Signing the pre-surgery paperwork giving consent to removal of ovaries and or fallopian tubes – or a full hysterectomy if found to be necessary – I thought, *Shit! This had better all turn out okay. I really want another baby and don't think I'll cope at all if the option is taken away from me.*

Thankfully, the cyst burst of its own accord in the days prior to surgery and nothing alarming was found from the biopsy taken during the procedure. To give my body time to recover, we waited a few months before having my Mirena contraceptive removed and trying for other baby. By now I was thirty-seven and Josh was forty-three, so I was acutely aware that it might take longer to fall pregnant than last time. I cut back on coffee, pretty much stopped drinking alcohol and made a huge effort to look after myself. I really wanted this to happen and wanted nothing else to hinder my chances or delay our plan.

Just as I was about to give in and see a fertility specialist, I saw those two lines. I am not a patient person. When I decide to do something, I want it to happen immediately, if not yesterday. I was so relieved we had fallen pregnant; my impatience was starting to overshadow my daily thoughts. As excited and happy as I was, I also felt incredibly nervous. I felt like I was pushing my luck with this fourth baby, but tried hard to brush those thoughts aside. I told myself I was being ridiculous: *everything would be fine.*

Chapter 3 The cherry on top

From the very beginning, I felt like my pregnancy with Miles was doomed. I know it sounds dramatic, but I had a strange feeling that something was wrong, which I voiced over and over to Josh. I started bleeding at nine weeks and was convinced it was all over. I was getting ready to go out for dinner with a bunch of girlfriends. Dressed and ready to go, I went to the loo just before leaving and saw the tell-tale signs of bleeding. My heart immediately sank. There is very little that can calm the nerves of a pregnant mother who has discovered she is bleeding. I wanted to stay home, but felt rude pulling out at the last minute. (I used to often worry about being 'rude' – that is one thing that has completely left me since I lost Miles.)

Thankfully, the bleeding stopped after a day or so. A scan showed that the yolk sack was full of blood and I was assured that this was not unusual and certainly nothing to worry too much about. Despite being told that everything was fine, I kept thinking that at any point, something terrible might happen. Every time I went to the bathroom, I expected to see blood. I had another new obstetrician, as the one I had with Bonnie had now retired. My new guy seemed nice, fairly relaxed and didn't seem overly concerned about my history of IUGR. He felt it was something we could talk about later if the need arose. I tried to be cool and adopt his 'take it as it comes' approach, but it did nothing to calm my nerves, which were on high alert after the bleeding.

We opted for a Harmony test, as well as the standard nuchal translucency screening and blood tests at twelve weeks. I wanted to reassure myself in every way possible. I was convinced we were going to receive bad news, but both sets of test results came back clear, with no issues detected. I rang the midwives to chase up my results, as I was desperate to know what they were. I asked the midwife on duty if these tests ruled out all possible issues. She said the twenty-week anomaly scan would show anything major, however it was very rare to encounter anything significant at that later stage, after our early, clear results.

Even after we received these good results at thirteen weeks, we didn't announce the pregnancy to the world. I was strangely self-conscious about having a fourth baby. A lot of people said things like, *You're brave* or *Better you than me.* I was sick of having to respond and wished people would just wish me well, without judging. To put it less politely, I wished people would mind their own bloody business! People also commented on the fact that Bonnie's pregnancy had been high-risk and asked if we were worried it would happen again. I wanted to answer, "Yes of course we are!", but I usually brushed them off with false optimism instead. I only told really close friends, and let the news filter out to others organically, hoping to avoid having similar conversations over and over. Even by eighteen weeks, I had people coming up to me saying, *I only just heard from so and so that you're having another baby. Wow! You're brave!*

As far as pregnancies go, apart from the bleeding at the start, it was pretty standard. Crushing fatigue, ever-so-glamorous constipation, and a raging addiction to Ben and Jerry's Phish Food ice-cream. The first flutters of movement were magical: that delicate *whoosh* and the first tentative little kicks began at about sixteen weeks. I was still nervous, still worried something was wrong, but the movement signaled that the baby really was there and was growing well. By about nineteen weeks, I was starting to feel confident that it would be okay. My bump was bigger than it had been with Bonnie, so I felt that this baby was growing well. People pointed out that I wasn't looking very big, but I've never had a big bump. I hadn't announced the pregnancy on social media and thought that perhaps I would announce it publicly after the big twenty-week anomaly scan.

I booked the scan for my birthday, for no reason other than it was my only kid-free and work-free day that week. The previous two weeks had been sheer chaos, with end-of-year school concerts and Christmas catch-ups. Work was also very busy in the lead-up to Christmas, so I thought it would be nice to get all of that behind me and head into the scan with a clear mind. I felt like I should start to make some effort to enjoy these milestone moments of my 'last' pregnancy. I'd been too nervous to relax and cherish it before now. I had forgotten to book the older boys in to vacation care, (school holidays had started the week before), and rang to organise it that morning, only to find it was fully booked. I rang Mum, but she had an appointment, so the boys couldn't go to her house until later. They were old enough to come to the scan and understand what it was all about, so I thought, *What's the harm? I'll drop Bonnie at day care and bring the boys along, they'll love it.* They could go to my mum's later, when I needed to do some client work.

The excitement of being allowed to come to the scan was evident on their little faces. When the baby's tiny form was projected on the screen, Ted said the baby looked like a duck face and kept asking the sonographer to tell him if it was a boy or a girl. I reminded him that we'd decided we weren't going to find out the gender this time. Ted was desperate for a boy. He'd conjured up this entire fantasy about he and his baby brother being the 'annoying ones' and ganging up on his older brother Alfie, together annoying the hell out of him. Ted had written letters to the baby and drawn pictures, saying how much he was going to love it and could it please be a boy, named Tom, after his best friend. When we'd told the boys that Bonnie was going to be a girl, Ted had burst into tears and yelled, "Change it! Ask to swap, I asked for a boy baby", to which we replied, "You can't change it Ted, it is what it is. There's no one who you can go to to change these things." Ted responded, "Yes there is, talk to the man, there's a man for everything." This became a running family joke and every time someone wants something impossible done, we say, "ask the man, there's a man for everything".

Between Ted calling the baby *duck face* and yelling out, "It is a boy, I've seen its willy!", (which was totally made up), the scan was not your usual calm, quiet one. Even the sonographer got the giggles and I had to breathe deeply and try to stop laughing, so she could capture the pictures she needed. I thought this distraction, along with Ted's constant interruptions, was why it was taking so long. At about the fifty-minute mark, she asked if the boys could go to the waiting room to watch TV. I instantly felt alarmed. Sensing this, she told me there was a problem with the baby's brain and she needed to call in the supervising radiologist to review the images. She was openly upset and deeply apologetic about the limited amount of information she was able to give me. I felt an overwhelming dread and hopelessness. The room was suddenly ice-cold. A few minutes before, Alfie and I had been pointing out the baby's fingers and toes to each other, while Ted was shouting out, "There's the willy!". In an instant, we had gone from utter hilarity to eerie silence. Shaking, I called Josh. After three previous pregnancies, I knew that the sonographer's response meant this was not an ordinary problem: this was going to be bad. I asked Josh to collect the boys, run them over to Mum's and head straight back.

I sat on the edge of the bed, alone, holding back tears, waiting for the sonographer to return with the radiologist. Each ten minutes felt like an eternity. I have no idea how long I actually waited. I was supposed to meet at a client's office to do some photography work at midday, so I texted to tell her I'd be late, even though I doubted the news would be good and knew I might not make it at all. When the radiologist arrived, he looked crestfallen. He was young, softly spoken and incredibly kind. He told me their equipment was not high-grade enough and I would be referred to an obstetric clinic specialising in level-two scans. As this was not his area of expertise, he would contact my obstetrician and organise the referral. The sonographer asked if I wanted her to load the baby's images onto a DVD. She could barely look at me. When she brought the DVD to me fifteen minutes later, I could tell she had been crying. She started crying again when she saw me, apologising for having to deliver such devastating news. At this point I didn't have a clue what was wrong with our baby, but could only assume that it was pretty bad.

Josh returned from dropping off the boys just as I was leaving the clinic. I couldn't speak, so he rang my obstetrician's rooms to ask them to book us in for the next scan as soon as possible. My doctor was in surgery. His staff said the soonest available scan was in two days. There was no way I could last that long not knowing what was wrong. I cancelled work, left the boys at my mum's, went home and cried. It was all I could do. Nothing could distract me from my worries and the tears wouldn't stop.

That it was my birthday was now irrelevant. I could barely stop crying, let alone contemplate celebrating. Darling Josh had other ideas: he had collected the kids from Mum's and nursery school, and had taken over the kitchen in a flurry of festive industry. Cocoa was flying everywhere, eggs were being cracked and chocolate souffles were made. I could barely eat. Every scrap of energy I had was directed at acting as normal as I could for the kids. I felt like I was watching my life from above. I was so grateful to Josh for his ability to keep it together and carry on as normal. I couldn't wrench my thoughts away from the news we'd received.

Our obstetrician didn't get in touch with us until quite late that evening. He explained that at the next scan I would most likely be offered an amniocentesis and what they had seen was an issue with the brain, the ventricles of which were severely enlarged. He told us not to be alarmed, that this was relatively common. In the same breath, he mentioned that at the next scan, they may talk to us about ending the pregnancy if the baby was deemed to be incompatible with life, at risk of severe disability or diagnosed with a life-limiting condition. We were both floored. Not only to receive this crushing information over the phone, but to also try to digest it without having any real idea of what we were dealing with or what the complications identified in the baby's brain might entail.

The next day I was booked for a longstanding lunch with a group of women who, like me, work from home or for themselves. It's our annual tradition to have our 'work' Christmas lunch together. I didn't think I could sit through a festive lunch, chatting about the year that was and future plans, but Mum suggested I take any distraction I could. Looking back, it is the last time I can remember being completely my old self. Since losing Miles, I feel heavier, more fearful, less free. The girl who slapped on a smile and went off to lunch is still there, but she's eternally changed. Once you experience just how wrong life can go, you're never quite the same again. This is not necessarily a bad thing. Once I emerged from the initial, crushing stages of grief, I was far more empathetic to others facing difficult circumstances and far less preoccupied by insignificant daily worries and frustrations. Grief helped me see the bigger picture and focus on what really mattered.

A day later, Thursday 13 December, we were sitting in the waiting room of the scan clinic. Tears fell unchecked down my face. I kept looking at the other women and their partners, their seemingly healthy pregnancies, and thinking, *I wonder if your baby will make it. Will mine be the only one that doesn't?* The scan took about forty-five minutes. There was no chit-chat, no polite questions about what names we were thinking of, or how old our other children were. It was straight down to business. I stared at my baby bobbing about on the screen, trying to take in every detail, but simultaneously thinking, *Don't get too attached, this is unlikely to end well.* I was wishing like mad this scan would dismiss all of our fears, that we'd be told to head home and have a Merry Christmas, with nothing to worry about whatsoever.

Towards the end of the scan, came the inevitable line: "I'll go and check with the radiologist on duty to see if we need any more images". The sonographer left the room. I knew instinctively. Josh reached out and held my hand and the tears started flowing again. The head radiologist came in and said, "I'm so sorry, there is something very wrong with your baby. The brain is hugely enlarged and there is also a heart defect, which I think indicates a syndrome". We were told that the next steps involved an amniocentesis right there and then, and a fetal MRI at the Women's and Children's Hospital in the city, as soon we could be booked in.

We were asked to sit in the waiting room while they prepared a room for our procedure. We were handed a coffee voucher for the adjacent cafe and I thought, *Are they mad? Coffee is the last thing I need. And is there somewhere more private we can sit?* I was nervous as all hell about the amniocentesis and wished we didn't have to wait amidst the hustle and bustle of the clinic.

After the amniocentesis, I went home and put myself to bed. Just for something different, I cried and cried, and cried. I was glad the boys were at their dad's; I couldn't have cared for them in any way, after the day we'd had. Josh collected Bonnie from nursery school and we muddled through the evening routine, waiting to hear from our private obstetrician, who would relay the results of the scan to us in detail. This was the standard procedure, as he was the referring doctor. He didn't call until 9pm. That call remains probably the worst medical care I've received in my life.

He told us he hadn't yet read our report or seen the actual scans, as he hadn't been back to his rooms, but he had spoken to the radiologist who'd reviewed our scan and performed the amniocentesis. He relayed her opinion, which she had given to him over the phone, that "if it were her pregnancy she would not consider continuing with it". We were floored, not only to hear this devastating statement, but to also be given such harrowing, life-changing news over the phone. To this day, I cannot understand why we were not called into our obstetrician's rooms late that afternoon or first thing the next morning, to be supported through this shocking turn of events in person. Josh asked him to call again in the morning, once he had read our report and seen the scans himself.

During this short phone call, he asked us what we thought we would do given the diagnosis – would we end the pregnancy? We replied that we had no idea, as we didn't yet have adequate information with which to make a decision. We didn't know what the diagnosis meant, but the comments of the radiologist filled us with despair. Josh said that with three children to care for and support, we would have to think very carefully about what we did. To bring a child into the world who was so severely disabled that they would need round-the-clock care to breathe, eat and stay alive would obviously impact our other children. If our baby could survive at all. If the damage was so extensive that it could not be reversed in any way, there was a possibility that the baby would die before or shortly after birth. All of this was still unknown.

I couldn't speak. Naively, I had never heard of ending a pregnancy so late into the second trimester. It went against every fibre of my being and I felt so disturbed by it, I was physically ill. It was not a 'choice' I thought I would ever face, or a decision I would have to make, my mind was having enormous difficulty processing it. I hoped with all my heart that the next step, an MRI, would give us a good result or more information about the severity of our baby's condition. The idea of making a decision to interrupt a pregnancy based on a second-hand opinion of one doctor, relayed over the phone by another doctor, was quite simply ridiculous. I needed every tiny bit of information I could get my hands on before even embarking on the 'decision'-making process.

Our obstetrician called back on Friday morning to let me know I had an MRI booked in for Monday at 9am. He told me that he'd read our report and it diagnosed 'severe hydrocephalous' resulting in squashed brain matter, and that the baby had a possible heart defect. He didn't elaborate in a meaningful way about what any of this meant, but told me to try to enjoy my weekend. By this stage I was starting to realise that we were in the care of an obstetrician who severely lacked compassion, and had an atrocious bedside manner.

When he had asked the night before what our feelings were on ending the pregnancy, I'd had no response, as I was shocked by the very notion of not continuing with a much-wanted pregnancy. To make matters worse, in the same breath he told us that if we were to 'interrupt' the pregnancy, it was not something he could assist us with, as he had made a decision earlier in his career not to perform terminations in any circumstances. I had read on his information pamphlet that he didn't perform terminations after a first-trimester diagnosis of Down's syndrome, but no other conditions had been mentioned. The pamphlet said nothing about his position on ending a pregnancy well into the second trimester due to a life-limiting diagnosis. Confused, I felt like I was being treated with disdain, that he was letting a personal moral judgment influence his actions as a doctor.

He went on to say that if we chose not to continue with the pregnancy, I would be handed over to the Women's and Children's Hospital and I would, considering my gestation, be induced to deliver the baby naturally in the care of midwives. He made no mention of handing me over to the hospital's Maternal Fetal Fedicine team, or any specific obstetric department. It seemed that I would be cast out into an unknown system and left to deal with this alone. We felt lost, completely uninformed and unsupported. He showed no sensitivity or empathy towards us. It was as though he was washing his hands of an ugly situation that was not to his liking, and it made an incredibly difficult time even harder.

During his brief phone call on Friday morning, he said something along the lines of, "If the MRI results from Monday morning confirm what we've seen on the ultrasound, I could book you in to end your pregnancy as soon as that evening." This was said without offering to meet with us to discuss our case, or arranging any counselling to inform us of the full implications of our baby's diagnosis – and before we had received the results of the amniocentesis.

I decided it might help to speak directly with the female radiologist from the clinic, who had given the opinion that if it were her pregnancy, she would not continue with it. I wanted to know what had prompted such a strong comment. I rang her rooms and was told she wasn't working that day. When I explained the reason for my call and the nature of the comment that had been passed on, the receptionist said she'd discuss it with the on-duty radiologist as, yes, she agreed that comment should not have been passed on in the manner in which it was.

The receptionist rang back later in the afternoon to explain that the on-duty radiologist was uncomfortable discussing the comment, as he had not been directly involved with our case. This was fair enough and I understood his reticence to get involved. He did contact our private obstetrician to discuss it and relay the fact that I had rung to talk through the comment and get some clearer information about our situation. Our private obstetrician still didn't call us in to his rooms, though I was clearly distraught and desperately seeking information.

I rang my friend Anna who had lost her baby ten years before. She suggested I ring a woman she knew who had lost a baby due to a brain abnormality nine years ago. Her friend's first baby had been diagnosed as incompatible with life and delivered at twenty-five weeks. I rang and told her all that I knew so far. She was shocked that I hadn't been called into my obstetrician's rooms or offered any counselling. She gave me the number of the head of genetic counselling for fetal abnormality at the Women's and Children's Hospital and suggested I call her first thing Monday morning for advice. She also suggested I change obstetrician as soon as possible. Throughout her heartbreaking diagnosis and subsequent loss, her obstetrician had supported her, met with her, hugged her and offered endless compassion. I was terrified of the road ahead but knew that the next step was to change doctors as soon as possible. My mind swung from believing with certainty that our baby would be okay, that he or she would be miraculously spared from this horrible twist of fate, to knowing that was a fantasy, and that our lives would never be the same again. I was already worried about how we would cope. How does anyone cope with the loss of a much-wanted baby? I thought back to when I was bleeding at nine weeks. When that happened I had thought, *Please not me. Please god, the universe, whoever controls these things, spare ME, spare my baby.* I thought I couldn't possibly cope with that kind of heartache. Now, these feelings returned, with a new intensity. I have been close to two women in my life who have had stillborn babies, so it was not a foreign concept. I had seen first-hand just how devastating it was. I knew from listening to their experiences that it was something that stayed with you forever, a loss you never got over. I didn't think I had the capacity to deal with it, but understood I might not have any choice in the matter.

Chapter 4 A devastating diagnosis

The weekend was a blur, the end of the year was hurtling towards us. I wanted to make sure Christmas, a little over a week away, was as magical as it had always been for the kids. Christmas presents were bought and wrapped, and Santa sacks were stuffed early, in case I couldn't do it later. I knew that unless a miracle occurred, we had some very tough times ahead. If the worst happened, I would not be out buying presents, making ice-cream puddings or taking part in our usual Christmas traditions. I was laying low, avoiding friends, refusing all invitations and screening phone calls. I couldn't talk about what was going on. There was no way I felt remotely ready to discuss what I knew, and I was so uncomfortable with the idea of interrupting a pregnancy, even if the MRI did determine that our baby was incompatible with life, that I felt too ashamed to talk about it with anyone. I was scared of being judged, that people might see it as a choice – though of course, it wasn't a choice at all.

Over the weekend I contacted a school mum who was a radiologist at the Women's and Children's Hospital. I wanted to learn as much as I could about our baby's condition. She explained that the MRI would give us more information, but I also needed to be aware that if the swelling continued, the baby's skull could increase in size. This would put me at risk of uterine rupture (spontaneous tearing of the uterus, causing the baby to slip into the mother's abdomen), which was life-threatening. I'd had no idea. I also spoke with my husband's uncle, a pediatrician, who helped shed some light on the hydrocephalus diagnosis. He explained that some babies born with this condition can be treated with a shunt after birth and go on to live normal lives, but this was usually only successful with milder cases that began later in pregnancy. Given that ours was considered severe so early on, our chances were not so great. I found it incredibly comforting to talk to as many people with some experience or expertise as possible, and gather as much information as I could – though of course, they didn't have my case notes, so couldn't review my specific situation.

Monday loomed. I couldn't sleep and everything upset me. An old friend of Josh's suggested to him that "perhaps it was for the best", that finding out now that the baby wouldn't survive birth, or would have severe disabilities and no quality of life, was a 'silver lining'. In hindsight, I can see that he was trying to look for a positive, to give us comfort in some way, but his comments hurt me deeply. When you're potentially facing the death of a child, you see no positives, no silver lining. There is no 'at least'. I wanted my baby, this exact baby, the one I was carrying. I wanted this horrible situation to disappear, and in no way did I feel that finding out now was a good thing. To me, it was simply a death sentence. It did not alter the heartache that would inevitably follow or make my child's life any less important or valuable. The comment implied, *It's a dud. Best to know now and get rid of it sooner rather than later.* It made me feel even more apprehensive about sharing the full story, in case people didn't get it. We were not making a choice or taking the easy option; we were also not dealing with a straightforward diagnosis.

On the day of the MRI, the thought of not getting enough data for meaningful results terrified me more than going through the procedure itself. I was worried that I'd move too much and they wouldn't be able to get clear enough pictures. I was so desperate for results that I barely breathed while I was in the machine. Straight after the MRI, I rang the senior genetics counsellor at the Women's and told her my story, explaining my dismay at the (lack of) care we'd received from our obstetrician and asking her if she felt it would be appropriate if I were to go to my GP and seek an urgent referral to the Maternal Fetal Medicine department within the hospital. She agreed it would.

My GP not only read the reports from my scan on Thursday, but also sat with me, hugged me and said the words I was desperate to hear. "Annabel, this baby is loved and whatever decision you make is the right one."

I'm very lucky to have had the same GP for over twenty years. She knows me well and had helped my through all of my babies, divorce, postnatal anxiety and so much more. I had been feeling like an utter monster, akin to a murderer, that we were having to consider not continuing with the pregnancy. Her words reassured me that anything I did next was out of love for this baby. She told me that this baby may never make it so as much as I felt I might have to 'choose' to not continue, the 'decision' may have already been made for me. She told me there was no wrong or right decision; whatever we did next was the best thing for this baby and our family.

A referral to Maternal Fetal Medicine (MFM) was faxed immediately. The relief I felt was enormous. An obstetricspecialist from MFM rang me soon after, at about 1pm, with the results of my MRI. She was incredible. It was like there was an angel at the other end of the line. This warm-hearted young obstetrician instantly put me at ease. She explained that yes, the baby's condition was very serious. The MRI showed that the baby had suffered a brain hemorrhage and as a result there was a blood clot in the third ventricle, which was causing the brain to swell dramatically with CVS fluid. They felt that this was indicative of a syndrome called NAIT or F-NAIT, in which the mother's antibodies attack the platelets of the baby, which carry the father's DNA: maternal antibodies perceive these to be a threat. As a result, platelets are diminished and the baby can have dangerous internal bleeding. In the most severe cases, this can occur in the brain. The condition is rare and not routinely screened for. Given that the boys were from my first marriage, it was thought that during Bonnie's delivery, blood from the placenta might have crossed with mine, and my body had registered the foreign DNA.

This was a bombshell, but also an answer of sorts, which is what we needed. She said I could come in for an appointment as early as the next day, or wait two days and be seen by the head of the department. I opted for the latter. The boys were spending the day at our friend's house on Wednesday and I'd booked a nanny for Bonnie, so I felt happy to wait one more day, knowing I had the kids sorted and would be meeting with the head of the department. I collected the boys from vacation care Monday and took them to their swimming lessons. Anna, my friend whose first son was born still, ten years before I gave birth to Miles, was there. Her children had their lessons at the same time as mine.

We sat and talked and I felt almost normal for an hour. Talking to someone who has been through the confusion and devastation of a bad diagnosis in advanced pregnancy is incredibly liberating. You can say anything – there is no judgement, no filter necessary, just complete empathy. I felt almost normal for an hour. Anna has been my biggest support since this began unfolding, and still is.

I told her that I felt like my obstetrician had been a complete asshole. Because we are mature adults, we changed his name to something unmentionable in my phone. He happened to ring while I was sitting there, and we fell about laughing hysterically as his new moniker flashed up. I let the call go through to message bank, not wanting to talk to him while I was out with the kids, and without Josh. I realised that no matter what lay ahead, I would laugh again. I would need to surround myself with people who understood and not let the darkness overshadow everything.

Ironically, when he called back later that evening with our MRI results (which had already been given to me hours before our obstetrician's first phone call, by the doctor in the MFM department) he gave us his most understanding and informative update so far. But by now, we had lost faith in him. The person we had been counting on and looking to for guidance had been truly disappointing and unprofessional. He had still not made any effort to meet with us and I wanted nothing more to do with him. I felt especially angry that even though he knew I had quite recently suffered postnatal anxiety after Bonnie, he not once asked how I was coping mentally, nor recommended any counselling services.

My father-in-law, a retired surgeon of forty-five years, offered his opinion when we told him about our experience: "He's a B-grader and should be reported." He was appalled that we had not yet been seen in person and suggested I make a complaint to the Australian Medical Association. But I knew I had bigger battles ahead, which deserved my energy far more. I did, however, write the obstetrician a very long letter explaining how and why I felt he had repeatedly failed us as our doctor. Given the seriousness of our baby's condition, I felt we should have been an absolute priority and seen immediately. I shared some recommendations on how to handle any unlucky couples he might encounter in the future, facing similarly gut-wrenching situations during their pregnancies. I kept imagining first-time parents encountering him, being pushed aside and insensitively handled during a deeply traumatic time. It had the potential to do lifelong damage.

He replied over a month later, after I'd had to ring his rooms to check that he had received and read my letter. He said he usually did bring patients into his rooms with cases like ours and wouldn't go into the reasons he didn't with us, as they would simply sound like excuses. He went on to say that my appointment with my GP to seek a referral for MFM was unnecessary, as he had already organised one. This had never been communicated to us. Without adequate communication from our private obstetrician, I still believe we had no choice but to take matters into our own hands. When I rang the MFM department to clarify the issue of the referral, they said that no written referral had ever been received other than the one from my GP.

I have not replied to him and never will. I will also never regret my course of action: I did what I needed to do for my baby and my own sanity. I needed to feel that I was in a position to find out every possible skerrick of information about our situation. My actions were also influenced by the outstanding medical care I had received at other times throughout my life. Doctors who had sat with me and carefully explained diagnoses and outcomes. Doctors within my own family and social network, who I know to be incredibly caring professionals who would never relay this kind of information by phone call alone. Anyone facing a trauma of this magnitude deserves to be treated with enormous sensitivity. At the very least, their doctor should urgently make time to discuss their situation in person.

The medical world can be intimidating and scary, especially when you're in great distress. We are taught to respect doctors, as we are teachers and other people in positions of authority. It can be daunting to stand up for yourself in this kind of environment. If you are being reasonable and not acting out of anger, it is your right to ask for a second opinion, or to change doctors if you feel you are not being heard. Nothing in this world is more important to a parent than their child, so we should never be afraid to go to whatever lengths necessary to get the answers we need. Many people will receive the tragic news that their baby has no heartbeat, or face a similar scenario to ours, which was weeks of tests, investigations, and an initially uncertain outcome. Others will receive a comparatively early diagnosis of a congenital abnormality after routine testing at twelve to fourteen weeks. They are all heartbreaking, unexpected and have the same outcome: empty arms. I assume that most mothers are heading to scans or appointments with great excitement, naturally anticipating good news and a chance to see how much their baby has grown. The joy of seeing your baby and its progress instantly evaporates if unexpected bad news is delivered. And this occurs in a foreign, sterile environment surrounded by strangers. The way bad news is delivered is so important.

Some women start to miscarry at home or at work, which I imagine would be confronting and terrifying in equal parts. They then need to seek medical support. How they are received and treated can have a huge impact on how they cope with the grief ahead. I started grieving my baby during the first scan, from the very second I realised something was wrong. This was just the beginning of an incredibly difficult time, which is why it is crucial that women (and their partners) are cared for by professionals who understand just how devastating baby loss is, and respond with adequate empathy. It's a scary mix of raging hormones, shattered dreams and broken plans – a time where grief and trauma collide head on.

.

Chapter 5 A 'decision' that is not a choice

That week, we were in the midst of a heatwave. Josh hates hospitals. They make him incredibly uncomfortable and I'd make a guess that if he never has to enter another one for as long as he lives, he'll be a happy man. Sitting on the sticky vinyl charts in the Maternal Fetal Medicine waiting room, flicking through the year-old gossip mags, avoiding eye contact with other terrified parents, Josh looked like he wished he could be anywhere else. We both did, because we wanted our baby to be okay, to be told to go home, that it had all been one big mistake.

The head MFM doctor explained our baby's condition to us in great detail. We were taken to another department in the hospital straight after, to meet with a neonatal neurologist. The neurologist was very clear: our baby basically had no chance unless the clot blocking the ventricles moved of its own accord. The damage from the hemorrhage and the swelling was likely to be irreversible and could indicate incompatibility with life. At this stage of pregnancy, important brain development was occurring, which our baby would miss out on completely. If it had been later in pregnancy, early delivery followed by surgery may have been an option, but at our baby's gestation period, it would not be strong enough to go through that.

The outcomes were bleak: our baby's situation was like that of an adult who had suffered an aneurysm and was being kept alive by a life-support machine. In our case, the placenta was the life support machine. Once removed from it, the baby may not survive. The doctor could see how torn we were by the diagnosis. He suggested we come back in a week, after Christmas, for one final scan to see if anything had improved. We would also have the full results of the amniocentesis by then. I think he could see just how painful this 'decision' was for me and that we needed time to absorb what had been explained to us so far. Josh, ever calm and practical, kept telling me, "You are not choosing to do this, you are simply acting on the cards you have been dealt."

I hadn't told friends what was going on. Lots of people had called for my birthday and were looking to catch up for a pre-Christmas drink (a non-alcoholic one for me obviously). I was ignoring them all. I couldn't bring myself to talk to people, let alone socialise. Telling people would make it real – and I wasn't strong enough to encounter adverse opinions. Being forced to 'decide' whether to terminate a pregnancy that's likely to result in a child that is incompatible with life is still an unspoken and taboo area of baby loss. And I still feel uncomfortable with the topic at times, even though I have lived it.

Christmas, like my birthday, felt completely hollow. We had organised well in advance that the boys were going off to their dad's at noon on Christmas Day, and they were going to stay with him for two weeks. The morning was full of great excitement: the opening of Santa's presents, the discovery of new bikes and the sheer joy that Christmas is for kids. I watched the boys whiz around the front driveway on their shiny new bikes, with Bonnie trying to keep up on her scooter, and felt completely dead inside. I couldn't soak up their happiness, I was so broken and empty. I felt like the grim reaper was hovering over me, waiting to snatch this precious baby away from our family before we got the chance to meet him or her. Sitting on the front step, I started crying.

"Why are you crying Mum?" asked Ted, as he rode past.

"No reason Ted, just feeling a bit sad, nothing to worry about."

"Is it because your baby is sick and it's going to die?"

"No darling, the baby is fine."

Ted is very perceptive and obviously quite the eavesdropper, but this still floored me. He had clearly sensed that something was amiss and picked up a few little soundbites along the way. Ted was obsessed with this baby and had been asking so many questions about it. If this baby didn't make it, his little heart would be broken too.

I love Christmas and adore cooking Christmas lunch and making a big day of it. But my heart wasn't in it, for obvious reasons. If I could have skipped it altogether, I happily would have. Luckily, Josh's entire family was on Kangaroo Island, off the coast of South Australia. We were doing a very small lunch at my parents' house, with just my older brother and his partner, over from Melbourne. I'd messaged my brother the day before, to organise a swim and a catch-up, so he could see the kids. I had an echocardiogram at the Women's at 4pm on Christmas Eve, to investigate an additional issue picked up in the baby's heart during Thursday's scan, so Josh brought the kids to see my brother. I told my brother in my message that things were not going well with the baby, and the only way I'd make it through Christmas Day was to not talk about the baby at all.

I wonder now how I will feel towards Christmas in the future. It was such a pivotal day for us, the year Miles was born. I had gone to such extreme lengths to hide my distress from the boys, until they went to their dad's on Christmas Day. I'd taken them to a movie the week before, sobbing through the whole thing in the dark, only just pulling myself together before we walked out of the cinema together, into the sunshine. I avoided school holiday hotspots, as I was terrified of bumping into people. I always feel obliged to tell people exactly what is going on, so I didn't want to risk seeing people and having to explain why I was so down, especially in front of the kids. But once we got through the Christmas Day – the last thing we were expected to show up for – Josh and I were free to hide away and no longer had to keep up our brave faces.

A few very close friends knew what we were facing. The lovely ones who took the boys for the day when we had our first appointment with MFM were an incredible support. My best friend was over from London, and I felt I could tell her the full extent of the situation. And of course, there was Anna, the friend who had lost her own baby ten years ago. Our next MFM appointment was on 27 December. Although I knew the outcome was unlikely to change with this final scan, I was wishing upon every star in the sky that it would. The amniocentesis results that came back on Christmas Eve had cleared us of all syndromes, infections, etc. The only possible explanations remaining for our baby's condition were NAIT (neonatal alloimmune thrombocytopenia) or a one-in-a-million brain hemorrhage.

Like many do when faced with this kind of tragedy, I began to bargain with the universe. I'm not religious, but I kept hoping that by some miracle, some twist of fate, our baby would be fine. I refused to believe this could even be happening. The *why us?* question played on repeat. What had we possibly done to deserve this? The answer was simple: nothing.

It wasn't fair. Even though you hear of people losing babies, you always think it won't happen to you. The odds will be in your favour, not against it. I wondered if I'd been 'chosen' because I am strong and as much as I didn't want to have to survive this trauma, I knew I would somehow cope if the worst happened. I suppose the other way of looking at it is, *why* not *us?* As much as we would all like to think we can pass through life without tragedy or pain, it is unlikely that we will. Many people are lucky not to experience earth-shattering grief until later in life. For Josh and me, it seemed very likely we would face it relatively young.

Someone said to me, "At least you have three beautiful children." I remember thinking, *yes, I am so, so lucky, but I certainly didn't need this utter devastation to make me realise that, or appreciate my living children.* I always have and always will. Having to share the custody of the boys and going through a high-risk pregnancy with Bonnie had already reinforced this. Like all parents, I found my children exhausting and exasperating at times, but I was also so grateful to be their mum. I was worried that if the baby didn't make it, the grief would crush me so much I wouldn't be able to parent my living children. I was also worried I'd feel so guilty that they lived but their little sibling didn't and wouldn't know how to make sense of the injustice of it. My mind was in overdrive, with so many conflicting emotions vying for attention. But once we had got through Christmas and waved off the boys, our baby and his or her future dominated my every thought, without interruption or distraction.

Chapter 6 Preparing for the worst imaginable thing

The final appointment brought no joy. The swelling of the brain was still extreme, the blood clot had not moved and there was absolutely no change in our baby's situation. Doctors are not allowed to tell you what to do, but in the kindest, simplest way, we were told there was absolutely no hope for our child. There were three doctors in the room with us reviewing the final scan, which in itself spoke volumes in a busy public hospital unit. The two female specialists who took me in for the final scan were so beautifully empathetic that I could not stop crying as they analysed the baby's brain and discussed the outcome. It was clear to us from everything said that there had been no change and was no likelihood of one occurring.

From this point forward, everything was a hellish blur. Paperwork was signed, bookings were made. I had to sign a piece of paper that would result in the loss of this precious baby. I suppose the best thing I can liken it to is a parent having to switch off their child's life-support machine. A task you never, ever imagine you will have to do; a task so dreadful and confronting that it beggars belief. In our case, I was the life-support machine and there was no tangible switch. In its place, there was a pill to swallow that would cause my placenta to stop working and induce labour. I still don't know how I physically swallowed that pill. *I didn't want to* barely scratches the surface of the torment within me. All I wanted was this beautiful baby, who I already loved so dearly, to stay with us.

In order to cope, I tried to rationalise it. I was so emotionally invested in my imagined future as a mother of four that I kept thinking it was all just a horrible nightmare. Josh was far more pragmatic. He knew we had no option, but as he admitted, it's much easier to take a practical approach if you're not the one who can still feel the baby kicking and moving inside you. I couldn't comprehend how the baby could be so safe inside me, yet have no chance of surviving once born. The stark contrast between what I could feel physically and what I was trying to wrap my brain around emotionally was sending me mad. I was also exhausted. I hadn't been sleeping and the emotional toll of the last few weeks had caught up with me.

Now that the final 'decision' (this will always be said in quotation marks, as to me this step was not a real choice or decision) had been made, I wanted to get the next stage over with. I was traumatised by the sight and feel of my pregnant belly. I toyed with the idea of asking a close friend to take some photos for me, but in the end, I didn't. I felt too self-conscious. Now I wish I had, but not going ahead with that influenced many other decisions in the coming days. I didn't want any more regrets. I was acutely aware of how limited our time would be with our baby and didn't want to miss another opportunity to create memories, especially due to decisions made because of my own awkwardness. I didn't want this to happen, I didn't ask for it, and couldn't control it or stop it. The only thing I *could* control was how I chose to handle it.

The day after the final MFM appointment was Josh's birthday, 28 December. We had stumbled through a month usually overflowing with celebrations and happiness, navigating my birthday, Christmas, and now had Josh's birthday, with New Year's Eve still ahead. These dates were meaningless to us this year. I did wonder how December would ever be a happy month for us again, as it had always been. How could we ever be happy during the month in which our baby died? But I am now confident that we will come to see it as a month to celebrate and remember Miles in. It feels nice that he's a December baby, like Josh and me.

We decided to go out for sushi (something I'd fastidiously avoided for the previous six months) and I needed to collect some things for the labour ward. It was incomprehensibly sad, buying maternity pads and other things for the labour ward, when I knew I'd be delivering a stillborn baby. I'd been through this ritual before: packing a hospital bag for me and my expected baby felt familiar. I'd always taken great care with this process and decided it would be no different for this baby. He or she was just as special and deserved the same care as my other children. And whether I liked it or not, I was about to be put into labour. I needed these items.

I was desperate to find a toy for the baby, a little talisman I could keep to remind me of him or her. Nothing seemed right: I couldn't find anything delicate or special enough. I searched and searched, and just before giving up, I found the sweetest little honey-coloured bear. When we got home, I rang the genetics counsellor at the Women's and Children's Hospital. I needed to know the gender of my baby before delivery and knew it would have been recorded from the amniocentesis. I think I would have been devastated regardless of the answer, as we were equally excited about having another boy or another girl. A sister for Bonnie would have been lovely – and what a combo two boys and two girls would be! A baby boy would have been equally wonderful: Ted was desperate for another brother, Bonnie was quite a tomboy, and we were already quite a boy-oriented household.

When I learned it was a boy, my heart broke just that little bit more. I don't know why exactly. I think in my mind, a boy was a mini version of Josh, and that was the one thing (biologically) we had not experienced together. In my gut, I had felt like I was having a boy from very early on in the pregnancy. The thought that I had known this by instinct made me feel genuinely connected to this child. I'd had also felt that something was not quite right from the start – and it turned out I was correct on both fronts. Maternal instinct is a truly strong force, and should never be ignored or dismissed.

I went through the older boys' baby things: the special pieces I'd put aside as keepsakes. I knew none of the clothes would fit, so I picked out three of my favourite baby blankets. My absolute favourite was a wrap with navy blue stars, which both boys were wrapped in after they were delivered. I have near-identical pictures of the boys wrapped in blue stars in hospital, and wanted the same for my third son. I also wanted to name our little boy before he was delivered. I was scared that if we left it until after he was born, we would waste the short, precious time we'd have with him in hospital trying to decide on a name. (We didn't have a good track record in this department: it took three days to name Bonnie, who was very nearly a Daisy). It was at this point that I realised Josh and I were approaching the situation very differently.

He had been shocked to learn that the baby would be delivered by induced labour. He had assumed that the baby would be delivered in 'a procedure', done under general anesthetic or by caesarean. He had no idea we would be given the opportunity to hold and cuddle our baby: a notion which repulsed and horrified him. I felt the exact opposite. I wanted to hold our baby, love him, have pictures taken and treat him just like my other children. I had carried him within me and it felt unnatural to do anything other than nurture him after he was born.

I brought up names and the only thing Josh wanted was for the baby's initials to match his late father's initials: M.J.B. Josh was happy to call him M.J., but for me that seemed like a shortcut, like we weren't bothering to give him a proper name, as he wasn't going to come home with us. Instead, I said I'd find a name to fit with the initials. I love to talk things over and over, but Josh doesn't. I texted him a list of suggested names (some which weren't M's or J's, but names I hoped he might go with anyway). He replied with the only two M/J names on the list: Marcus and Jack. These names didn't mean anything to me, but I was determined to go in with a basic list to work with. I swapped the Jack for Joshua, as that is Josh's full name, and stuck with Marcus.

I didn't want to name our little boy something I would frequently hear in playgrounds or at school. The thought of hearing his name called out seemed too cruel. I have a cousin named Mark so was unsure of Marcus, I wanted a name that was unique but also very 'us'. Naming a baby who is not going to live is not easy. I would happily have named him any of the names we'd started talking about together before we knew we'd lose him, but none of them were M names and given it was Josh's only request, I wanted to fulfil it.

Chapter 7 Saying hello and goodbye in the same moment

What do you do the night before you go to hospital to deliver a stillborn baby? There is no guide for it, and apart from continuing to breathe in and out, I can offer few meaningful suggestions. *Beaches*, a movie I had watched a thousand times as a child in the eighties, was on TV. It's not something I would watch now, nor something Josh would ever think of sitting through, but we put it on. I cried the whole way through. I swallowed a sleeping tablet, sent a prayer of hope to the sleep gods, and I'm pretty sure I cried in my sleep all night. The next morning, the thought of picking up my hospital bag, getting into the car and walking into that hospital seemed impossible. Josh, Bonnie and I drove there together. The plan was for Josh to drop Bonnie to my parents once I was settled, then come back.

Hopping in the car, popping the seatbelt around my bump for the very last time, I was overwhelmed with sadness. As Josh turned on the ignition, the Pharrell Williams song 'Happy' came on. Oh, the irony! I started laughing out loud. The past few weeks had robbed me of my sense of humour, and certainly my happiness, but I caught a glimpse of both. I think of Miles whenever I hear that song now. Perhaps it was his little way of telling us that one day we would be happy again, and giving us his permission to be so.

Walking into the hospital with a two-year-old was a great distraction and made what seemed so unnatural feel a tiny bit normal. We were taken to our room at the end of the labour and delivery ward, 'away' from the noise of crying newborns, and introduced to the midwife who would be looking after us. She turned out to be a friend of a friend, which could have been bad or good. She carefully mentioned the connection – a friend of mine from the mother's group I was in with Alfie nine years ago – and I instantly felt comfortable with her. She was in the middle of a difficult divorce, something I could relate to, we bonded over that. As sad and horrible as what lay ahead was, I felt I was in good hands. She treated me with absolute kindness and compassion, which helped to minimise the trauma ahead.

I had given birth three times before (two inductions and one spontaneous labour) and each time, the epidurals had worked in different ways. In my first labour, I had refused one until late and ended up so dosed up, I didn't feel a thing at the end. For the inductions, the epidural was suggested from the get-go as induced labour can be far more intense and come on fast and strong. In both of these deliveries, the epidural had worked for the first stage of labour, but by the time I felt like I really needed it, I had run out of time for a top-up. For this labour, patient-led analgesia was the only option I had. It is pain relief dispensed via a drip, re-loaded by pressing a button at five-minute intervals. I didn't have the energy to question why, and just accepted that this would be all I was getting.

Josh came back from dropping Bonnie to my parents as restless as ever. Knowing how hard he finds hospitals, I suggested he go and have lunch somewhere. I had just had my first round of tablets, so knew nothing was going to happen in a hurry. After the second dosage of tablets, my labour progressed very quickly. I wanted to stop time. I didn't want to deliver this baby. That would mean it was over, that he really had died, and there was no way of reversing or changing his fate. It was as intense and as painful as all of my other deliveries. I had naively thought that because I was delivering a preterm baby, it would somehow be physically easier. By some small mercy, it was faster, but in no way did that dampen the pain.

The thing that still haunts me is the silence of the delivery room. No excitement, no reward after a painful labour, no first cry. The first of many lost firsts. No first tooth, first step, first word. Our baby's life began and ended the second he was born. During the final excruciating stage of labour, pushing went against every instinct. The contractions felt like my body was failing me. The experience was truly traumatic. I don't think I will ever get over or come to terms with it.

The midwife gently wrapped up our little boy and handed him to me. He was beautiful: tiny and perfectly formed. He looked so much like my other newborns, just smaller, darker, and still. The first thing I said to Josh was, "He looks just like you." Later, Josh told me that this broke his heart. To watch the son he hadn't wanted to see or hold arrive as a perfect little version of himself made his baby's existence seem very real. Our enormous loss was immediately apparent. For Josh, the baby had been an abstract. He hadn't felt him move inside his tummy, or had him live and grow inside him for almost six months. But the moment his baby was earthside, he could see that he was his son, his child – but one he would never see grow, or get to know.

I knew instantly that this baby wasn't a Marcus: he was too delicate. I searched my brain for a different 'M' name and stumbled upon Miles. It suited him. It wasn't a name I'd considered and I had only ever met one Miles (spelt Myles), which appealed to me. I wanted our little boy to have a unique name. When I first held him, I tried to soak up every detail of his little face. I could see he would have been handsome and quite possibly tall, like his dad. He had very long legs, a button nose like his sister and ears like mine. I couldn't get over how lovely he was. I'd been terrified that

I would be repulsed by him, unable to hold him or love him. But I felt the opposite. Knowing how short our time together would be, I wanted to make the most of it.

My placenta had other ideas: it was stuck. The second midwife who was assigned to us, an absolute angel, tried a few things. She was almost apologetic. An obstetrician was called in and tried to manually extract it, but after some uncomfortable prodding and pulling, it was decided I'd need to go to theatre. I remember signing forms, agreeing to various things, talking to the anaesthetist and everyone saying how sorry they were that I would have to go through surgery on top of labour. By this stage, I couldn't have cared less what they did to me. They could have amputated an arm for all I cared: I felt dead inside and was physical and emotionally at rock bottom. Surely whatever was next – surgery, recovery, after pains – could not be harder than what I had just endured.

An orderly came in to wheel me down to theatre, a big bruiser of a guy with tatts and piercings. "Hello love, I'm Marcus, I'll be taking you through to theatre." I couldn't believe we'd almost given Miles the name of this gentle soul in a gruff casing. This confirmed we'd picked the perfect name for our little boy. He was definitely a Miles, not a Marcus.

The surgery felt surreal. Waiting in recovery afterwards was torture. The spinal block I'd been given had a greater effect than intended. I had no feeling up to my shoulders and ended up unable to walk until midnight. The lovely anaesthetist apologised and said it often happened with smaller people, as the dose sometimes had a greater impact. I'd delivered Miles at 5:45, was in surgery by 6:30, and was still in recovery at 8:30. I was freezing, itchy, starving and above all heartbroken. How had this happened? Why had this happened? Had it really happened at all? I just wanted to get back to my room and see Miles. Josh had gone home while I was in surgery to feed the dog and bring me back something to eat. I felt like I should be incapable of such a mundane task as eating. I had just lost my baby: how could I still have my appetite? It was the first of many, many times I felt guilty for how I felt or for doing something I wanted or needed to do. I didn't know how to act. There was no guidebook for what was ahead, and I had no idea how I was going to make my way through any of it.

So that is our story, and Miles' story. A baby boy we so desperately wanted and through a cruel twist of fate, had to say goodbye to. The days, weeks and months ahead were the hardest of my life. I was scared the loss would break me. That I would never be the same again, or would remain in the first, shocking stage of grief forever. Words cannot adequately describe the horror of it.

If you have picked up this book because you have lost a baby, or if you are reading this in the hope of supporting someone who has, I hope that the following sections of this book provide you with some comfort and helpful suggestions. I have included some stories of others who have experienced baby loss in different ways, as well as interviews with health professionals. I talk about how I processed my grief, what worked, (and what didn't), what upset me, what comforted me and what I was feeling throughout it all.

It's a hopeful story: I was determined to survive, even if some days I didn't believe I would and on the some of the really early dark days, I didn't even know if I wanted to. Everyone responds to and recovers from a tragedy like this differently, but I hope hearing someone else's experience brings other baby-loss parents a little bit of comfort, eases their isolation, and makes them feel like they're not alone.

Part 2 Support through baby loss

Chapter 8 The taboo topic of baby loss

Over and over again while researching this book, women said to me, *I didn't know how to begin talking about my loss, I felt like I was being overly dramatic or too sensitive, I had to campaign for my baby's worth and meaning,* or *I felt like had no right to be grieving at all.* All of these comments broke my heart. For some archaic reason, and despite it happening to so many women, baby loss is a taboo subject – an event that is usually shared quietly, privately and often only in detail with those who have also experienced it. The death of a baby in utero is one of the few deaths within our society that is not routinely announced publicly. This may be because it is so traumatic for the bereaved and because we are yet to create a safe space in which to communicate it openly.

Community awareness about stillbirth is minimal and many people misunderstand and undervalue the emotional and physical impact of miscarriage. Funding for research into the cause of both stillbirth and miscarriage is lacking, as they are sadly viewed as inevitable potential outcomes of pregnancy, rather than a medical crisis to be investigated. The ongoing psychological impact the loss of a baby has on mothers and families is immeasurable and we need to help reduce this and stop unnecessary suffering.

As someone who grew up in the 1980s, I have vivid memories of Red Nose Day, in support of SIDS (sudden infant death syndrome). We would take a two-dollar coin to school to buy a red nose to wear for the day. We all knew we were giving money to help scientists and doctors find out why some babies suddenly died in their sleep: this fact wasn't hidden. We all knew that some little babies went to sleep and never woke up. Sadly, we don't have open conversations about babies lost in the womb, as we were encouraged to do with SIDS. This needs to change.

I only recently discovered that (as of 2017) for every baby lost to SIDS, thirty-five are lost to stillbirth. That is six babies a day, in Australia alone. The rate of stillbirth, unlike the rate of SIDS, has not dropped significantly in the past twenty years, and in my opinion, the information (and in many cases, the support) offered to women who have had a miscarriage has not evolved adequately either over the last few decades. Many women I have spoken to feel that their loss is minimised and (wrongly) think they're at fault. The Red Nose Organisation now contributes significant funds and resources to support research into baby loss during pregnancy as well as neonatal death. Red Nose also offers support to anyone who has suffered the unexpected loss of a baby or a child, be it through miscarriage, medical termination, stillbirth or after birth. While in many cases miscarriage cannot be prevented, new research is emerging and gaining momentum. There is also strong evidence that the rate of stillbirth could potentially be reduced by educating women of signs to look out for during pregnancy.

Due to the exceptional work of the Red Nose organisation, the rate of deaths from SIDS has reduced by 85% in the last twenty years. In 2017, 87 babies were lost to SIDS. In this same year, 2107 babies were lost to stillbirth, and an estimated 100,000 plus to miscarriages. According to some statistics, there is one miscarriage every three and a half minutes. That amounts to a lot of heartbroken parents. The death toll in 2017 from motor vehicle accidents was, tragically, 1225. Despite the fact that the rate of stillbirth is almost double that of the road toll, information to help educate parents and reduce the rate of preventable stillbirths is not communicated in a consistent or ongoing way. Conversely, public awareness about road safety is broadcast far and wide in government funded campaigns to help reduce the rate of accidents. We drive cars fitted with multiple safety devices, are legally required to wear seatbelts, adhere to the speed limit and know not to drink and drive. This information is communicated via television commercials, radio and on social media. By comparison, simple practices such as counting kicks and monitoring a baby's movement, which can in some cases help prevent stillbirth, are not spoken of broadly or even directly between health professionals and expectant mothers. In no way do I wish to pit the impact of one loss against another, but these figures highlight the lack of public awareness and education surrounding stillbirth.

The Adelaide-based charity Still Aware is Australia's only charity exclusively dedicated to raising awareness of stillbirth. Through education, action and prevention, it aims to see a 20 per cent reduction in preventable stillbirth by 2025 and to lift the level of stillbirth understanding to that of SIDS. This organisation is empowering women to monitor and record their baby's movements in utero and to take action if any changes occur. Due to the work of this incredible charity and so many more, I hope over time we will change and evolve the dialogue surrounding miscarriage and stillbirth. I am optimistic that the next generation will possess both the awareness and the confidence to speak openly of any worries they have during pregnancy.

In my first pregnancy, I spent so much time thinking about what we would name our baby, and what kind of cot and pram to buy. It seemed so important at the time, but in the greater scheme of things, such preoccupations were inconsequential and pointless. There was no mention that anything could go wrong with the pregnancy. People don't want to burst your bubble of innocence and happy anticipation. We brush aside and bury deep the ugly reality that not all babies make it, which reinforces the taboo. Sharing is not for everyone, but we do need to give future mothers the tools to cope with what may befall them. Babies are lost and it is crucial that women in the future do not face this heartache without some prior knowledge of what is involved both physically and emotionally. We owe it to them to make sure they do not feel alone and isolated in their grief.

If I'd had a miscarriage before doing research for this book, I would have had no idea what to do. I would probably have called my husband and my doctor, but apart from that, I would have had no idea what lay ahead, what the physical process was, or what would happen to me and my baby. I shudder at the thought that women will continue to fall down this rabbit hole of baby loss completely unaware of what it is like and without the comfort of knowing what their options are. And what I dislike even more is that people will continue to feel that their grief is unworthy and not to be shared, because this topic has such a stigma attached. By sharing our stories, we create a safe environment in which other women feel safe, hopefully giving them the confidence to tell their own stories, knowing that they will be met with understanding and support.

Kristina Keneally, former Premier of New South Wales, tragically gave birth to her stillborn daughter Caroline in 1999. She has campaigned tirelessly since to raise public awareness about stillbirth and was instrumental in coordinating the 2019 'Select Senate Inquiry on Stillbirth', which helped to secure much-needed funding for research, prevention, education and the support of bereaved parents. Kristina has spoken about the stigma and silence surrounding stillbirth: "Remaining silent has meant we don't talk about it. It's meant we don't address it. It's meant that stillbirth has been a tragedy people have suffered in silence. We viewed it as a private tragedy, not a public health problem. And it is a public health problem."

Baby loss as a whole seems to finally be coming out of the shadows and I can only hope this helps people talk about it more freely. That is why I tell my story. I hope other people will feel that they, too, can speak out as much or as little as they feel comfortable with. I hope they see that they won't be dismissed as being overly emotional, self-indulgent, or too absorbed in their grief. Baby loss is a very real loss and it's time to recognise just how significant it is and how big the ongoing effects are. We need to look after our mothers, give them the care they need, equip them with the information before and the tools after to best cope with the loss of a baby at any stage of pregnancy. It also needs to become routine practice that women are told how and when to monitor their baby's movements and not to hesitate to report changes. At the end of this book, I have listed several charities that offer counselling services and information about pregnancy loss at various stages. There is incredible support out there and many passionate volunteers who work tirelessly to make sure people do not endure this heartache alone.

Chapter 9 Baby loss in early pregnancy

For this book I spoke to many women who have suffered miscarriages to build on my understanding of baby loss beyond that of stillbirth and develop a deeper consideration of what they endure. There are some obvious physical differences however I believe that many, if not most of the feelings are the same: the emptiness, loss of hopes and dreams, and the sense of isolation.

Both miscarriage and stillbirth are confronting physical ordeals. Miscarriages can occur naturally, however it's also common that surgery or medicinal intervention is required to ensure the pregnancy has passed safely. These processes and the decisions relating to them can be terrifying and confronting, especially when coupled with heartache and shock.

Like some of the women I spoke to who miscarried before 12 weeks, you may not have told family and friends about your pregnancy before the point at which your baby died. To lose a baby, and then endure the grief that follows without people knowing, denies women adequate support and places them in the incredibly confronting position of having to simultaneously announce a pregnancy and tell people that the baby has died. Everyone responds differently to miscarriage; some people are able to work through their loss and rationalise it quickly, while others are overcome with grief. There is no set way to react and grieve; however you feel is valid and it's important that you give yourself permission to fully embrace the emotions within you. Some women have said that the impact of their loss didn't hit them until they endured a second miscarriage or were navigating a pregnancy after the loss. We are all so different, but none of us should have to go down this path alone.

To be completely honest, I didn't think stillbirth and miscarriage were similar when I first lost Miles. I felt that because stillbirth was less common and occurred later in a pregnancy, it was more traumatic and harder to cope with. I soon came to realise that pain cannot be measured by gestation, size or time. Nor can it be quantified by how you delivered your baby or how you were able to bond with your baby afterwards. How you respond is related to you as an individual, how your experience has affected you, and such a thing should never be compared with others. I can willingly raise my hand and say that initially I had it wrong, very wrong.

To think that so many women have been through miscarriage and not had adequate support makes me feel uncomfortable and also quite ashamed of my own ignorance and lack of understanding. I can now see that we are all mothers who have lost a child. The details of when and how do not dictate the depth or intensity of the feelings that follow.

Studies have shown that post-traumatic stress syndrome, depression and anxiety are relatively common after miscarriage. It is an event that can have ongoing implications in a woman's life, and as a society we need to get better at acknowledging the trauma and pain of miscarriage. Women's grief should not be brushed off with clichés like, *lucky it was so early, there must have been something wrong with it anyway,* or *at least you know you can get pregnant.* These simply aim to push aside and belittle the pain, they are an attempt to shift the focus to something positive in a time that for those enduring the loss, is likely to be incredibly dark. Women are also inclined to blame themselves for a miscarriage, when most of the time it had absolutely nothing to do with anything they have done.

Miscarriages often go unexplained, with no cause ever found, which could lead the mother to assume that perhaps it was something she did, when in reality, it was most probably the result of something occurring on a cellular level that sadly resulted in the pregnancy not continuing – something that none of us can ever have any control over.

Another common feeling after miscarriage is failure. A sense of inadequacy that their body wasn't able to create and sustain a viable pregnancy. Miscarriage and stillbirth have many things in common; one of the most heartbreaking is that the death of your child occurs within your own body, or shortly after leaving your body. Usually there is nothing you can do to prevent, control or stop it from happening. It is also highly unlikely that it has happened because of anything you have done or through any physical fault that is under your control. It is simply a tragic event, the outcome of which you cannot alter.

Instinctively as mothers, we want to keep our children away from harm and this begins in early pregnancy. At this early stage, it is our job to carry the baby and keep it safe. I suppose this is why the loss of a baby can feel like a failure; it was your body in which the child lived, but this alone cannot protect them completely or change their course. You could not have done anything differently and, hand on heart, most mothers know that, but feelings of guilt can run wild. So even though it is understandable to blame yourself for the exercise class you took, the cold chicken salad or the tiny sip of champagne, please don't. A miscarriage is highly unlikely to be your fault.

Sadly, miscarriage is relatively common, which in no way minimises the pain felt by each woman who endures it. It seems strange that such a common occurrence is not spoken of openly. This has prompted me to give a great deal of thought into why we have to hide our pregnancies until we reach this safe zone of twelve weeks. Is there ever really a safe point? If women do share their news early and then miscarry, I have heard of such comments being made as, "Well it was very early, she probably shouldn't have told anyone yet". This is utterly irrelevant. A baby has died. A mother has endured immense physical and emotional pain and needs support. It also implies that if your pregnancy news becomes sad, it would be better off for everyone if you didn't share it at all. If you haven't told anyone that you are pregnant in the first place, you then won't have to follow this up with the sad news of your loss. After losing a baby at the stage of pregnancy I did, it was impossible to hide the news. Most people knew we were having a baby. Losing a baby early on is often kept quiet, forcing women to handle their heartache in secret. Forcing women to return to work when they are still in the initial throes of grief, not to mention also recovering physically. Some women are able to use what limited sick days they are entitled to, but very little else is offered, especially to women who hold casual positions.

The way the impact of early pregnancy loss is often dismissed is incredibly unfair. People saw Miles as our child, not a medical incident or a failed pregnancy. Miles, however, is not all that different to a baby lost at eight or forteen weeks. I felt love for Miles as strongly at six, eight and twelve weeks as I did when he was born. From the minute I saw the two lines on a pregnancy test and his heartbeat at the first ultrasound, he was my baby, the next family member. I cannot imagine having to endure the grief that came after without having the option and opportunity to speak of it openly and publicly. Sadly for many who encounter miscarriage, their grief is disenfranchised and not given the same level of understanding.

Medically, miscarriage is sometimes treated in a very clinical manner and spoken of in terms of statistics and procedures rather than emotions and feelings. Perhaps the language surrounding it is efficient and medical by way of necessity: The medical world does need these definitions and guidelines for treatment in order to work safely and efficiently to look after patients' physical wellbeing. But terms such as 'blighted ovum', 'evacuation of products of conception' and 'incompetent cervix' are impersonal, and can have derogatory connotations which dehumanise the loss. Support or counselling is not routinely offered after a miscarriage and in the setting of an emergency department, a miscarriage is not seen as a medical emergency, unless it is an ectopic pregnancy. I can see how this would make someone who has had or is having a miscarriage feel like their loss is being treated as a common and insignificant event. Physically it may not be medically high-risk or rare, but emotionally the implications are enormous, long-term and incredibly personal.

It is also important that governments and health organisations begin to see the ongoing effects baby loss can have on families who encounter it and in turn begin to train the staff who will care for and counsel patients on the front line. I can only imagine that it is deeply traumatic and confronting for professionals in these positions and they too need to be adequately educated and supported. If doctors, midwives and sonographers are not given adequate guidance as to how to deliver news, how to communicate with patients and how to best manage these situations, how can we expect them all to do so with an appropriate level of sensitivity and empathy? By speaking of the ongoing psychological impact of good care versus poor care, I hope we will help to create protocols by which a patient's emotional needs are taken into consideration as much as their physical needs. I imagine that 99% of health care providers are instinctively empathetic and do their absolute best to support women through this kind of ordeal, but sadly some women are not cared for appropriately and this can add to the trauma.

It seems absurd to me that as a woman nearing forty, no one had ever told me what it felt like physically to have a miscarriage. I had wrongly assumed it was like an extended heavy period, which is a common misconception. I had no idea of how drawn-out and painful it can be. I never knew that some women have contractions, go through a process very similar to labour, are at risk of hemorrhage and pass large blood clots. To go through this at home, without medical support, would be utterly terrifying. Friends who'd had miscarriages had quietly shared their news, but I had never felt it was appropriate to ask them what they had gone through physically. I knew that they were struggling emotionally but assumed they didn't want to share any other details of their experience. Perhaps they had wanted to, but felt uncomfortable and didn't know where to begin. Perhaps I never asked the right questions. I'm sure I am not alone in this and that many people are scared of asking the wrong thing and overstepping boundaries. We have a long way to go in finding the right balance.

Movements like *I am 1 in 4* and *I had a miscarriage* will hopefully, over time, lift the lid on the silence and empower women to start speaking openly of early baby loss. Women (and men) need support and should not feel like they have to remain quiet. It will not suit everyone to shout their story from the rooftops, and nor do I expect everyone to be as comfortable speaking openly as I am, but it would be nice to think that in the future we are all afforded the opportunity to share without fear of judgement.

Some of the ways I sought comfort after losing Miles may not be relevant or meaningful to everyone, but I hope that overall my sentiments will resonate with others and bring comfort, and perhaps some ideas about how to remember your baby. I hope that as you read about how I felt and how I grieved you will think, at times, *Me too. Thank goodness I'm not the only one who feels this way.*

Chapter 10 Miscarriage, Eleanor's story

A heartbreakingly honest and raw Instagram post about baby loss caught my attention. It was beautifully penned by beauty editor and founder of Gritty Pretty, Eleanor Pendleton, about the miscarriage she and her husband sadly endured. The heartfelt way in which she shared and spoke of her grief moved me deeply, so I reached out to her to ask if I could include her story in my book. She was incredibly willing to do so and we arranged to speak soon after.

Her Instagram post featured a beautiful poem by Christy Ann Martine

Little dove I love you so
but I know you had to go.
So spread your wings
and fly my love,
soar above the world my dove.
Paint the sky in indigo,
let your graceful colours flow
and I'll search the sky
for your rainbow.

Eleanor went on to share the utter anguish which followed her loss: "In January this year, my and my husband's world was turned upside down. The little life inside of me I loved so deeply so quickly had its own heartbeat and when it stopped beating unexplainably, our world stopped spinning. In the weeks that followed my pregnancy loss, my way of taking control was to commit to grieving healthily and privately. I took a few days off work (albeit not enough), making space for the life we had loved and lost — the baby of our hopes and dreams. I confided in my beautiful husband, my family, and my closest girlfriends. I saw healers, acupuncturists, my doctor and a psychologist to help process our loss. I tried to control a situation I had zero control over. I struggled to surrender and accept that our loss was caused for reasons that were completely beyond our control."

I asked Eleanor what those early days were like. "When I look back now, those immediate days after are a complete blur. We miscarried on 27 January and I remember it like it was yesterday. It was the day after Australia Day. We had been at the beach the day before having a barbecue with friends and I felt pregnant. I told my best, best friend as I'd seen her that day. Then the following day, I started bleeding in the morning and I think I just knew. I just had this awful, awful feeling. It wasn't right. And I tried to put it out of my head and I said to my husband, 'Look, I just need to go out, we need to go to the beach. I need to have a swim, I just need to get in the ocean.' I got home and the bleeding had continued and it was very, very clear that I was in the middle of a miscarriage.

"It is devastating. I'm very aware that everyone's loss, in particular miscarriage can be very different or some people can experience a missed miscarriage and have that devastating experience of finding out in the sonographer's office. We didn't have that, we had a natural miscarriage. Neither way is better, it's all really, really shit. So my husband took me to the hospital, we went to emergency and they took my bloods and confirmed that I was in the middle of a miscarriage. The whole thing is such a blur.

"I just remember when it did happen and we were back at home. I went to the bathroom and it was very clear what was happening and I cried like an animal cry. I couldn't ever recreate that sound. It was like a primal scream almost. My husband and I held each other and we just cried and cried and cried. It was awful.

"We had to book a scan for an early pregnancy loss assessment. That was a few days after because it was a public holiday. So I couldn't actually go back to the hospital until maybe three or four days later. Then we went back to the hospital in that strange stage of grief where you've lost your baby, the baby you wanted but then everything has to follow, the medical appointments and so on.

"I kind of remember, I think for the first few days I just laid in bed. I don't remember. I almost don't remember it. I felt a deep sadness I've never felt before. I've never really experienced that level of grief. And I think, miscarriage, pregnancy loss and stillbirth, it's the closest type of grief you can have because that life is a part of you. My first few days were just spent in a daze; I'd never felt so dark in all my life.

"And somehow you still function, somehow you get to the hospital and you still have your assessments. I met with this beautiful nurse and she sat there and cried with me, she was divine. It was lucky that she decided I didn't need a D&C because I was passing naturally. She felt that it was best to let nature take its course and let my body do what it was already doing. So I think I just spent those first few days in this weird, weird bubble. You're just functioning and you're breathing and you're waking up. It's kind of like you're not there, but you are.

"And it's hard to find the words, I guess, but I remember journaling. In the days that followed, I wrote a letter to my baby. I just wrote pages and pages and pages. In the first few days it's hard to think about anything else – the first seven days for me were the darkest I've ever, ever experienced. I just felt like I had to be completely wrapped in darkness. By the end of that first week, my husband said, 'I think we need to do something to say goodbye.'

And it was definitely a form of healing and for the two of us. So we just went down to our local beach and we popped a beautiful rose into the water and that was really nice."

Like many women, Eleanor was searching for answers: "I remember going onto my phone and you go down that stupid rabbit hole and you find these ridiculous forums. But you're just trying to find out why has this happened to me? What is wrong with me? Why did my body do this? Is there hope? Will I fall pregnant again and have a baby? All those things. And I remember, being like, I'm an intelligent woman, a very strong and capable one but I remember at one point I just felt so hopeless that I googled, 'Will I ever be happy after a miscarriage?'

"I think for me, I'm such a control freak with elements of my life, I run a business and I have control over what happens in my life. I felt unable to control a situation for the first time in many, many years. It took the control out of my hands. I couldn't stop the miscarriage, I couldn't prevent the miscarriage. I couldn't bring that baby back. And I think that's what I struggled with the most. But then I tried to use that sense of no control to control my grief. I decided that whatever I would feel, I would feel it. I've never been one to suppress emotion. When I feel emotion, I feel it. I am not scared of it. So when I would sit there in fetal position, I needed to be left like that for a while.

"I told my best friends and my family who we had told that we were pregnant and I leaned on them as hard as I could. They got me through it so much. My husband got me through it. We were surrounded by a support network who made sure we were eating, as at that stage I was only just able to get up in the morning."

Eleanor also found huge comfort in seeking professional help. "I went to speak with my GP, who then referred me on to a grief counsellor and psychologist. I took that upon myself, and my husband and I both went for the first couple of sessions and then I just kept going back. I always kind of tried to control it. I just was like, okay, I need to do whatever I can to get through."

"I think that's the thing. We all respond to grief so differently and everyone's experience of loss is so, so very different. And I think what I've learned is there's no right or wrong way, but if you can do anything it is to feel whatever you're feeling. I definitely went through bouts of anger. I just remember being really, really fucking angry and saying to my husband, 'We are good people. You're healthy. I'm healthy. Why the fuck did this baby die?' And I just remember being so angry, but I had to, I knew I had to feel it. And once the anger had passed, then it was just like a deep sadness and learning to feel that too.

"I felt at the same time, even though I had moments of feeling quite lonely, I always felt supported. I had the most incredible, beautiful husband and the most amazing network of women around me. Sadly, most of my friends have experienced loss. I kind of had this weird fear when I was pregnant the first time that I was going to miscarry, I was really anxious that I would. After the miscarriage I was like, did I manifest it because I was always scared and did I bring that upon myself?"

In her Instagram post Eleanor made some really important observations about grief and how other people react to it and how they can best respond to someone who has lost a baby. "One of the things loss has taught me is that YOUR grief can make OTHER people uncomfortable. People will naturally say what they feel will best comfort you; always coming from a good, kind place. Before I lost my baby I never truly understood what a woman who had suffered a miscarriage was going through. Now this chapter is part of my story, it's part of my truth." Eleanor shared the following recommendations of what to say — and what's best not to say to a woman or couple experiencing loss:

DON'T SAY:

'This one just wasn't meant to be.'

DO SAY:

'Feel whatever you need to feel and for as long as you need to. Be kind to yourself.'

DON'T SAY:

'At least you know you can get pregnant.'

DO SAY:

'I'm so very sorry for your loss.'

"For me, this one stung the most. Why? Because I believe no loss of life, of any kind, should EVER be comforted with the words 'at least' opening a sentence.

"If you don't know what to say simply do this: write a sympathy note, send a meal delivery, allow that person to make space and acknowledge their baby's life that was lost; the family they thought they were going to have and the memories they thought they were going to make. Everybody grieves in their own way and every person's loss is dealt with differently."

After her miscarriage Eleanor had to continue to have blood taken multiple times to make sure her HCG, the hormone levels which rise incrementally in early pregnancy, were returning to normal. In the middle of taking blood, one nurse asked her how many weeks pregnant she was even though the form clearly stated 'bloods post pregnancy loss' and Eleanor quite naturally burst into tears and said, "I lost my baby." The nurse didn't apologise or say anything at all after this: "She had nothing to say and I remember that devastated me. Much the same as comments made by well-meaning friends who haven't experienced loss and don't understand the enormity of what you're dealing with, whereas when you have been through it, you know how to handle those situations with the utmost sensitivity."

I could relate so much to Eleanor when she said that "when you are sitting in the rawest part after your loss and you wanted this baby more than anything, you planned for this baby more than anything, and you've lost this baby, just to have to have anyone, it doesn't matter who it is, whether it's your close friend or a stranger or an acquaintance, to have anyone say anything that's possibly dismissive, it kind of almost sweeps your loss under the rug. I think it really, really hurts and I found great (offence).

"That's why I actually made those kinds of recommendations in my (Instagram) post because I understand that those people generally are coming from a really kind, beautiful place and they only want to make you feel better, and if they could take away your pain, they would. But there are just simple things that I think should never ever be said. Those two particular things for me, the 'you can get pregnant' and that 'it wasn't meant to be', those ones, I just don't think they should ever be said. You would never say if someone died of cancer, 'Oh, at least they had a good life'."

Another question / comment which was particularly painful for Eleanor after her loss was, "When will you have kids?" She wrote: "I would become filled with such anger that they felt they could ask any woman such a deeply personal question that I'd often snap back telling them that it was none of their business (even though deep down I knew they only meant well)." This question is so painful to navigate after loss or if you are struggling with infertility, it can cut deeply, just as being exposed to other pregnancies can. "I'd see a pregnant woman crossing the street and burst into tears in public. I'd hear an ad on the radio for infertility and want to smash my fist against the car dash. Seeing pregnancy announcements on social media became increasingly hard. I'd speak to someone who would joyfully tell me their baby was due in September, like our baby was, and I'd smile, put on a brave face and offer them my sincerest congratulations, feeling a pang in my broken heart."

The response to Eleanor's post was immense. She invited other women to share their stories in the comments below it and was overwhelmed by the visceral outpouring of grief that followed. She felt privileged that she had been able to speak openly of her loss and had been supported unwaveringly by those around her, as many others are not as fortunate.

"I felt so much sadness for the women who contacted me and said they were going through it alone or they had never told a single soul. The only person who knew was their partner and they couldn't even tell their parents. So many women contacted me and said that they grieved in solitude and they really regretted that. I was dumbfounded by the amount of women who contacted me saying that." The responses reinforced the very reason she decided to so bravely share her story with her social media community.

"I thought long and hard about whether I would share my loss with you all. At first, my answer was simple: No. I wasn't ready. But throughout my sadness and developing anxiety that now, six months later, I finally feel on top of, I also felt dishonest by not sharing my truth. I felt I had to pretend I was okay when I simply wasn't. I'm not ashamed of my miscarriage — no woman should be. So today I've decided to use my platform to let those know who have experienced it or are currently experiencing their own loss: you are not alone. In Australia one 1 in 4 of all pregnancies will end in miscarriage. As the majority of my 80,000 followers are women, many of you will have experienced a loss of your own. If you haven't (and I hope you never do), it's highly likely you know someone else who has.

"By sharing my own story, in my own time, I hope I can help break down the stigmas surrounding miscarriage. Miscarriage isn't a dirty word. We shouldn't feel alone or afraid or uncomfortable for talking about it."

We also spoke about the stifling taboo that surrounds baby loss and infertility, especially given that Eleanor knows only too well "it's so ridiculously common. I know they say it's one in four, but when we were at emergency, the doctor said to me, 'It's probably more like one in three.' And that sense of shame, the shame that follows, it's so strange. I remember my husband, Matt, and I were talking about it. We were just like, it's sort of strange that couples and women in particular feel that afterwards, it's such a weird archaic thing, it's so bizarre. I think the more that people are willing to talk about it, and I think it is slowly happening, but the more people can talk about it, slowly I think those walls of taboo can come down. A lot of people assume that it's so easy to fall pregnant, and then you reach that stage of your life and you realise it's nowhere near easy."

Trying to move forward after loss is incredibly difficult and requires a lot of energy. "People would ask how I was doing and I'd lie saying, 'I'm good thanks'. There are steps forward and many backwards, grief is a long and arduous journey."

In the months following her loss Eleanor says she, "slowly but eventually found joy again. I laughed with my husband again, I danced at friends' weddings. I drank Champagne (a lot). I threw myself into work. I tried to forget about our pain. Then, just when I thought I was getting 'better', like the rising tide that grief is, it would hit me like a crashing wave all over again, smashing me to the ground like a raging shore dumper."

For both Eleanor and me, the desire to have another baby was a strong and undeniable urge after our losses and trying to fall pregnant again was an integral part of our healing process, even though this in itself brought with it different fears and a sense of guilt about the baby who wasn't able to stay with us. "My heart in particular breaks for women who haven't been able to have children following loss. Human beings are so resilient but for me my form of healing was, I just have to get pregnant, I need a baby in my hands, in my arms for the rest of my life and that's the only way I'm going to get over this. I can't see another way of moving on or recovering from miscarriage." We both agreed that any babies born after loss were because of our angel babies, not instead of or a replacement for them.

We talked about navigating the due date of the babies we lost and both agreed that it is a date filled with sadness and intense emotion. "I'm definitely nervous about my first due date coming around. I don't know how I'm going to feel on that day or if I'm going to do anything." These dates can bring up so many painful memories of the days surrounding pregnancy loss. Looking back is still hard. "It's an awful time, I don't think anyone can put into words what it's like when you're in that really, really, raw part. I think it's healthy to feel it. It's a healthy way of processing all of the emotions and it's the best way that you can deal with it. Anyone who isn't able to process loss or suppresses fear and all of their emotions so to speak, I think it definitely extends their grieving process."

Eleanor spoke so openly of the unwavering support she had from her husband Matt. "I do think that we grieved differently and now six months down the track I see the beauty in it and I'm almost glad that we did. But I'm also very grateful for the fact that I have the most beautiful husband who is so in touch with emotion. We have always had such a very open communicative relationship and we can talk about anything, so he didn't shut down or suppress his feelings or anything like that. We talked about our loss as much as we both needed to and I feel really lucky in that sense."

There were of course a few little bumps in the road, which is completely natural during every couple's journey after loss. Eleanor recounted one occasion that still fills her with feelings of deep shame and regret. "I do remember and I feel terrible about it, that maybe a few weeks down the track he seemed okay. I just remember being so angry, so this was obviously my stage of anger, and I remember being so angry and saying, 'How the fuck can you just be okay? You can go to work and you can still go surfing and you don't give a fuck about our baby!' And afterwards I felt disgusting. I felt so bad that I'd said that to him because he looked gutted. When I said that he replied, 'That was my baby too.' I still feel so bad for this moment of anger".

"I think it's only normal that they grieve differently. I remember Matt saying to me, 'I am obviously devastated too', and I've never seen him hurt the way he did the day we lost the baby. But he did say to me, 'You are my number one priority.' Given that we don't have living children yet, he just said to me, 'My focus is on you.' He focused everything he had on looking after me and making sure I was okay, and I think therefore he was directing his grief in a different way.

"I definitely believe that men and women grieve differently and I don't blame him in any way for grieving differently. I think we should grieve differently because we as women are different. I don't think it's physically or biologically possible for anyone else to be closer to that life than us. When that life has grown inside of you I think it's only natural that we are so, so deeply connected and that we grieve much harder."

After hearing Eleanor's story and talking to her so openly and candidly about her grief, I felt less alone and could relate so much to how she felt. Her bravery in sharing her loss on Instagram no doubt also brought a great deal of comfort to many women. Not everyone is able to tell their story and sharing publicly takes a great deal of courage. Knowing this, Eleanor recognised this in her post: "I'm fortunate to have a voice and a large female community on this platform, so I'm sharing my loss publicly for the women who can't or don't want to but need to know there are others like them – just like me."

The tide is slowly turning and I hope in the near future we will all feel comfortable in sharing our stories and not feel that we have to bury them alongside the hopes and dreams we held for the baby we lost. Thank you so much Eleanor for telling your story.

Chapter 11 A little life, not a little loss

I feel, and truly hope that society's response to miscarriage is starting to change. In time, miscarriage will surely no longer be seen as women's business which should be kept quiet, nor as an unfortunate medical event. The World Health Organization published a study on miscarriage and stillbirth in early 2019, which shone light on the long-lasting emotional effects miscarriage can have on women. Titled 'Why we need to talk about losing a baby', the introduction reads:

"Losing a baby in pregnancy through miscarriage or stillbirth is still a taboo subject worldwide, linked to stigma and shame. Many women still do not receive appropriate and respectful care when their baby dies during pregnancy or childbirth. Here, we share your stories from around the globe.

"Miscarriage is the most common reason for losing a baby during pregnancy. Estimates vary, although March of Dimes, an organisation that works on maternal and child health, indicates a miscarriage rate of 10-15% in women who knew they were pregnant. Pregnancy loss is defined differently around the world. Every year, 2.6 million babies are stillborn, and many of these deaths are preventable. However, miscarriages and stillbirths are not systematically recorded, even in developed countries, suggesting that the numbers could be even higher.

"Around the world, women have varied access to healthcare services, and hospitals and clinics in many countries are very often under-resourced and understaffed. As varied as the experience of losing a baby may be, around the world, stigma, shame and guilt emerge as common themes. (sic) Women who lose their babies are made to feel that should stay silent about their grief, either because miscarriage and stillbirth are still so common, or because they are perceived to be unavoidable."

Reading something so powerful and compassionate on the topic of baby loss strengthened my resolve to keep sharing my experience after losing Miles. To see a global health organisation as influential and respected as WHO recognise baby loss as a traumatic life event gave me confidence and helped to validate my feelings. I also felt that it addressed the ongoing impact baby loss can have and challenged the stereotype that because it is common, it should therefore not be so difficult to deal with. The study also identifies themes of guilt and blaming oneself for miscarriage, as well as sharing many stories from around the world. It says that after experiencing miscarriage, women face many mental and emotional hurdles.

"All of this takes an enormous toll on women. Many women who lose a baby in pregnancy can go on to develop mental health issues that last for months or years – even when they have gone on to have healthy babies.

"There are many reasons why a miscarriage may happen, including fetal abnormalities, the age of the mother, and infections, many of which are preventable such as malaria and syphilis, though pinpointing the exact reason is often challenging.

"General advice on preventing miscarriage focuses on eating healthily, exercising, avoiding smoking, drugs and alcohol, limiting caffeine, controlling stress, and being of a healthy weight. This places the emphasis on lifestyle factors, which, in the absence of specific answers, can lead to women feeling guilty that they have caused their miscarriage."

Other common themes identified in the study were the silence and stigma attached to baby loss. Many times, I felt there were no opportunities or welcome environments for me to talk about how I was feeling after losing Miles and this increased my feelings of isolation and despair. My comments were sometimes met with a tilt of a head and a sad face, which indicated sympathy, but nothing more was said to invite further conversation. After a while, people stopped asking how I was, even though I was still feeling incredibly sad and working out how to find my way through everyday life with the added burden of grief.

Also noted in the report is the general reticence people have towards talking about death and dying. "As with other health issues such as mental health, around which there is tremendous taboo still, many women report that no matter their culture, education or upbringing, their friends and family do not want to talk about their loss. This seems to connect with the silence that shrouds talking about grief in general."

The study identifies ways in which those supporting the bereaved can help them and what they can say and highlights the importance of compassionate medical care. Couples need sensitivity and empathy, not to be treated as medical statistics or routine procedures. The final statement sums everything up beautifully: "The unacceptable stigma and shame women face after baby loss must end".

Chapter 12 Best practice for early pregnancy loss

I interviewed Associate Professor George Condous, who founded the first and only Acute Gynaecology Unit in Australia, which is based in Nepean Hospital in Sydney and utilises ultrasound as the first point of contact for women with emergency gynaecology as well as early pregnancy complications, primarily miscarriage and ectopic pregnancy. I wanted to find out what he thought was 'best practice' for the care of women who realise they have encountered an urgent problem in early pregnancy, or have begun to miscarry their baby. I was curious to know if there were standardised national procedures in place or if women were at the mercy of the healthcare facilities they presented to. I also wanted to ask him about what training was given to doctors in this area and how we can best train healthcare professionals to give compassionate and tactful care during a traumatic time in a person's life.

George is passionate about the emotional and physical wellbeing of his patients and recognises that pregnancy loss is traumatic and that it is natural to grieve for this loss. In his opinion, training in how to offer appropriate support to patients when delivering bad news "should happen at medical school." He noted that "although psychiatry was one of our core subjects in fifth year and we did speak a bit about the concept of the grieving process, it's not very well taught and it's not necessarily well delivered either." George surmised that the care patients receive is therefore dependent on the individual nature of their doctor and his or her own personal experiences, their exposure to adverse situations and baby loss specifically. He noted that this care is also "usually based on whether someone has good interpersonal skills or otherwise. It's a lottery for the patient, and for their partner, and so from that perspective I would think that training would need to be looked at from medical student days onwards." He feels this is important in all areas of medicine and would hopefully have a positive "impact on the delivery of news in relation to cancer diagnosis, delivery of news in relation to a relative dying", and many other diagnoses doctors deliver daily.

George also feels that it is vital "when dealing with people who are going through a loss to balance your response. You don't want to be apathetic, because obviously that is inappropriate, you don't want to be sympathetic because then you're almost over-compensating and becoming part of the grieving process, but you need to be empathetic and so getting that balance right sometimes just doesn't happen. It's about knowing the difference between sympathy, empathy and apathy, there is a spectrum and you want to try and hopefully pitch it in the right part of that spectrum."

From my own experiences, both good and bad, I know firsthand just how big an impact the way your doctor delivers distressing news can have. In a situation that is already traumatic, not being shown adequate empathy can compound any fear, guilt, confusion and isolation the patient may be feeling, and that is the last thing someone about to lose a much-wanted baby needs on top of grief and heartache.

George also feels that for anyone who endures a pregnancy loss, it's really important for them to hear from a medical professional that they should not blame themselves. One of the things he always says is, "You haven't done anything wrong, it's not your fault." George is well aware that many women feel intense guilt after the loss of a baby and they need to be reassured they have not caused

it, and in most circumstances they couldn't have done anything to
stop it from happening. If this sentiment is given by someone with
vast experience in this area, it may carry more weight than similar
comments made by friends and family wanting to reassure women
who may be feeling responsible.

I also asked George if women who have miscarriages are
routinely sent to or offered any counselling or support from social
workers. He felt that this happened on occasion but not routinely,
as in general, women are less likely after early pregnancy loss to be
offered emotional support. It is often up to the women themselves
to seek support and George felt that this is why it's so important
"'to get support networks like The Pink Elephants Network out
there" and make sure women are aware of the counselling services
they offer.

George has worked in and studied early pregnancy loss since
completing his training in obstetrics and gynaecology in London,
after which he worked as a Senior Research Fellow at St George's
Hospital. There he set up the hospital's Acute Gynaecology unit
and upon returning to Australia, he saw the vast difference between
services and care available to women in Australia in comparison to
what is offered in the UK. George notes that the "problem with
some of our early pregnancy services is that it's different to the
UK. In the UK they tend to be walk-in services whereas here (in
Australia) you need to be referred from an emergency department
or your GP."

The impact of this is most evident because as George recalls, "In
the UK what happens is that there is a dedicated service. It's usually
run by midwives and there is a lead consultant who usually looks
after the whole unit and so there is consistency in the approach
to women regardless of whether they have an ectopic pregnancy, a
pregnancy loss or a pregnancy which will continue, so it's always

very protocol driven in that sense. It works well as there is consistency." A walk-in service also means that there is no need for women to seek a referral before presenting to an early pregnancy loss unit.

By contrast in Australia, he observes that there is very little routine or standardised care offered when a woman starts to miscarry a pregnancy. "In Australia, for example, someone might come to an Early Pregnancy Unit (EPU) and be seen by a very junior doctor, they then get sent to radiology, perhaps in the fetal medicine unit where ultrasound is done and they are having to wait with heavily pregnant women also having ultrasounds, then they go back to the EPU by which time their consultant may have left as by now it's the afternoon and they see someone who has just started their shift, who has no idea what has been going on. They are then reviewed, (but not by the lead consultant who runs the service) and probably told to come back the next day. They are then usually seen by a different consultant. So if you present with a miscarriage say on a Monday, you might go to surgery, if you present on a Wednesday that person may give you medicine to discontinue the pregnancy". There is no uniform approach, it is dependent on the consultant on duty.

From his perspective, the issue with this is that "when you've got such a varied approach, these women are not being looked after particularly well. Then you throw into the mix that they're going through a grieving process and the whole thing is disastrous. But that is the pathway." There are some alternatives to this but they are not geographically available to everyone. The only option for many may be to present to an emergency department or your local GP. The care in his own Early Pregnancy Unit is very different to this. "Where I am at the Nepean, because I am the lead consultant we have the same approach to everybody, Monday, Tuesday,

Wednesday, Thursday and Friday. So everything is the same, and women get managed the same way and we are lucky because we've got good services with our physiological support across the road from us. I'm lucky because we have the same doctors on everyday scanning as well.

"I still think that we could have midwives involved and getting them to be involved with the scanning and the management because they tend to see that much more often, they're well versed in it and they're motivated to look after women from that perspective as with all aspects of pregnancy, but that comes with funding. Also the whole early pregnancy area because it's part of gynaecology and not deemed to be part of obstetrics has different training. The training in it is not great and the understanding of the process is not great and the byproduct is poor care for the couple."

After talking to George and learning about the compassionate and consistent way patients who access his EPU are cared for, I feel even more strongly that we need a routine national approach to how women are supported and treated medically and emotionally before and after miscarriage. Women need to be educated about the various options available to them and counselled about what they should expect to encounter, both physically and mentally, whichever path they choose to take. Sadly many women present to emergency departments only to be told to go home and return to a different department for an ultrasound the following day as their situation is not considered a medical emergency, unless an ectopic pregnancy is suspected. While I completely understand this from a clinical perspective, I can imagine it would be terrifying for a woman who is losing a much-wanted baby.

As a result, women are sometimes left to miscarry alone, with little guidance and a lack of understanding of what to expect. I asked George what he would recommend women do in areas where there isn't an Early Pregnancy Loss Unit. Is it better for women to present to their GP or an emergency department? He felt that given "there's always a lot of horror stories associated with the emergency departments, I think unless someone is really unwell and bleeding significantly it's probably better to avoid EDs But then again, sometimes people think that they're having a miscarriage when they might have an ectopic pregnancy and under those circumstances being in an ED is probably not such a bad thing as you will get a full assessment just to make sure there are no signs that there could be something like a ruptured ectopic. But generally speaking, I think that in an ideal world there needs to be accessibility to units that are not necessarily linked to private health insurance because these things happen to everyone and not everyone has a private obstetrician or GP they can call or see immediately. So unfortunately that means that the ED is the first port of call for many women." George hopes that in time and with greater funding we will see an increase in units dedicated to early pregnancy loss run by consultants specially trained in this area.

In 2007 after a woman sadly miscarried her baby in the toilets of the Royal North Shore Hospital in Sydney after presenting to the ED with a threatened miscarriage, an inquiry was launched to determine how women could be better treated in such a situation. As a result, a policy directive was created by New South Wales Health to implement protocols for care. Overall, however, we have a long way to go in addressing this issue. In the meantime, George feels that if women having a miscarriage had better information about what to do or who to call, it would be a very positive step in the right direction.

The Pink Elephant Support Network has excellent information on its site about the different pathways available to women who are faced with delivering their baby in early pregnancy, or when they suspect they are beginning to miscarry a pregnancy. Their guide to miscarriage treatments and procedures can be found alongside extensive support resources on their website. Their aim is to guide and support you through the emotional and physical aspects of early pregnancy loss.

Chapter 13 TFMR the last taboo

Termination for medical reasons -TFMR (or as I like to call it - the last taboo of baby loss), is a deeply painful experience, yet so many people are unaware that it even occurs and many who've been through it are afraid of speaking openly of their experience for fear of judgement. Making the heartbreaking 'decision' to end a much-wanted pregnancy goes against logic, but when a baby is given a life limiting or fatal diagnosis in utero it's a scenario many face.

Abortion is a divisive and emotive topic usually focused on ending an unintended pregnancy (please know I am steadfastly pro-choice). But by its very nature it is fundamentally different to ending a planned and much wanted pregnancy after severe fetal abnormalities are found, yet legally and medically they are bound together. Many women I know who were faced with TFMR had never heard of it until thrust into their own living nightmare of enduring it firsthand.

I've had messages from women haunted by their experience who've never been able to speak openly as they're terrified people may wrongly think they took the 'easy option' or that their grief is not welcome in the baby loss community (it absolutely, without question is). TFMR is a topic which needs to be talked about more freely as it is utterly traumatic and if women are afraid to share their stories they won't get the support they desperately need as they grieve for their baby.

Leading Melbourne obstetrician Professor Lachlan de Crespigny is quoted as saying "In 30 years I have had zero patients who've come to me for an abortion late in pregnancy that hasn't been an agonising decision. They go through such heart-rending stuff to decide what to do." To have the strength and compassion to say goodbye to a much-wanted child to spare them from immense pain is a selfless act of love and never a decision undertaken lightly.

To walk out of a routine pregnancy scan with the knowledge that your beautiful baby is unlikely to survive after birth is gut-wrenching. To go through natural labour to deliver a child who cannot stay is harrowing. To do all this without telling your story for fear of it being misunderstood adds a huge burden to an incredibly dark and distressing time.

In Australia there are still obstetric specialists and maternity hospitals that will not treat patients who decide to interrupt a pregnancy after a fatal or life limiting diagnosis is given. I firmly believe that if you enter a specialist area of medicine, i.e. Obstetrics, you should be willing to give care to your patients at every single stage of their reproductive journey.

If as an OBGYN you feel that abortion is a procedure you are not willing to perform I feel that morally it would be far more logical to choose a different speciality rather than cherry-picking the 'good' parts of a particular area and deciding to forgo the difficult and uncomfortable elements. As you can probably tell I have a very strong opinion on this which has been influenced by my own experience.

If doctors order screening tests during pregnancies but are only willing to continue to care for a patient if the results are favourable I feel that they have no place in this field. To hand over a patient in a time of crisis after unfavourable results are delivered implies judgement which during a traumatic time is highly likely to cause additional psychological damage.

TFMR remains largely unspoken, this is understandable as society doesn't make it an easy topic to raise. But it needs to be talked about so that those who are faced with one of the worst decisions imaginable do not feel overwhelmed with shame and feel forced to remain silent.

I hope one day I will be able to update this chapter to say that TFMR's are now officially referred to as 'medically interrupted pregnancies' or 'compassionate/genetic inductions'. I hope that protocols surrounding the contentious objection of doctors who are morally opposed abortion are reformed, regulated and managed in a far more transparent and empathetic way.

I hope that on a woman's pregnancy record they don't write 'TOP' (termination of pregnancy) in big bold words with no explanation, as the very sight of this line on my own pregnancy record in reference to Miles made my eyes well and my chest tighten every time I saw it. I am pro-choice but I never felt in any way that the word termination or abortion could adequately explain the complexity of my situation or give the TFMR experience the gravity or respect it deserves. Nor does it reflect the deeply painful process parents face in saying goodbye to a much wanted and much-loved baby in unexpected and harrowing circumstances.

Chapter 14 Delivering your baby

When you are faced with the fact that you are going to have to deliver a baby who is incompatible with life, unlikely to survive after birth, or a baby whose heart has stopped beating, you are not only in shock and heartbroken, but you are also required to make incredibly important and confronting decisions about how you will do this and what you will do once your baby is born. You have a plan for your baby and visions of the future, but these must now be cast aside. You are thrust into a new reality, one you haven't asked for and it feels like a living nightmare.

Most commonly, babies born still are delivered vaginally in a hospital setting. In some cases when it is deemed medically necessary, due to previous caesarian deliveries or other medical factors, a caesar is recommended to avoid serious complications and danger to the mother. In Australia, a stillborn baby is classified as having been delivered after twenty weeks gestation or weighing more than 500 grams. A baby born between twelve and twenty weeks is considered a late miscarriage or mid-trimester loss.

If you are in the private medical system the obstetrician who has managed your pregnancy may attend the delivery. However, if you are in the public system, as I was, it is most likely your baby will be delivered in the care of midwives. If you fall into the latter category, the thought of meeting a complete stranger and having them help you through such an ordeal may feel incredibly uncomfortable. This is because the whole situation *is* uncomfortable and unfathomable, to say the very least. But be assured the midwives who are rostered to attend stillbirths are true angels. From the stories I've heard from women who have had to deliver their still babies, the majority have done so with kind and compassionate care by their side.

In some hospitals, there are bereavement midwives who are specially trained to care for mothers who are delivering a stillborn baby. If you are unsure of what to do, reach out to a midwife or an organisation like SANDS (Stillbirth and Neonatal Death Society), which supports women through all kinds of baby loss. They have seen and heard the devastation and may be able to help guide you to hold, meet and ultimately mother your baby after he or she is delivered, or if this is not possible, find other ways to say goodbye. Midwives can help dress and wrap your baby, put together a memory box, take photos for you and give you as much support or as much privacy as you need. Alternatively, if you feel like you are not being handled with adequate compassion, request to see the ward matron and ask to be placed in the care of someone else.

Don't be embarrassed to ask for help: healthcare professionals will not judge you, as they too feel heartbroken for your baby, you and your family and want to make a truly dreadful time as gentle as possible. There is nothing else quite like giving birth to a baby you know will not be coming home with you, so feel at peace with the fact that these incredible professionals have seen this before and are here to help you.

I put the question of pain-relief options to an online post-baby-loss support group I'm part of and the responses varied greatly depending on gestation and private or public care. Overall, it would seem there is no uniform approach, nor a reason why some women are offered every drug imaginable and others are only offered gas and air. It would seem that each patient is at the mercy of their healthcare provider, and this means that options vary greatly between public and private care, as well as the policy of the hospital in which they deliver. I feel women should be given information and access to whatever is going to make a deeply harrowing ordeal more comfortable for them and they should not be forced to endure what the policies of each individual labour unit recommends.

Some women in the group said they needed to feel the pain and rejected any pain relief offered, as enduring the pain was their way of honouring their baby. For them it was a physical act which in some small way illustrated just how much they loved their baby. Others worried the physical pain would overshadow the situation, so they knew they would benefit from pain relief to enable them to endure the emotional toll of birthing their baby. There is no right or wrong way, and I feel so strongly that whatever pathway will serve you best emotionally is the one to take. Ultimately, we face the same conclusion, regardless of how we go through it, and we will need to find the strength to say goodbye to the precious child we have just delivered.

When Miles was delivered, I was overwhelmed with fear, horror, love and pride. I was expecting a warm, screaming newborn, in its place I was handed a still, silent infant. There was no flicker of life, no suggestion that some miracle would occur and he would start breathing. He was already gone. Nothing can quite explain how gut-wrenching this is and I still can't find the words to adequately describe what it was like. In a time you were expecting life, you see and feel death. I had an overwhelming feeling of "What now? What am I supposed to do?"

You kind of know what is expected of you when you deliver a breathing baby. You hold the baby, feed the baby, send out texts announcing this exciting, happy news, share pictures. What on earth are you supposed to do for a baby who has already passed away? You are emotionally at your absolute lowest or perhaps even completely detached from the reality of the situation. I was worried

I wouldn't have the strength or the capacity to make any rational decisions. In this moment it seemed inconceivable that I would have to say goodbye, that I would never get to see, hold or feel my child in the future and watch him grow. The hospital room had an ambience, feel and scent I associated strongly with the arrival of my other children and I had vivid flashbacks of when they were delivered, which compounded the tragedy of Miles' death. Everything seemed so familiar, yet utterly foreign at the same time.

Josh and I also felt differently about what we wanted to do and how we wanted to handle the situation. Josh was content to never hold, be photographed with or spend time with Miles. While I didn't understand this, I had to respect it. I felt the opposite. I didn't want to put Miles down. It did feel strange holding a tiny lifeless baby, perhaps even awkward in some moments, but I knew I needed to do it. Maternal instinct overran the confronting parts of it. I felt almost like I was playing with a doll, something I had not done with genuine intention in thirty years. I've played dolls and had imaginary tea parties with my children and their toys, but always as the facilitator, not the one invested in the fantasy. With Miles, I felt that this was almost what I was doing but it was now my turn to play make-believe.

I wish I had done more with him and for him, but am at peace with what I did do, which I think is all that counts. I wish I'd bathed him and bought some tiny preemie clothes to dress him in rather than using the lacy dresses they have for all stillborn infants in the hospital. These are beautiful hand-sewn gowns made lovingly by volunteers for stillborn babies. As beautiful as they were, they didn't feel like anything I'd dressed my other babies in. But I don't dwell on these things, as there are already too many what ifs and if onlys to deal with and I don't need to add any more to the list. Instead, I wrapped Miles in the same blankets as his brothers.

Carefully swaddling him in the same way as I've always wrapped my babies. It's a process I know well – tight corners and smooth lines, tucking the extra fabric up and around to secure them in their bassinet. Miles looked no different to the others bundled up like this and I love the pictures I have of all my boys swaddled in the same blue stars.

The thing for which I am most grateful are the photographs we had taken by the most beautiful volunteer from Heartfelt Photography. This is an organisation that arranges for professional photographers to visit bereaved parents in hospital and take pictures of their baby or child. Elizabeth took not only the most precious images, but also gave us an enormous amount of comfort by sharing her story of baby loss with us. Fourteen years before, she had lost her first child in very similar circumstances and then studied photography so she could volunteer with Heartfelt and do something in her son's honour. Hearing her journey and her need to do this for her son reinforced the notion that a loss like this would be life changing, eternal and enormous. To hear how she had retrained and redirected her life helped me accept that it was okay to feel as broken as I did. It made me see that it is normal to yearn for ways to remember your child and find ways to include them in your life going forward.

Josh didn't want to stay overnight at the hospital, it was simply too confronting and upsetting for him to contemplate sleeping in a room with his lifeless baby boy. I knew there was no point in insisting he stay, but, absolutely needed to be in the room with Miles. Thankfully, given my surgery and that fact that I still had no feeling in my legs after the spinal block, I would not be discharged until the following morning. For some people, it feels better for the baby not to stay in the room with them, which is also completely understandable. I knew I was on borrowed time so I wanted to make the most of every possible moment with Miles.

Josh brought me dinner, carried me to the shower and helped me wash before lying with me until I fell asleep at about midnight. I slept until 5am and when I woke up, I popped Miles in bed with me. I know it's against 'safe sleeping' rules but I've always loved bringing my babies into bed with me for a cuddle in the morning, so it felt right to do this with Miles. I held him in the crook of my arm, both of us lying down and tried to soak in every little detail of him I possibly could. The sun rose and I felt like we had had our special moment together. It would never, ever be enough but it was better than nothing. My favourite photo of Miles is the one I took at about 6am, just as I watched the sun come up over the Adelaide Hills. We don't have many memories together, but if I had to pick one, this would be the one I cherish most.

Josh arrived back at 8am, Elizabeth from Heartfelt was coming at 9am. I showered, dressed, tidied up the room (my midwife Jo thought I was mad doing this) and took some of my own photos of Miles. I'd taken my camera in just in case, but had assumed I wouldn't have the strength to do this. I didn't want to regret not taking my own pictures, especially as photography is such an integral part of my life. I felt cocooned in the safety and privacy of my hospital room and was dreading leaving it, so it felt good to have something to do, a distraction of sorts.

All that morning, my internal monologue was trying to rationalise the inevitable goodbye I was going to have to say. I was having so much trouble working out how on earth I was going to walk out of the hospital and leave Miles behind. I knew he had died, I knew he wasn't coming back to life but I just couldn't imagine letting go physically and leaving him there in the hands of strangers. In the end I had to set myself a time to leave, or I knew I'd have wanted to stay forever. I sadly thought, "What more can I actually do? I've held him, kissed him, loved him, photographed him, what else is there to do?" There is not much more you can do. All that is left is your love for your baby, even if like me you are desperately searching for something more tangible, another physical way of mothering and remembering them. Josh was desperate to get back to Bonnie. I was so numb that this wasn't on my radar. I was too broken, too exhausted to turn my mind to anything other than Miles at this point. I wanted all of my energy to go into him and didn't feel I was capable of giving attention to Bonnie.

Noon was the time I set myself to leave. We had to sign forms for an autopsy, for memory boxes and footprints and legal documents to hand him over to a funeral home. Prescriptions were written, medication given to stop my milk from coming in and all that was left was to say goodbye. I couldn't fathom how was I supposed to do this. Once the doctors and midwives had left our room, I sat up with Miles and held him for about half an hour before putting him down in his cot for the last time. Josh came and stood behind me, with his arms tightly around me and said, "Go well, Miles. We love you and you will live on in our hearts forever." His words were perfect. Until that point, I hadn't been able to work out what Josh was thinking or feeling. I felt he was going through the motions to support me, but I couldn't read him or work out how he was feeling. He had seemed almost devoid of emotion. His words told me that he was just as broken and that just because he was handling it so differently, didn't mean he saw Miles any differently to me. We had both lost our son, we were both heartbroken. How this looked on the outside was so different but how we both felt inside was undeniably similar.

I almost had to run out of the hospital. Once I'd given Josh the nod that I was 'ready' to go, I had to leave immediately. One friend told me that after she lost her baby early in the second trimester and had to have a D&C, she jumped in the car and yelled at her husband to drive! She needed to get away from the hospital as fast as she possibly could. I had visions of being removed by security in three days' time if I didn't just leave right then and there.

Walking out of the dingy hospital, having been in artificial fluorescent light for twenty-four hours, into glorious high-summer sunshine felt like a slap in the face. It was completely at odds with how I was feeling. People were still going about their daily business, birds were still chirping and the world was still turning. I felt like my world had stopped, and it was shocking that life went on, whether we wanted it to or not. Time doesn't stand still for anyone else, even if for the bereaved it has come to an absolute standstill.

Home alone while Josh collected Bonnie from my parents, I wandered about the house unsure of what I was supposed to do with myself. I'd just given birth, I was exhausted, hurting physically and emotionally void. Each other time I'd given birth, I'd had a baby to care for. I knew the drill and my arms ached to do these things, but I had no baby to do them for. I think even as a first-time mum, your natural instincts kick in. I had to sleep holding a teddy bear for weeks, as I felt a physical hole in my body where Miles had grown and needed something to fill my empty arms. I felt disoriented; not being pregnant, but despite being postpartum, having no baby to care for. This was one of the many things I felt so confused by. I was a grown woman, now a mother of four, why was I sleeping with a toy? It felt so strange that I think I even tried to hide it from Josh. There are not many people I could talk to about how I was feeling, and in the early days, you don't even know what it is you need to talk about, let alone contemplate how to come to terms with what has happened.

I certainly had no idea how to act or feel: all I knew was that never, ever, before in my life had I felt so sad. The heavy darkness almost choked me, it was a permanent lump in my throat and it physically hurt. I felt like my entire life had ended, and the thought of ever recovering was unimaginable.

I felt like that for a long time, but eventually, without me even noticing, bit by bit I started to piece myself back together. It wasn't an easy process. As one friend said, "You've been handed a shit sandwich, and now you've got to eat it." And that's what I did, day by day, until a little bit of sunshine let itself back into my life and as time passed, the sunny days overtook the dark ones.

Chapter 15 Getting to know grief and what it's really like

The first weeks and month after losing a baby during pregnancy or soon after birth are truly dreadful. Words like numbness, disbelief, shock and heartache come to mind, but these alone are not enough to describe how horrific it feels. It is an experience that takes over every fibre of your being.

We escaped to a seaside town called Black Point four days after Miles was born. I needed a change of scenery, the promise of some fresh air. And I needed to be alone, or at the very least, feel like I had some control over who I saw. It was during this month that I came to realise what a beast grief is, and that I was embarking on a very long journey to recovery. I was slowly learning to accept that this loss was something I'd never get over but would instead need to learn to live with.

In the midst of this, my body was going through the standard post-birth recovery process. My milk came in, I bled heavily for weeks, my stomach was enormous. I was exhausted and emotional – *so* emotional. It was like I'd been cast into a no-man's land of hormonal imbalance. My pregnancy had ended abruptly and prematurely and while those hormones were not in competition with the postpartum ones, neither of them seemed to know whose turn it was. My post-birth hormones had not quite caught up on the fact there was no baby, as the urge to nurture after birth was there and it was very strong. That's why, when everything goes to plan, Mother Nature is a genius. We are flooded with hormones afterwards which help us care for our child, but when there is no baby to nurture, these instinctive urges have nowhere to go and it feels like Mother Nature is being a right old cow.

I felt like an uninvited house guest had turned up on our doorstep, with the intent of casting a dark shadow over all aspects of our life. This house guest was called grief and I knew I was going to have to get used to him being there for some time. I had a feeling he might be a permanent guest and a pervasive one at that. As to be expected, this overbearing house guest followed us when we escaped town to Black Point; he followed me everywhere. I felt like he omitted a fine grey mist that permeated the air I breathed, seeping into each ounce of my soul. No part of me seemed to be untouched.

We knew going away wouldn't change how we felt, but hoped that a change of scenery might give us some peace and quiet. I continued to cry a lot, sleep a lot, read a lot and much to my surprise, I ate a lot. By the end of the first month after losing Miles, I weighed more post-pregnancy than I had while pregnant. How's that for bad luck? I don't think I have ever hated my body more. I'm not sure if it was comfort eating or some kind of subconscious way of keeping my belly round, but I sure went hard on the chocolate bars! I knew this was a superficial worry, but it bothered me. I was torn between wanting to get rid of the baby weight and wanting to keep it as a memento of what I'd been through. I was bemoaning my weight gain to Josh, who like all good (read 'smart') husbands replied, "You're beautiful, haven't gained an ounce." But he also said, "Please, on top of everything else, don't start hating your body." But it's really hard not to feel resentful of your body; in some way, it's natural to feel like it's let you down. My appetite in the first few weeks really surprised me. I had assumed I would feel so miserable that I would be unable to eat. What I was and wasn't able to do physically, and emotionally, continued to surprise me.

Five days after I gave birth to Miles, I went horse riding. If you'd offered me one million dollars to guess what I'd be doing five days post-birth, I would never have guessed I'd be riding a huge black horse in the summer sunshine. I'd grown up riding and I saw a lady walking two beautiful horses along the beach we were staying at. I approached her to ask if I could help her exercise them to which she replied, "Absolutely, I'd love a hand." Fast-forward twenty-four hours and there I was, galloping along a deserted beach atop a giant black thoroughbred. I felt free and alive and remembered thinking, "I will be okay, this has happened but I will be okay. I just have to survive and keep my head above water." By stark contrast, I spent the entire next day on the sofa crying, but that was how the month rolled on. Amazing days, terrible days and absolutely no idea or indication of which order they would fall in.

I feel there should be an amnesty for all things said and done in the first weeks and months after baby loss. Quite simply, you're not yourself. Things that normally wouldn't offend you will offend you greatly. You may lose the ability to make simple decisions, perform basic tasks and partake in your regular activities. I lost my sense of humour and patience for many people and situations. I couldn't believe they were still living their lives as per usual when mine had imploded. The world moves on without a pause, even though you feel as though you've fallen into a deep dark hole from which you will never see sunlight again. One day I caught myself smiling and laughing and thought, *Wow, I never thought I'd feel like this again.* I'd thought the heavy grief would last forever: in the initial stages, it consumed my every thought and everything I did.

In this first month, grief as an emotion and a process took me by surprise. Although I had experienced grief on different levels throughout my life, I had never encountered anything like what I was dealing with after we lost Miles. I had lost a much-loved grandmother in my twenties, a close friend at almost thirty, and dealt with the end of my first marriage, but none of these experiences prepared me for how I felt after losing a baby. It was the darkest pain I have ever felt. I didn't have any skills or experiences to lean on, I had no idea how to cope or how to help myself navigate the heartache. I hated the grief. I wanted to fast-track it, to control it, to get back to being my old self as soon as possible. I didn't want to feel like this forever, but at the same time I wanted to stay close to Miles and grieving for him made me feel close and connected to him in a very intimate way.

Our fast-paced modern society is not very good at dealing with the ugly, hard, unglamorous parts of life. We want life to be fun, successful, carefree, a continuous stream of happy memories. Instagram is flooded with images of 'perfect' pregnancies, stories of effortless entrances into motherhood and carefully curated pictures of beautiful babies attached to their mother's breasts. A picture of a stillborn baby in the midst of all of this seems too harrowing, too great a contrast and not in keeping with images of the 'perfect' lives of others. We tend to glorify our successes and hide our sadness, which is not conducive to helping the bereaved navigate their loss or giving them a safe place to share their stories. Sharing once is hard enough, sharing repeatedly can be misinterpreted as attention-grabbing or ongoing wallowing, when really, it's a way of honouring a life that was lost. When a baby lives, we celebrate them. I felt when my baby died that in sharing his picture, I was at risk of being told to move on.

Some people feel that images of stillborns must come with a 'trigger warning' notice. I loved my pictures of Miles, I thought he was beautiful. But even I was only brave enough to share a picture of his little feet and a black and white picture of him at a distance in his hospital cot for fear of turning people away. I thought, "No one wants to see a picture of a dead baby, that's far too macabre", and very few people asked to see one. When a loved one dies, we usually have many pictures of them to choose from and select from a highlight reel. When a baby is lost before birth, the only pictures we have of them are post-death, or on an ultrasound. Our society does not know how to handle and publicly acknowledge the loss of a baby, and those of us who have lost a child can struggle to find the confidence to share their images.

What has struck me greatly is the huge contrast between how the bereaved mothers are supported today by society as a whole and how they were treated a hundred or so years ago. In times gone by, death in infancy and pregnancy was far more common, due to lack of hygiene and medical conditions. But rather than this making people less sympathetic, people spoke of it openly and society encouraged the many rituals surrounding it. I did a road trip with my older boys when I was first pregnant with Miles, heading interstate to Victoria to visit Sovereign Hill, a replica town built exactly like a mining settlement during Australia's gold rush in the 1850s. We did a lamplight tour that focused on death on the goldfields, which was commonplace and at times pretty gory. Walking around in the soft lamplight in the eerie stillness of the night, we visited the town's undertaker. He showed us coffins and carriages and explained how many families set aside money each week to cover the costs of funerals. Visiting the schoolhouse, the local nurse told us all about the terrible diseases that ravaged the goldfields and led to many untimely deaths.

A spooky tour of the goldfields at night was like a giant Halloween hunt for the boys. While they were taken with the stories of men who fell down mines and were run over by coaches, I was fascinated by the attitudes towards mourning and how different they were to today's. Little did I know just how personally it would resonate with me by the end of the year. It was considered poor form not to openly mourn and to not bury your loved one appropriately, and if able, extravagantly. No one was expected to 'move on', or 'get on with things'. It was universally understood that the mourning process was a long one and not to be rushed.

Nowadays some people think you will bounce back within a week, a month, a year. They seem to think that a loss is something you can get over or, my most hated expression, 'find closure' on. To still be mourning and grieving months later alarms people. Some think perhaps you're not trying hard enough to cope with what has happened, or you have become depressed and anxious as a result of too much grieving.

From my experience I decided there was no such thing as grieving too much. Those feelings were inside me and they had to be felt, and felt fully. I was not putting them on, or drawing them out for too long, I was dealing with the situation I had encountered. I didn't see any benefit in shelving or suppressing my feelings, as I knew they would come back later if I didn't acknowledge them. The weight of expectation that I should be better in X amount of time did not sit well with me, and I avoided meaningful conversations with anyone who I sensed had this attitude. I had lost a child, it was normal to miss him forever. I was not wallowing in my sorrow, I was processing the trauma that had come my way in whatever way felt most natural to me.

What did inspire me in this first month was a man I met on the beach at Black Point. He didn't mention his story, nor did I mention Miles when we met. Instead, we talked about what he'd caught when out fishing and how good the weather was. I knew he had lost his wife to ovarian cancer five months earlier; she was only 37, about the same age as me, and they had two beautiful sons together. I watched this man loading up his boys and their friends onto his boat, whizzing them around, taking them fishing and giving them the best summer imaginable. I thought he was incredible. I also thought, "How is he functioning?" He had gone through such a tragedy and from the tiny glimpses I caught of him he seemed so good, so happy, so together.

I knew that inside he was likely to be incredibly sad and ever so heartbroken, but he was putting on a brave front for his children and the outside world. It made me realise that there are many people around us who are carrying within them an immense sadness every day, and we can't always see it as they hide it so well; that perhaps the best therapy is to throw yourself back into life as much as you're able. To make a decision to be happy, to make the choice to live your life as fully as you can. You can still be sad, you can still be devastated, but there is a lot to be said for embracing joy and letting it sit beside your sadness. It is not a case of feeling one or the other: they are not mutually exclusive; they can sit side by side and have a simultaneous impact on your life.

This acceptance that both the sad days and the happy days are as important as each other and not in competition, that it's not a case of choosing one over the other as they both have their place, helped me move forward.

Chapter 16 Grieving and feeling alone

Initially I didn't want to talk people, as I didn't have the energy. I also felt like no one would be able to help me. Friends and family would be so upset for us, but what could they really do to help? To one friend who asked what he could do, Josh said, "Get us a living baby". Dark, I know, but short of this there was nothing else we wanted or needed. We had a house full of food, I absolutely did not want endless deliveries of flowers arriving, I didn't want company and I felt that no one could offer us any meaningful advice. I came to realise I was wrong about this last one, as unbeknownst to me, there were people around me who had also experienced baby loss and could genuinely understand how I was feeling. Many stories I had never known, a few I did and over time, I realised that so many people had been here before and their stories did help. I was just too raw at the beginning to see it

It is such a silent loss. When you give birth to a living baby, people fall over themselves to visit, help, and cannot wait to impart their knowledge of newborns, stories of breastfeeding and recovery from birth. There is not much to offer when a baby dies, beyond saying "I'm so sorry". Advice and suggestions from those who have not been through something similar sometimes falls flat causing offence, rather than bringing comfort. You can't ask friends about what to do with your milk when it comes in and how to stop it, as it's unlikely they have the answers. Your birth story may not feel like something to share and celebrate, as its end was a tragedy. You can't bond over sleepless nights, as yours are not from a baby waking, crying and needing to be fed; they are the result of your endless crying, nightmares and inability to sleep.

The loneliness of this feels enormous. The few friends I did reach out to hadn't experienced baby loss first-hand but they showed great empathy and kindness. When I could bring myself to talk about it and tell my story, they listened and cried with me. I was too scared to do this at first, scared of the raging torment of emotions inside which I thought could drown me if I started to acknowledge them. So I found that although I felt so alone, people did want to listen and hear my story, no matter how difficult it was for me to tell or for them to digest. In the end, talking did help. When I was talking to people, it felt like an out-of-body experience. I didn't feel like myself, I couldn't believe it was my story I was telling, that this had actually happened to me. But each time I told my story, I felt the teeny-tiniest bit better, and these minuscule pieces accumulated over time and I'm sure ultimately helped me heal.

One really close friend offered to tell me some funny stories from a recent party she'd been to with lots of our mutual friends. Previously I would have loved to hear them and have a good laugh with her, but I could not think of anything I was less interested in. She was looking for ways to cheer me up, but I had no interest in or capacity for the outside world. Nothing is going to "cheer you up" when you've just lost a baby. I felt my life was in ruins and very few things amused or entertained me. This terrified me. I had always been social, chatty, cheerful and strong, now it seemed I was a different person, and a broken one at that. This compounded the feeling of isolation because I thought I might never return to being someone even remotely similar to who I had been before losing Miles. Not only did I feel out of sync with my friends, but I also felt out of sync with myself.

It is also very hard to talk about a child who no one has ever known. As the mother, you know them through the love you feel for them, which has been there since the minute you found out you were pregnant. You love the changes they will bring to your family and the knowledge that this little person growing inside you is going to be with you for the rest of your life. Conversations surrounding the death of loved ones others knew are also heartbreaking, but there is more for the conversation to focus on. For example, if a grandparent passes away you can reminisce about your memories of them baking cakes with you or visiting special places. You can talk about their likes and dislikes, the funeral arrangements, how other close family members are coping. With baby loss, the memories are harder to share as they lived mostly in your hopes and dreams. The love is just as big but it is likely that only you and your partner felt this fully. Others may have been very excited about your impending arrival, but to them it was not yet part of their everyday thoughts, whereas for you it very much was. Each time I've been pregnant my babies have occupied most of my thoughts. Should I have eaten that? Was that a kick? I wonder what he/she will look like? I hope this baby is okay?! I can't imagine anyone else gave your baby much daily attention: for them it's an abstract person, one they will meet and grow to love once he or she are earthside.

For me, accepting the fact that not everyone would 'get it' helped immensely. Even the midwife in the hospital said, "I cannot imagine this pain". Half of the comments on my Instagram post announcing Miles' arrival started or ended with *"I have no words"*. People have no words, no idea what to say. Saying this is better that a glib line like *"count your blessings"* or *"perhaps it was for the best"*, and it is a statement made out of pure kindness, as people are not trying to pretend that they understand. However, it compounds your sense of isolation, as you feel that *NO ONE GETS IT*.

I had very few people who I could ask, *"what got you through this?"* I did have my close friend, Anna, to ask and even we differed in our grief. She lost her first baby and returned home to an empty, silent house, desperately wondering if she would ever be the mother of a living child. I returned to a house with a loud, magnificently boisterous toddler who wanted Mummy - the old, fun, happy Mummy as well. I felt that because of this I was forced to step out of my grief on many occasions and prioritise her even when I didn't feel strong enough. I could not imagine how my friend would have felt managing her grief in an empty home with the added grief of not knowing what her future held in terms of motherhood.

In these very early stages of grief, support groups were too much for me to contemplate. I couldn't see my friends let alone face a room full of strangers. I did attend an afternoon tea held by SANDS (miscarriage, stillbirth, & newborn death support) about seven months after Miles was born, so perhaps my early feelings of isolation were self-imposed to an extent, though I don't think I'm unique in having a reticence or shyness to attend a group counselling session or get-together with other bereaved parents.

In the early days I did go back to see my GP, to touch base and tell her how I was. Having struggled with depression and anxiety in the past, I wanted to put it all out there in case they reared their ugly head again after this trauma. It is hard to distinguish grief from depression and anxiety, as they are similar in so many ways. My GP explained to me how grief may never leave you, but its most intense symptoms will ease over time. She also explained that whilst depression and anxiety can manifest after a trauma, grief is a natural and expected reaction. This gave me hope. I felt that I'd have half a chance if I stayed aware of myself and kept trying to gauge whether I was grieving or slipping into something more serious.

For me, grief brought feelings of loneliness, numbness, disbelief, shock, hopelessness, exhaustion, fatigue, anger and embarrassment. These are very hard emotions to talk about at the best of times. They make it hard for you to manage day to day, let alone in the wider world, which brings me back to that feeling of isolation. You can't partake in normal life as you are simply not up to it, and normal everyday tasks can feel enormous, even simple ones like cooking or driving. Talking to people was an effort, not a carefree exchange of news. Initially I didn't have much genuine interest in what other people were up to, (and as horrible as this sounds) I didn't have the capacity to care either. I thought that compared to what I was experiencing, their lives were very vanilla, full of superficial fun and frivolity, and I had no interest in hearing about what they'd been up to. It seemed completely at odds with my heartbroken state of being.

Building up the courage to leave the house, for fear of breaking down once out and about, was daunting. I felt like a shadow of my old self and found mindless tasks as simple as showering, getting dressed and heading out the front door to be arduous. This is a very lonely space to be in, so if you don't have a friend who has been through this, try to think of one who you can sense will be very understanding and start talking to them. It won't make everything go away, but it may help you build up the confidence to talk to more people, to say your baby's name, and to start telling your story, one step at a time.

In these very early stages, online support groups can offer the support and understanding you may feel is not available to you in your immediate circle. They are safe places to vent, ask questions and share your grief in a like-minded community. The Bears of

Hope private Facebook group is an active network of bereaved mothers who have lost babies at any stage of pregnancy or in infancy. If you do not feel ready to participate and post something about your baby and your own experience, reading other's thoughts and the responses of the group members can make you feel less alone. Very few topics are off limits: among many other things, people ask about birth, postpartum recovery, relationships, trying to conceive again. The group is also closed to non-bereaved parents and closely monitored by administrators to ensure that all commenting remains kind and supportive.

There is also a strong community of bereaved parents on Instagram who I have found to be incredibly supportive. The hashtags #ihadamiscarriage, #babyloss, #stillbirthsupport and many more can lead you to people experiencing similar pain who in many cases give you the validation and connection you crave. I have met some incredible women through Instagram who are like minded souls. They understand what I am going through and help me dispel any fears that I am being irrational, too emotional or too caught up in my grief.

Initially I didn't think I would ever be capable of talking about Miles, but when I did, I felt immeasurably better for it. I was scared of being too vulnerable, but being vulnerable is the best way to open up the conversations, which in turn will hopefully help you feel less alone. I learnt my limits early on and knew if I pushed myself too hard, I'd fall in a heap. Small steps in the right direction helped me to reconnect with friends and let go of my self-imposed isolation. It really wasn't as scary out there as I'd first thought.

Chapter 17 How to announce your loss

After losing a child, the idea of then having to tell people seems like a double blow. If you're anything like me, the last thing I wanted to do was text, talk to or see anyone, let alone have to share this dreadful news. Telling people would also make it very real. I wished it wasn't real, that it hadn't actually happened: my mind was struggling to accept that what had happened was true and irreversible. I think until the initial shock and numbness wears off, many others feel the same way.

Josh suggested I tell people the same day we arrived home from hospital, to get the next part of this terrible process over and done with. I scripted a text to send to close girlfriends, which in itself felt torturous. I wasn't quite sure how people would react. I was worried they wouldn't understand how devastated I was and would underestimate my grief, but I was also worried that hordes of people would start calling or worse still, want to come and see me. I didn't want any visitors. I felt too fractured and bewildered to handle anything like that. I wrote:

Our beautiful baby boy Miles was delivered stillborn yesterday.

We are heartbroken and beyond devastated.

I will forever see an empty seat at my kitchen table and wonder what our gorgeous boy would have been like and grown to look like.

I don't have the strength or energy for calls or visitors at this stage and please, no flowers.

As full as our hearts are with the gorgeous children we are so lucky to have, they are breaking for the one we have just lost.

He was growing and developing beautifully but sadly suffered a brain hemorrhage in utero.

He was tiny, perfect and will always be loved.

The minute I pressed send, the replies started flooding in. People were shocked, stunned by the news and devastated for us. A few friends told me later they had a tiny giggle in the midst of their sadness that even in the middle of this trauma I was being bossy and giving instructions about not visiting or sending flowers. About ten years earlier, a close friend's husband had died suddenly. We all pretty much moved into her house overnight and stayed there for the next few weeks. Someone was with her every minute of the day to support her and make sure she was never alone. I couldn't fathom a situation like that. I didn't want to deal with anyone else and also didn't want people to see me in the state I was in or to start turning up on our doorstep.

One of Josh's best friends did come over immediately. He cried with us and told me about what the grieving process had been like for him when he'd lost his mum three years earlier. I felt daunted by the grief ahead, but from talking to him, I knew it was important to face it and not try to shove it into a box never to be opened. He also told me that it was okay to do whatever I needed to do to make myself feel a little bit better, that it was totally fine to withdraw, to seek solitude and to prioritise my own needs first.

As mentioned previously, we decided to get out of town. All I was doing was lying in bed or on the sofa, crying. I said to Josh "I'm bored of staring at the same four walls and crying, I'm bored of crying! It would be nice to cry somewhere else, preferably with a better view." A friend very kindly lent us her beach house at Black Point where some other very close friends were holidaying at their own shack. They were what I call "safe friends": people who just get it. Friends who didn't expect conversation (or anything) out of us, but were there to offer company and support if we needed it, or felt up to it. Josh was happy to be around people and do things, whereas I wanted to curl up in a ball and hide. At Black Point, we could each do our own thing when we wanted to and I wouldn't feel the guilt of holding Josh captive to my grief.

In these first few days of grief, everything felt scary. I went for a walk alone along the beach and my legs felt like they were made of concrete. I was terrified of a simple stroll along the shoreline, walking at a snail's pace, staring at my feet and ignoring the beauty of the coastline as I willed myself to walk another metre, then another one after that. A small beach walk felt like a hike up the toughest of mountains: I didn't think I was even capable of getting to the other end of the cove and turning back. Most of all, I was worried I'd run into someone I knew and have to make conversation - or worst of all, tell them the news. I still looked pregnant and later that day, I did bump into someone I knew while we were sitting on our friends' front verandah.

Susannah, Josh's friend's sister, bounded up.

"Hi! How are you? How are you coping being pregnant in this heat?"

I realised our news hadn't reached her.

"You don't know do you?" The poor girl looked bewildered.

"No, what's happened?" she asked

All I could say was, "We lost the baby", before I started crying.

Susannah started apologising and crying with me. I said to her, after a minute or so,

"in all honesty, this is a good thing, If I had to bump into anyone and tell them, I'm glad it was you".

Susannah is the kind of person who does not shy away from awkward conversations or situations, she instinctively knew how to respond. This incident made me realise that I had to get the word out somehow as there was no way I could go through the process of running into people over and over and telling them what had happened. I needed to broadcast this far and wide for my own sake. I also wanted to make sure our story - Miles' story - was told correctly. I hated the idea of gossip spreading like wildfire and misinformation being shared.

I initially felt that social media was inappropriate - too modern perhaps - but Susannah and I talked it through and came to the conclusion that it was today's version of a newspaper announcement, or town crier if you like. There was nothing wrong or tacky about posting about Miles on Instagram. I'd done posts on Facebook or Instagram for all of my other babies when they arrived, so why should it be any different for Miles? I drafted a post, pulling lines from the text I'd sent my friends. I tried very hard to express the fact that to us, Miles was our fourth child, and despite never knowing him, we wanted to celebrate him and remember him forever. I agonised over sharing his picture and in the end I posted a carousel of pictures, starting with his little feet, then my four babies as newborns, my three boys all wrapped in their stars, Bonnie when she came home from the NICU - and finished with a picture of all of us, when Miles was in utero on Christmas morning.

If you need a way to share your news, social media can be a very useful way of reaching many people. For me, the relief of sharing the news of Miles on Instagram was instantaneous, as I had barely spoken to anyone since we lost him. I felt like I'd have to explain it to people. I couldn't even fathom how huge it was - and it had happened to me. I now look back and see that my fears were natural. I was grieving, my brain was completely muddled and at this early stage I was unable to rationalise what we were going through. If even I couldn't comprehend my situation, it was natural to assume others wouldn't get it either. People did get it and also understood my desire for Miles to be celebrated, not treated just as a tragic life event we would turn the page on and forget. My Instagram post (read along with the words borrowed from my earlier announcement via text):

"Saying goodbye to Miles is the hardest thing I've ever done. Stillbirth is devastating, overwhelming and most people's worst nightmare. My initial reaction was to hide, if I didn't tell people, maybe this wasn't happening. If I didn't talk about it perhaps the all consuming grief and heartache would disappear too. It's hard to know what to say.

But I feel this takes away from the simple fact that a much loved and much wanted baby boy was born. The arrival of each of my other children was announced with great joy, this is obviously so different but our beautiful Miles deserves to be celebrated like the others.

We will always love him and miss him, Miles is part of our family and will live on in our hearts forever. So wherever you are this evening, please pop a cork and raise your glass to our beautiful little boy."

I was overwhelmed and hugely comforted by the responses I received. I was moved by stories people shared of their own losses and felt keenly that I was not as alone as I'd initially assumed.

One friend sent me a message asking if she could help me by telling people about Miles on my behalf. This was such a beautiful, practical offer of help. I had gone bananas spreading the word: once I started, I just kept on pressing re-send to everyone I could think of. Between the messages I'd sent via text and the Instagram post, I felt confident I'd managed to tell most people who I felt needed to know. If the idea of sharing the news is beyond comprehension, delegating this task to a relative or friend would be a very sensible thing to do. If you cannot imagine dealing with replies, they can handle these for you to see later, when you feel ready. Some people may choose to create a new email address or Facebook/ Instagram profile for this very purpose. It will keep all of the responses in one spot and save you the pressure of immediately responding.

I also found that social media, in particular Facebook, was a minefield of reminders of my loss. Feeds have the potential be overflowing with friend's pregnancy announcements or updates of their progress. News of new arrivals and pictures of sweet newborns are also likely to appear. Scrolling through one morning, advertisements for maternity wear and pregnancy guides kept flooding my feed. I furiously whizzed past them, only to be hit with another advert for elastic-waisted jeans, which to be honest I still needed to wear: just not for the intended purpose. Clearly the algorithm hadn't caught up with my news: it was still pushing content out to me based on the topics I'd been googling for the last six months. I switched off from Facebook for a while: it was too upsetting and I didn't have the appetite for it anyway.

I couldn't find the fortitude to reply to the majority of texts and messages I received, it was too exhausting and emotionally draining to repeatedly find the right words. My mind was full of my own torment and I didn't have the capacity to draft multiple responses. One thing I did end up doing was draft a fairly generic message on my phone in the notes section, which I copied and pasted as a reply to many. It was something along the lines of: "Thank you so much for your beautiful message and words of support. We are heartbroken and as to be expected, will take some time to process this trauma. We appreciate your support." To those who wrote specifically "How are You" I generally replied, "Up and down, there are good days and bad days, a long road to recovery ahead".

Very early on I remember getting angry with Josh. He was on the phone to his brother who asked how we were going. He replied, "We're okay, fine thanks." I know it's a standard response, especially for your average Aussie bloke, but I was horrified. I was so far from okay it wasn't funny and the thought of someone thinking I was okay terrified me. If they thought I was okay would I have to act okay next time I saw them? Would they tell other people that apparently we were okay? The expectation alarmed me. I said told Josh, "please whatever you say, do not tell people that I'm okay. I'm not and I'd rather you say, she's finding this all really hard or we are still very up and down." The thought of saying anything less seemed misleading and to me it trivialised and glossed over our loss in order to put others at ease.

It is hard to say to people that you're hurting: it's raw and honest and not something we necessarily do with ease. We are conditioned to say, "Hi, how are you?" and generally expect the reply to be "Good thanks, and you?" even if it's not the case. I also hated being the downer, the negative element in a conversation. It was high summer, everyone was celebrating the new year. I didn't want to drag them down with my sad story but sometimes you have to. That's life and we shouldn't always have to pretend that we're coping well.

It's okay to hurt, especially after losing a baby. I think people need to recognise just how fragile women are after baby loss and that they need immense support and understanding in the months and perhaps years that follow. Sharing intimate details of your loss is certainly not required and not for everyone. You may find it easy to talk about your baby far and wide, or like many people I spoke to, have great difficulty finding the words, knowing where to start, or trusting that you have supportive and empathetic ears around you. How you choose to share is deeply personal, so never compare yourself to what another bereaved parent is doing. We all have our own way.

The amount you feel able to share is in no way a reflection of the depth of your grief. For many people, mourning privately in isolation is the only way they feel comfortable, though this in itself brings its own challenges. I imagine like any parent, whether your baby is born alive or still, the desire to talk about how perfect your precious little baby is would be ever-present. It is an announcement we, as bereaved parents, wish we didn't have to make in the first place. To add to insult to injury, our society is not very good at allowing conversation on this topic to flow freely. However you choose to initially communicate the news of your baby, it need not set the tone of how you wish to go forward. You may find your voice and need to talk later on, or alternatively retreat and seek isolation after speaking openly at first. Do whatever works best for you and feels right at the time: it's your story, your heart and your baby.

Chapter 18 Having a funeral or a memorial

A huge question to contemplate after losing a baby is, "Will you have a funeral or a memorial?" The answer is particularly hard, as the funeral of a stillborn or miscarried baby is most likely something you have not attended or encountered before. When someone older dies, it is assumed a funeral or memorial will be held. With babies lost in the womb, this may not always be the case. It's a huge decision to make in a time of shock. I thought, who would want to come to Miles' funeral? Will people find it macabre and uncomfortable that we are having one? I also didn't want people feeling they needed to come home early from their summer holidays to attend.

I questioned whether I could emotionally cope with a group of people, or the effort organising a funeral would require. I was so confused that I decided to do nothing formal at this point in time. I wanted Miles cremated and had already bought a beautiful silver box for his ashes and had it engraved. Beyond this, everything else felt too hard, too awkward, my grief too personal. I thought that perhaps in a year's time I would have the strength to organise a memorial of sorts but in the all-consuming first stage after loss, organising a funeral was incomprehensible for me for many reasons. I am sure it is something that could be delegated to a close friend but even the thought of doing that was too much for me.

I called the funeral home we had chosen to help us with Miles' cremation five times before I finally built up the courage to talk to someone. Each time, I would hang up before someone answered.

I couldn't work out how I was going to get the words out. I didn't want to say the words, 'I am ringing to organise my son's cremation'; they just seemed too horrible, too bizarre. When I did make it through, the man I spoke to was incredibly kind and professional, which helped enormously. He assured me that the little silver box I had chosen would be appropriate and that he would take care of all the communication with the hospital about transporting Miles' body to the funeral home once the autopsy was completed. I was so relieved that this would all be taken care of for us.

I organised a time to deliver the box and sign paperwork, but as the appointment loomed, I knew I couldn't do it, so I asked Josh to go for me. I couldn't face the funeral home and didn't want to have to have anything to do with the arrangements. I had made sure he had a beautiful silver box with his initials engraved on it as his final resting place. But I was incapable of making any more decisions beyond that. Josh was more than happy to do this for us. I would not have been able to cope with the conversations that needed to be had, to decide on what kind of coffin Miles would be transported in from the hospital, to settle the account for this process we wished we had no need for.

No one asked if we were having a funeral, which did make it easier. I don't think anyone could bring themselves to ask the question as the answer was simply too sad. Some people were surprised we had to make a decision about cremation or burial, it had never occurred to them this would happen after a stillbirth. I suppose many see it as a medical event and assume hospitals deal with it all, as they once did. And many people didn't realise I had given birth to Miles.

I have spoken to parents of lost babies who had private funerals, just the parents, and others who had large wakes or smaller, intimate gatherings. I think it is best to go with your gut, do what feels right. If you don't know what that is, there is no rush to make a decision. You can do something when the time feels right.

A lady I spoke to who lost her daughter almost forty years ago told me that she regretted not having an open funeral for her child. She had a closed service, with just her husband and living daughters. For her the thought of her difficult and opinionated mother-in-law saying or doing something dreadful at the funeral was too much to bear. The best way of avoiding this was to invite no one. She still feels this decision influenced how others perceived her daughter's death and the significance of the loss to her family. Perhaps if they had been there to bury and farewell her daughter, they may have had a better understanding of just how real she had been and how much her life had meant. By keeping the service closed, her narrative stayed private and stopped potential conversations before they had the chance to begin.

A funeral need not be a somber, depressing occasion. Some families choose to hold a 'celebration of life'; a party at which their baby is remembered with joy and gratitude. A chance to reflect on the richness their baby's short time on earth brought to their lives and the legacy their child has left. It may be a beautiful opportunity to cherish those around you and focus on just how much there is to be grateful for. A chance to acknowledge both the sad and the happy parts of your life.

In the case of a miscarriage, you are not legally required to have your baby's remains buried or cremated, but can discuss options with the hospital or your doctor about what you would like to do with your baby. After a stillbirth, you are legally required to decide between a cremation or a burial. This can take place with or without a ceremony, or you can postpone the ceremony until later. Some hospitals also offer services for babies of all gestational ages. They are placed in a special memorial with other babies taken too soon, though you can ask to take care of your baby's remains privately.

I felt immense relief once Miles' ashes came home. I can't explain why, but having him home with us brought me huge comfort. He sits up high in a shelf in our living room, in his little silver box, at the feet of a bronze horse that has long been a favourite ornament of mine. It feels right to see him up there. Anyone visiting our home wouldn't know he's up there unless we told them - and for now, that works for me.

There is a beautiful Japanese tradition for remembering babies lost in the womb called mizuko kuyo, which is growing in popularity worldwide. Japanese Buddhists use little stone or marble statues of Jizo, the protector of children, to take care of the soul of their unborn child on its journey to the afterlife, (which they refer to as paradise). Buddhists believe that during your life you amass good karma, which protects you when you die and guarantees your passage to paradise. Babies lost in the womb have not had the chance to do this, so Jizo helps them by smuggling their little soul inside his bright red coat and bonnet. The famous Okunoin Cemetery in the Koyasan mountains of Japan is home to hundreds of these statues and parents leave little toys and snacks to comfort their children in the afterlife. Jizo statues are easily found online and I like the fact that it is something that can stay with you throughout your life; it can be given a place in your garden and taken with you if you move. Many people place these ornaments in their garden and replace the statue's red coat and bonnet on their child's anniversary each year.

I still have an urge to do something for Miles, but until I find the right time and feel ready, I am content to wait. I suppose it is the same as grief: there is no timeframe, no set of rules. In many ways,

I have wondered if going through the motions of a funeral might have helped ease my disbelief about the situation we were in. When his body was still at the hospital, the thought of him being alone and handled by strangers upset me deeply. I felt he should have been with us. My desire to be near him was strong and I couldn't drive past the hospital he remained at for the autopsy, as I didn't trust myself not to run in and demand to see him. I remember asking Josh where he thought Miles' soul had gone, where his spirit was. Josh responded, "In our hearts." He felt that the body was merely a vessel and Miles lived on within us, forever in our hearts. This, like absolutely everything at this time, made me weep. To think of him as a part of both of us forever was beautiful.

This also made me feel unready to formally bid him farewell. There was no pressure from others to have a funeral. We were essentially alone in this. Anyone attending a funeral was there to support us, not necessarily say to goodbye to Miles. I know friends and family see him as a beautiful little boy they never got to meet and are so sad they never had the chance to, but I can't imagine they needed to say goodbye to him like we did. Perhaps I'll never be willing so say goodbye in a formal way, only time will tell, but for now he is at home with us, where he belongs.

Chapter 19 For the love of Lucia: loss in infancy

Some stories touch your heart and stay with you long after you first hear them. Lucia's story is one of these. A beautiful angel, who grew her wings at only ninety-nine days, never uttering a word but sharing a message of love and gratitude which inspires many. Sally, Lucia's mum, bravely shares her story as she believes that Lucia's brief life held a meaning far greater than any age, or time can measure. Her legacy is this; life is precious, live more, love deeply, be kinder and take nothing for granted: life is fragile, and sometimes tragically short, cherish it and your loved ones as breathing, living and loving is a precious gift.

Lucia passed away from a rare, terminal, genetic condition which was diagnosed when she was twelve weeks old. Two weeks later, she flew from her family's embrace, having known nothing but love. It's hard to imagine such heartache. Sally possesses immense strength; dedicating herself to sharing Lucia's message and raising money for The Royal Children's Hospital Melbourne, in particular the Pediatric Cardiology Ward. Three-hundred friends and family came together as 'Lucia's Angels' to run the Melbourne Marathon in her honour, Sally running the full forty-two kilometers with her twin sister Suzy by her side. Sally found comfort in doing something to raise money and awareness for other children with conditions similar to Lucia's. While nothing can take-away the pain and heartache, creating something positive did give her a sense of purpose.

The passing of time has also helped Sally begin to live again after losing Lucia.

"There is just a huge process and it takes time. I am only a few months into this journey and am still in complete shock. I get waves of anxiety and sadness that hit me daily - multiple times a day. I'm sure this will happen for the rest of my life but to a lesser degree." For Sally it's crucial to keep busy. "I'm a doer and I'm always keeping myself busy, so I haven't really stopped since her passing. I do take moments to stop, and reflect, feel all of the grief, and let it take over but once I am done, I turn to the next task at hand and move ahead. This is not something anyone has a rulebook for. You need to take each day as it comes. Minute by minute, and breath by breath. At some point start to live again, don't feel guilty for laughing or smiling, as your loved one would want you to do this, and to keep enjoying the precious moments you have. Your baby is here with you every day, all around you, and if you're open to the signs, they will visit you. I also try to think that with each day that passes I get closer to one day embracing Lucia in another life."

When it comes to losing a baby, Sally hopes that others know, they are not alone, that they should use all the help they can get, and take all the time they need. Going away after Lucia's funeral also helped. Sally, her husband, and their little girl Sophia went to Bali. At first this felt bittersweet and impossible, but Sally believes it gave her a chance to reflect, to let everything out, and to grieve hard without the distractions of everyday life. It need not be a holiday, or a far-flung location, but the chance to retreat from your usual environment, may create space for you to grieve without outside influences. It can be confronting, but hugely therapeutic, as often, when you slow down, emotions which have been kept at bay come out in full force, demanding to be dealt with.

Outsiders could easily presume that Sally is coping incredibly well. She is a positive, dynamic woman, with an infectious zest for life. But like all bereaved mothers she has dark moments: days when the grief hits her head on and consumes her entire being. There is no quick fix, triggers are everywhere, and no amount of love, family, work or business can keep them at bay. "Everything is hard, living is hard. Triggers are what they are, but I get the choking feeling at random moments, driving the car, in the shower, going to bed, walking, in the supermarket, anywhere and everywhere. Significant dates will be hard I'm sure, but every day is too." Life goes on but is lived with a shattered heart.

Talking about Lucia is hugely important to Sally. Telling snippets of her story, and constantly including her, just as she would have been included if she were alive. If someone doesn't mention Lucia, Sally will, she loves her being recognised; she's not physically here but that doesn't mean her story is over, her legacy lives on. Sally created a WhatsApp group full of 'Lucia's Angel's' team members. Friends have posted about how the light had peaked through the clouds whilst they were running or how a butterfly had flown beside them which made them feel as though Lucia was there with them. This gave Sally a safe place to post in if she was feeling low, she could share a short video of Lucia or unashamedly talk about how she was feeling. As a result a strong supportive community was built. Additionally talking to a professional grief counsellor both with, and without her husband was also essential.

Sally coped by making sure she "was doing things for the mind, body and soul." Sally took on the incredible challenge of training for a marathon in under 6 weeks having never run one before. She knows this isn't for everyone but the simple act of moving her body and doing something physical gave her a goal to work towards. It doesn't have to be a marathon, "even if you get some girls together and go for a short walk or something like that, it's about doing something with purpose, it can happen organically, and you don't have to raise hundreds of thousands of dollars - it's not about that - if you raise ten dollars from a cup cake stall on your street it's just about getting together with people and being busy. What the marathon did for us, apart from the endorphins you get from running, was get me outside, get me focused on something, and it brought together an amazing community of friends and family who were given a way to help me and pay their respects to Lucia."

For her soul Sally sought the guidance of healers and mediums. One reading was so profound, it gave Sally the clarity she'd been searching for. It gave her a sense of calm and a feeling of being deeply connected to Lucia. For Sally, the sense of life being out of her own control sparks deep anxiety and fear; such feelings were heightened by the sudden and unexpected loss of Lucia. During a colour reading Sally chose shades that showed an angel, and a trumpet, (symbolising a messenger). These signs reinforced Sally's desire to keep sharing Lucia's message. The third colour Sally chose, told her to live in the moment: that eventually, everything would be okay, she just had to bear with the feeling of life being out of control as eventually this would subside.

Sally was told by one healer, "not to fall into the trap of being addicted to sympathy." She thought these were harsh words for a grieving mother, but at the same time they resonated. The loss of a child is one of the worst tragedies you can endure but it reinforced how important it was to Sally to "get up every day, put a smile on, draw on her strength and be grateful." When she posted on social media about how she was feeling she was "never looking for sympathy. I want people to have empathy but not feel sorry for me, I've never wish for that when I post, I'm just putting my raw emotion out there."

In the early days Sally found it incredibly confronting when people said to her "you will never get over this, you will just learn to live with this." It was the last thing she wanted to hear, to imagine that life would always be like this, so achingly sad. It made her mind spin with depressing thoughts. In Sally's words, trying to live without Lucia "is torture, facing the day is challenging and the feeling of life going on is utterly gut wrenching. Some days are hard, the others harder...." Grief is so overwhelming, at the beginning it's hard comprehend how anyone can survive it.

In the short time Sally had with Lucia, after discovering her terminal condition, she made some beautiful memories. Giving Lucia her first taste of ice-cream, christening her surrounded by family and friends and treasuring every last moment. Her twin sister, Suzy, was an incredible support. Helping to organise the christening, overhauling Lucia's hospital room to make it warm and colourful, and most of all showering Sally with a sisterly-love which showed no bounds.

Below are some of the beautiful words Sally spoke at Lucia's funeral:

It seems only yesterday that we were celebrating the birth of our darling daughter... and what pure joy and magical moment that was. Pete and I felt the happiest we ever had in life with the most divine baby Lucia the sister to Sofia; our family was perfectly complete.

The birth of a new baby is one of life's absolute joys. Anyone who has loved a baby comes to realise how precious that tiny little life is. Full of vulnerability... potential... and pure, unconditional LOVE. For this reason, it is hard to find the words to express our immense heartbreak.

To be standing here today, and addressing you in this format, is utterly shocking... and so very surreal.... It is a position that no parent could...or should ever be prepared for.

Our world was turned upside down on the day we were told our beautiful baby girl had a terminal condition.

My head did not stop spinning and was filled with questions that any parent might ask… How can we fix this? My poor baby. What has happened? Why my daughter? This can't be true? How can we fix this?

Every day since this dark cloud set upon us, I've woken to wish that this has surely been just a terrible nightmare. However, waking in a hospital room alongside our baby girl fading away, was the realisation that our worst nightmare was in fact, a reality and the anxiety and panic would set in.

At moments during these past weeks, strength has prevailed… and we've found incredible joy in continuing to celebrate the delights of newborn baby life… only to be hit with an overwhelming sense of grief…. in knowing that these "firsts" in her life, may likely, also be her "lasts"

Lucia, you were so strong, so pure, and so beautiful. You were with us for such a short time… but the impact of your life has been immense and more than most will make in a lifetime. The ripples of your dear life will be felt for an eternity.

You knew nothing but an abundance of love and you gave it back to us in so many ways.

You had a sparkle in your eyes

Your whole face lit up when you smiled

You loved to nestle in, and fall asleep in our arms

You especially loved to fall asleep on my shoulder and I will miss your soft, sweet breath on my neck…

My heart aches knowing I won't get another cuddle with you

Lucia, my darling angel I will never forget the moment you left us….

We were surrounded by a circle of loved ones… we were crying… and your skin was on my skin. While you were embraced in my arms… daddy was holding your hands… and with every final breath you took, Daddy told you "fly away angel"…

I kissed your forehead as you slowly slipped away from me, I could feel your beautiful soul and spirit fly away to a purpose greater than this lifetime...

Surrounded by peace.... and by the greatest love... you went to a place where you will always watch over your Mumma, Daddy and sister Sofia.

The light shone so brightly that afternoon... and the heavens opened up to welcome you, my dear angel, Lucia.

Lucia, your message to us is as clear, as it is profound...

Cherish this lifetime.... every short moment of it....

LIVE MORE, LOVE HARDER, BE KINDER ... and take NOTHING for granted.

Get down on the floor to play with kids, read the extra story or catch up with friends, tell loved ones you care, show your kindness to strangers, work less, stress less and ultimately live more – THIS IS YOUR LIFE.

I ask ALL of you here today, to make a promise to yourselves, to live by her message... and please spread it."

Lucia's legacy will continue to shine bright - her devoted mother will never let it fade. It's hard to comprehend how something so positive can come out of such devastation. Such positivity doesn't erase the sadness or ease the pain but it does give it purpose. Lucia's story shows us just how precious life is, how important it is to cherish what you have - from the mundane, to the magical - as it's all miraculous.

Chapter 20 How the reactions of others can affect you

I dwell on what other people say. Josh doesn't: other people's opinions are like water off a duck's back to him. In grief, I became even more sensitive and reacted strongly to a few things I would otherwise not have blinked at. A friend of ours sent me, Josh and another one of his mates a group text with a picture of his young daughter driving his boat and pretending to drink a beer (kind of inappropriate, but he was taking the mickey out of himself). This was three days after we'd lost Miles and my first direct contact with him. I'd texted him the day before we had Miles to let him know what was happening and he'd sent love via Josh after Miles was delivered, but we hadn't been in contact directly since Miles died.

I couldn't understand why he thought I'd be up for a 'funny' text so soon after losing my child, or why he thought I was ready for some group chat banter. Josh laughed and said it was a funny photo, while I blew up completely and thought it was the most insensitive thing I'd ever received. I was appalled that someone who hadn't texted directly to acknowledge Miles' death was instead texting me in a group chat. Looking back now, I can see that this man who loves us all dearly was probably just trying to cheer me up as he knows I have a close bond with his daughter, but at the time I felt like he was saying *chin up, ha-ha, all back to normal now, look at us enjoying summer as per usual.*

It scared me that anyone could think I could handle such normality. I was terrified that I was going to lose myself, my sense of humour, my ability to withstand simple interactions. The thought that you've been robbed not only of your child, but also your humour and your sense of self, is overwhelming. But in the first stage everything hurts like hell, just living hurts. People around you need to tread carefully and be mindful of just how sensitive loss parents can (understandably) be. I didn't expect others to stop enjoying their lives, but I needed them to understand that I couldn't be expected to be a part of normal life for the foreseeable future.

People may have perceived me as being too sensitive or too reactive, but I don't think you can really be any such thing when grieving and trying to make sense of tragedy. How you feel is how you feel. If someone close to you does something that makes you feel uncomfortable or unloved, pointing this out to them is not overreacting or being ridiculous. You are just trying to articulate how you feel, and how their actions or inactions made you feel. Some people may find this confronting, especially if they did not realise they were being insensitive or can't understand how their comment or actions could cause offence. But I don't think we should ever be ashamed of the way we feel or necessarily suppress it to keep the peace. If people are continually told that the way they feel is 'too much' they will shut down and hold back from expressing their true emotions. Burying your feelings is never healthy and does not help you move forward.

In these early days, I felt especially lost and wished there was some kind of resource available that would help guide me. I was fortunate in the saddest of ways to have the endless support of my friend Anna, who'd lost her baby 10 years earlier. I spoke to her almost daily and she was my sounding board. I wanted her to tell me that what I was feeling and doing was normal (and she did). Not to humour me, but because she knew what I was going through and understood that whatever I had to do in order to cope was essential. She reassured me that whatever got me through was okay: the tears, the anger, the loneliness, the confusion, the denial. All natural. I felt like anyone who hadn't gone through this pain couldn't possibly understand it. As late-term pregnancy loss is quite unusual, this meant that most of my friends could not begin to imagine what I was dealing with.

What I did find, however, was that if I opened my mind to other people's pain and experiences I realised that while we had all encountered different things, our pain held many similarities. I was initially quick to dismiss someone who wanted to tell me about their cousin's friend who had miscarried at twelve weeks as it felt so different to my experience. But over the following months, I could see that sharing these stories helps to break the silence surrounding baby loss. Perhaps if we all spoke more openly about the heartbreak it causes, we would all be better able to support each other through our losses, despite their differences. If we all talk about baby loss more often, perhaps it will help remove the sense of loneliness so many women feel. I came to accept that people weren't trying to compare losses or rate them on a scale: they were simply saying *you are not alone.*

Some people's reactions really surprised me. Acquaintances at my boys' school would just about turn and walk the other way when they saw me approaching. I thought, *Shit, I'm that girl now. That person who no one knows what they should say to so it's easier to avoid me altogether.* By contrast, others came up to me in tears, to engulf me in a big hug and say how sorry they were. Both reactions are emotionally charged, compounding a time that was already so intense, it was a bit like walking around with my heart exposed. A quick school drop-off or trip to the shops became difficult. I wasn't just grabbing milk, I was bracing myself for the off-chance I'd be expected to engage in conversation about a raw, gut-wrenching topic in the middle of the dairy aisle.

I was acutely aware that my story was a hot topic of conversation both at school and within our social circle: not in a negative or gossipy way but because people cared and because it was such sad news. People often asked our close friends how we were going. In fact, this was more frequently the case than people asking us directly about how we were coping. I was a living, breathing example of many people's worst nightmare, so it was understandable that people were curious. During pregnancy and the newborn period we all worry something might go wrong, but we have a naive certainty that the 'something horrible' won't happen to us. The reality of it is far too brutal to imagine. We think that if we do all of the right things and follow the rules, we will be safe. But sadly, that alone is no guarantee of a good outcome.

For a while, I felt like every time someone saw me for the first time since I lost Miles, speaking to me was something they needed to tick off their to-do list. They knew the moment would come and were probably nervous about it but once they'd eyeballed me and said their bit (or completely ignored it and acted like nothing had happened), they were able to get on with their lives. Tick, done. The bereaved, however, are left to do this over and over and over again. Facing multiple interactions is exhausting and emotionally draining. I'm not in any way saying *don't talk to the bereaved mother - please always do!* Saying nothing is way worse. But be aware that she may already have had this conversation five times that day, or even that morning, and it's a lot to handle. She may not have the strength or energy to go into anything in detail: perhaps she has just done that with someone else, and is now running on empty. Or perhaps, like many times when I was walking kids into their classrooms and trying to get them settled, it isn't an appropriate time for her to stop and talk.

One of the nicest things that happened to me was when I ran into people and they sensed it was not a great time to talk, so they gave me a quick hug or said, "I've been thinking of you" and let me get on with my business. Often this was followed by a message or phone call to say something like, "I could see it wasn't a great time to chat, please know I'm here for you whenever you need to or want to talk." That opened the lines of communication and I knew without any hesitation that this person acknowledged my loss and was there for me, when it suited me. To reverse this, I often quickly said to people, "I'd love to talk but I'm not quite ready, I'll let you know when I am." It's a delicate balance: I was well aware that many good friends wanted to show their support and I didn't want to push them away. But I didn't always have the headspace to take them up on the opportunity at the exact moment they offered. Sometimes I was having a relatively good day and didn't want to burst my own bubble. (It was guaranteed to burst of its own accord at some point, so it was nice to enjoy some respite on the days that for some reason felt lighter.)

At about the one-month mark, after we'd come back to town, I felt overwhelmed by the number of people who wanted to catch up with me for a coffee. Some were people I'd never had coffee with before, but I think they wanted to do something to check that I was okay and to offer their support. The invitations came from kindness and goodness, but I found them a lot to deal with. I barely had the energy for my own family and oldest friends, so to have multiple catch-ups all over the place was something I couldn't even fathom. There were old close friends I still had to call back, organise to catch up with, presents I needed to thank people for, and in the midst of a muddled grief-mind, it was overwhelming. I felt rude rejecting people, but needed to make sure I didn't overload myself.

What really helped was when people gently guided me. Messages that began with, "please don't respond" or "I'm sure catching up and talking about Miles is hard, so I'd love to see you and am happy to talk, not talk or do whatever feels right for you." This took the pressure off me. I don't love being the center of attention, though it's something I've never shied away from either. I hated the idea of a catch-up that was specifically organised with the intent of seeing me and checking in on how I was going. The pressure felt immense. I was worried I'd cry throughout the walk, coffee or lunch, and it'd just be an uncomfortable, depressing experience for everyone.

I guess that's where true friends come in. They don't care if it's "all about you" – that's what they're there for, to listen and support. I knew my friends wouldn't be offended if I needed to postpone, or if I wanted to go to something but didn't want to talk about anything other than the weather. I found that usually once I built up the courage to go out and started talking, the initial tears would ease and I'd feel better for opening up even if it was hard to do so at first.

What left me feeling the worst was when I was with a group of women I knew reasonably well, either socially or in a work setting, and no one mentioned Miles: especially if it was the first time I had seen them or spoken to them since he died. I know people avoided talking about Miles or asking how I was going for fear of upsetting me, but nothing could upset me more that what had already happened. He was always on my mind, so by not mentioning him, people weren't sparing me pain - they were making me feel uncomfortable in my grief. There was never a time that I wasn't contemplating what had happened, especially in the early days. Miles and my memories were with me every waking moment.

If after an initial meeting people avoided the topic and didn't
check in on how I was feeling, I felt really funny about that too.
It seemed like there was a large blue elephant sitting in the corner
of the room, waiting to be acknowledged. I'd think - *Are they going
to say anything? Is it my role to bring it up? Should I be the one to
raise the topic?* I didn't expect a long conversation, but a simple
"how are you going?" would have gone a long way in removing
any awkwardness. I wasn't expecting anyone to give me the magic
answer to my problems, or make a statement so profound that in
an instant I would feel better. I wasn't even looking to others for
the simplest of advice: just support and acknowledgement of what
was happening in my life. As the months wore on, this expectation
or hope subsided and I no longer took offence when no one
mentioned Miles. I had become more comfortable in my grief and
it no longer dominated my every single thought.

You may find that gearing yourself up for each interaction and
each outing feels like an act of bravery. I had to pep myself up
to go out, to talk to people and engage with the real world. It
did get easier, but it was like ripping off a million little bandaids.
Anticipating people's reactions, managing their response to my
situation and making conversation felt intimidating. I often felt I
had to guide people, as it didn't come naturally to them, or I could
sense they couldn't think of where to begin. At first I didn't know
how to answer basic questions like "how are you?" or "are you
feeling any better?", so I came up with some standard lines to take
the pressure off, like "It's been tough and I have a long way to go".
Strangely, I found that some of the less close people in my life were
good sounding-boards. They were not so emotionally entwined as
my close friends, and could talk to me without fear of bursting into
tears. It gave me the chance to practice talking about Miles in a less

emotionally charged situation. That said, I actually loved it when people did start crying, as it showed me how much they cared.

Social occasions were also difficult which as a naturally social person was hard for me at first. Socialising and grieving are not natural bedfellows. It's a bit like when you're struck down with a nasty cold: the last thing you feel like doing is getting dressed up and heading out. Doing so when grieving is not all that different, as you may have understandably lost the stamina or inclination for such things. Celebrations such as baby showers, gender reveals and, christenings are likely to add another layer of dread. Let's be honest - the thought of these may be as appealing as sticking a fork in your eye. If for your own emotional wellbeing, these occasions are too much, it is okay not to go to them. You should never have to push your own sanity or jeopardise your recovery for the sake of another. If you were to ask someone with a broken leg to run a marathon with you and they declined, I can't imagine you would push them to justify their decision or insist on their participation: it's just not something they're physically capable of. We need to afford the same compassion to people's emotional capacity. If an occasion is going to be too hard to endure, you are entitled to say no and should not feel that you need to give a reason.

If you feel guilty for not attending, as I did for one friend's birthday lunch, skip the lunch, (or the bulk of the event) and join the group for a drink after. Doing this meant that I was only out for a little over an hour, and I didn't run the risk of feeling overwhelmed. It was a good compromise and in the end I really enjoyed heading out, seeing some friends and feeling more like my old self for a little bit. Self-imposed isolation can be very draining.

Some invitations were an automatic *no* from the get-go. I was asked if I'd like to join a group on a day trip to a seaside town to visit a friend's newborn baby. Everyone was travelling down in one car, so I would have no control over the duration of the outing should it all get too much for me. I had no interest in exposing myself to a day-long group situation that could also be full of triggers.

I tended to prefer smaller groups. I caught up with a beautiful girl for a play in the park with our youngest daughters, who were the same age. I had run into her on Josh's birthday, the day before I delivered Miles. I messaged her after his birth to tell her what had happened. She replied with such beautiful words that I felt like she was a safe person to reach out to later. She seemed to get my pain. In one message, she told me about an article she'd read that said that a heart can physically break during trauma, as it affects the muscle tissue. This made so much sense to me. About nine weeks after Miles died, she reached out again to see if I'd like to catch up. We grabbed coffees and headed over the road to a playground. She immediately said, "How are you? I've been thinking of you constantly." I burst into tears and said, "It's really hard and even harder to talk about, so thank you for asking."

We had a huge, open, honest conversation about what I wanted to do next, my desire (obsession) to have another baby and how exhausting it was to manage my grief amidst motherhood and work. It was akin to talking to a counsellor: she was happy to let me chat and workshop my ideas, without feeling the need to fix things for me or try to cheer me up.

Losing Miles has helped me to identify people I feel connected to, and not feel shy about reaching out to them. You get a sense sometimes that someone will be able to cope with what you're feeling. They may not have been your closest friend in the past, but they might be the right person for you in this moment. Not all of my friends could handle what had happened to me. Rather than resent this, I focused on what they could and did do for me and sought out the company of others to fill any gaps. Not everyone is going to understand your grief or respond to it how you would like them to, but in the end not everyone is equipped to do so.

I found it hugely comforting when people acknowledged my grief initially via text, card or email and then, when I was ready, over the phone or in person. One particularly close person did not make contact with me directly in any way, apart from liking an Instagram post about Miles. Other than this, there was no text, no phone call or mention of Miles in later conversations. This hurt, but as time went on I realised they were simply not equipped to deal with this level of tragedy or didn't realise how necessary it was for them to reach out to me. Even though it would most likely alter our relationship, I didn't feel anger towards them - just disappointment. I can appreciate that it's an uncomfortable conversation to have for many, but for me, it was hugely important that people, (especially those close to me) stepped up and found the courage to say something.

With a topic as taboo as baby loss, the reactions of others can range from incredibly compassionate and comforting, to deeply hurtful. I tried to not let the reactions of those who disappointed me get me down. Instead I focused on thinking about how over time, we could try to change how people respond. How could we teach future generations that the loss of a baby in the womb or soon after birth is a very real and significant loss of life and that saying nothing to the parents causes additional pain? Perhaps it changes one step at a time. Each time someone responds to your grief with outward kindness and compassion, others around them will hopefully see that it's not so scary after all, and can have a truly positive effect on those suffering. I always thanked people for mentioning Miles or asking how I was going.

I also took great comfort in knowing just how far we have come as a society. In previous generations, when women gave birth to still babies, they were often not told the gender, given the chance to hold their baby or offered any opportunity to say goodbye to their child in a meaningful way. Babies were whisked away, treated as medical waste. Mothers were told to move on, have another one and get over it. Thank goodness that is no longer the way baby loss is dealt with. I can't imagine the additional trauma this would bring.

Chapter 21 How to begin moving through grief

Many of us are expected to or need to return to our 'normal' lives very quickly after losing our babies. I had no choice but to re-enter the real world exactly a month after Miles died. Some people may have to return to their commitments far sooner than this. The school run stops for no one, kids' sports are a never-ending whirlwind and school lunches don't make themselves. The boys had new teachers, new classes to settle into and my work commitments recommenced.. I didn't cope with any of this very well.

In the midst of all this activity and busyness, my recovery was stalling - or worse, going backwards. It was a terrifying and confronting time, as I wanted to feel better, but was convinced that I'd never be able to handle the ins and outs of my life as I had before. Once the initial shock wore off the cold hard reality of what had happened began to set in with a brutal permanence. I was no longer cocooned by disbelief and denial: this was real and it was horrible.

I had lost the capacity to juggle. I was slower, sadder and not my best self. There is a quote from writer Toni Morrison which beautifully sums up that time: "pain can be greedy, leaving little room for anything else." Josh kept having to remind me there were going to be good days and bad days, that I just needed to roll with it. If I needed to step back or cancel an appointment or meeting, that was fine. If I didn't want to talk to another parent on the school run, I should pop on the dark sunnies, give a quick wave and move on. Everyone would understand. The initial numbness that shock brings had worn off and was no longer protecting me.

I felt like life was moving in slow motion: each day was an eternity. It was as though I had aged twenty years in the space of a month. Small tasks seemed formidable and fraught with danger. As one friend said, there were probably a lot of extra cogs turning in my brain that I wasn't aware of. The exhausting grief process seemed to have no end: a truly depressing thought. The idea of being stuck in this fog forever was daunting, but I had no idea how to get out of it and certainly on many days, I didn't have the energy.

I wanted a quick fix, but there wasn't one. The only thing to do was to keep moving forward, one step and one day at a time, and not shy away from what I was feeling. I would say to Josh, "I'm sick of feeling like this." I felt guilty that I was no longer the busy, efficient person I'd been. The best advice Josh gave me was to embrace the good days and make the most of them, as usually these were followed by down days. When your step feels that little bit lighter, embrace it. This doesn't mean you're moving on or getting over it: it just means you're giving yourself a little break and a chance to regain some energy.

I was never someone to prioritise self-care and felt guilty doing things for myself. Our house was a mess. There was so much I could see needed doing, but had to resign myself to living in chaos. After losing a baby, you come to realise that an overflowing laundry basket or dirty toilet is actually not so bad and certainly not important. I tried not to put too much pressure on myself to cook every night and go back to how I was before Miles. I hoped one day I could but for now I didn't need the added burden of feeling guilty for not being a domestic goddess - or even a semi-functioning adult. Simply getting up and making breakfasts, packing lunches and getting kids to school on time was enough. If then I got home, felt exhausted, needed to lie down and have a cry, or mindlessly scroll through Instagram for an hour before starting work, that was okay. It wasn't going to be forever. That is all easier said than done and I am my own harshest critic, but the sooner I allowed myself to let things go and stop to take care of myself, the better I felt.

Not everyone will be in a position to take time off work or do less within their household, but I think it's important that if you can't step back a little, you explain your limitations to your family and your work colleagues. You may feel like you're failing or not pulling your weight, but other people are unlikely to see it that way. They will probably think you are incredible for doing what you already are doing, or for just getting up, having a shower and leaving the house in the morning. The sooner your worries are out in the open, the sooner people can act with compassion towards you. The modern world moves so fast that people often don't stop to consider how people are going after a tragedy. You might feel like your loss happened yesterday, but to them it could seem like months or weeks ago. A gentle reminder that you're still grieving helps everyone and makes it easier to communicate how you're coping, so if you need to step back a little they are understanding of why.

A few women I spoke to felt they could not return to their old job or work after the death of their baby. Some found their workplace to be filled with too many reminders and triggers of their loss or its culture unsympathetic to what they were dealing with. For others, the pressure to resume their role in a professional environment and to be as fast paced, efficient and driven as they were previously felt immense, as they were no longer that person after their baby's death. Others wanted to dedicate all their energy to falling pregnant again.

Things that used to mean a lot to you may now feel insignificant and no longer inspire any sense of positivity or achievement. Some careers, such as childcare and midwifery, may expose you to too many triggers, making a return to your previous role totally out of the question. Of course it comes down to what will be financially and emotionally realistic in your individual situation, but I don't think anyone should feel they are failing if returning to their old role is not something they can contemplate doing.

While you are on leave, you have the mental and emotional freedom to think about your baby and your experience whenever you want to or when the need arises. Returning to work, you will have to shift your focus and put your energy towards other topics, in addition to managing your grief that is a huge mental burden to juggle if you're not ready: it is challenging to switch off difficult emotions on demand. You may find yourself exposed to triggers you hadn't anticipated, which will catch your breath and cause tears to well in your eyes. It may be as simple as a quarterly meeting, which causes you to reflect on the last one you attended when you were still pregnant. It might be something more obvious, like a co-worker going on maternity leave, or a work baby shower, or something incredibly confronting like a meeting to discuss your position and role within the organisation, (especially if arrangements had already been made to fill your position whilst you were on maternity leave).

In a workplace you will also encounter the good, the bad and the ugly in terms of how people respond to grief and loss, and all of these variations are unavoidable. Some people may know how to welcome you back and help you feel at ease, while others may act like nothing has happened, make no mention of your baby and expect you to be your old self. Some workplaces will allow you to take personal leave or sick leave after a miscarriage. After a stillbirth or the loss of a baby in infancy you may be eligible for government-funded maternity leave and legislation has just been passed to ensure workplaces offer the same entitlements. Returning to your role may be complicated for various reasons- or returning may be problematic if you have already made significant changes within your household based on the leave you anticipated. For example, older children who had been in childcare whilst you were working may no longer be booked in as you had expected to be at home caring for them along with your newborn. There are many factors and I can only hope in time that workplaces implement kind and compassionate policies to help women navigate these additional curveballs.

To me grief felt like a dark heaviness had settled on my shoulders and within my heart. Everyday tasks became arduous, my memory was muddled and my mind was working overtime to try to make sense of what had happened. I was worried people would expect me to bounce back to being my old cheerful and chatty self when I no longer had the bandwidth for idle smalltalk or gossip. Topics which used to interest me now seemed pointless and insignificant. I'd find myself among a group of people whinging about something I deemed trivial and I'd feel like yelling out "who gives a shit, my baby died, get some perspective!" In time I could thankfully handle normal, natural conversations like this without feeling resentful of how straightforward and easy I perceived other people's lives to be. I came to realise that they were just passing the time with polite conversation - and who knew, perhaps they too were holding onto sadness in their hearts, grinning and bearing their way through day-to-day life just like I was.

Managing my emotions around my children took a lot of energy. It wasn't that I felt I had to always be 'up' around them, but I didn't want to scare them. Children of these ages feed off their mothers' moods so much; I was very aware than my grief could rub off on them. I didn't want to alarm them by being inconsolable in their presence, or completely detached and distant. And let's face it, as lovely as kids can be, they are not always very sensitive to their parents' emotional needs (and nor should they be). It is our job to protect them, teach them resilience and calm their fears; it's not their job to do that in return for us. So while I was exhausted by having to put on a very brave face for the children I was ever so grateful that I had to get up each day, slap on a smile and function for a while for their sake. I needed to keep putting one foot in front of the other and getting on with life. It would have been easy to stay curled up in bed for a very long time, but I knew that ultimately this would do me no good. It would delay facing the inevitable pain which I'd need to work through eventually.

Getting up and motivating yourself to move forward is not a simple thing to do, but it's an important one. In a household without living children, some find a much-loved pet gives purpose, as can a hobby, a fundraising goal, or a memorial garden which needs tending. Whatever it may be, try to embrace it and allow yourself to savour the happiness and comfort it brings. I still had really terrible days where I would want to go back to bed after dropping the kids at school. This kind of day would take me straight back to the day we lost Miles and the weeks that followed. I'd feel like I'd physically had the air sucked out of me and I could not breathe, it felt so raw. I dreaded these days at first, but after a while I stopped fearing them. Afterwards I'd feel completely drained but strangely refreshed, like I'd managed to get something out of my system.

What I found most shocking was how hard the sadness could hit me seemingly out of the blue. It usually wasn't as random as I thought, there was often a trigger I didn't recognise until I was feeling less emotional: I could have a few okay days and then it was as though a massive rain cloud moved above me and poured down. I found this especially hard as time moved on. I felt like people thought I should have moved on by this stage, that the timer of my grief clock had gone off, and I was expected to pack it all away in a neat little box and move on. However, the feelings and flashbacks on some days were so strong, it was like I was still in the hospital, holding Miles and saying goodbye all over again. I found it hard to believe that this had actually happened to me. That it wasn't a cruel joke, a trick, a nightmare: it really had happened and nothing on earth would bring my baby back. There was no magic button, no second chance. This thought pattern alone was exhausting. Life moves on, but your loss stays the same. That is a hard thing to accept. I didn't want to forget Miles, but I did want to move on in some way. I was tired and missed being my old self.

People find comfort in so many different things: walking the dog, going to yoga or having a warm bath and a cup of tea. I wish I was more holistic, but I find it hard to unwind. Most people I have spoken to eventually found one small thing that helped them through their grief. One friend of mine started running. She'd run in any conditions - pouring rain or strong winds - and as she pounded the pavement, she'd let the tears run unchecked down her cheeks. Another poured all of her energy into her dogs, smothering them with endless love and attention. For me, work was the answer - and lots of it to keep me busy. I needed days off when I felt exhausted and swamped by my sadness, but overall having a sense of purpose and a goal to work towards helped immensely. It was a 'fake it till you make it' situation.

So apart from watching *Outlander* and crying, my self-care routine was pretty simple. I didn't go to anything I didn't feel up to going to. I didn't reply to every email, text and card I received, and pushed any fear of being perceived rude by not doing so to the side. I tried to go to bed early, I read a lot and treated myself to the occasional massage or pedicure. Self-care doesn't have to cost money; it can simply be about setting boundaries. The best and biggest thing for me was learning to say no, and not feeling one single bit of remorse about it. No, I don't feel like doing that. No, I'm not going to go to that. I used to be an absolute yes girl to everything. I had lost the energy for this and realised that you don't need to go to and do everything or be everything to everyone. I deliberately dropped off the face of the earth when it came to things that were no longer urgent or necessary and I was happy with that.

Self-care may also be as simple as putting a distance between yourself and people who you feel are not understanding or compassionate, or putting up some boundaries with people whose attentiveness is too much. There are many ways to look after yourself and at the most basic level it's about trusting your gut and doing things that bring calm, not chaos. For me, prioritising my own needs and putting a safe distance between myself and people or situations that didn't help my recovery was essential. Moving forward through grief takes a lot of time and energy, so casting aside things and people who don't help isn't selfish. Making yourself the priority is a survival mechanism.

There is a Winston Churchill quote which resonated with me: "If you're going through hell, keep going". It is simple, but powerful and certainly sums up what ultimately worked for me. I just had to keep putting one foot in front of the other, even when I really didn't feel like it. There were breaks along the way - steps sideways and steps backwards - but overall, I kept trying to keep going. How each person will face this is truly unique to them. Fatigue and exhaustion are hard to shake with a low state of mind, so rather than try to conquer it all in one bite, my best advice would be to treat yourself with kindness and allow yourself the time to gently find and restore your energy, to climb your way out of the darkness one small step at a time.

Chapter 22 Grief is a rollercoaster

As the weeks and months rolled on, I found that certain events or the lead-up to significant dates could set me back terribly – all of a sudden, I would feel like I was back at the very beginning of this nightmare. Over time I got better at preempting these and putting coping strategies in place. I started seeing a psychologist about six weeks after Miles died. Even though I didn't feel like I was suffering from clinical depression or anxiety, I knew I was not myself. While I knew I had to feel anxious and sad in order to move forward, it was so hard, uncomfortable and daunting. I worried about something dreadful happening to my husband and living children, as I'd lost my naïve certainty that life was simple.

I told myself I was seeing my psychologist, Brooke, as a preventative measure. But while I thought I was coping pretty well, I needed the support of someone neutral and specially trained in this area. I felt that if from the start I'd had someone to talk to, someone to workshop my thoughts with, I would be better equipped to handle the really tough days. I knew there were many more ahead of me and didn't always have the strength to cope with them alone. The worst thing would be to bury it all, only for the pain to rear its ugly head later, which I knew was inevitable if I didn't start dealing with it here and now. If you don't have access to a counsellor or psychologist, there are many organisations who offer counselling services to bereaved parents at no charge. I have listed these at the end of the book. Most of them are run and facilitated by parents who have also lost a child, so the support they offer is both understanding and compassionate.

Regardless of how far along your pregnancy was when you suffered a miscarriage or stillbirth, your baby's due date will have been indelibly stamped in your brain. This date is likely to remain with you always. My due date was the fifteenth of April, which I had been looking forward to with excitement and a touch of anxiety, but mostly happiness. The date then became shrouded with sadness and longing, as it would never mark the arrival of a living, breathing child. It served only as a reminder of what I had lost.

Similarly, I paid a lot of attention to how many weeks along I should have been. I was so excited to be six months, and at twelve weeks, I was thrilled to have made it through the first trimester. Regardless of gestation, I felt like I was always aiming for the next stage, the next step to bring me closer to my baby. I used to think each Tuesday, which was the exact day when my pregnancy rolled into its next consecutive week, *I'd be twenty-eight weeks now*, or *I'd be thirty-five weeks now*. It was a devastating reminder of what I wasn't. My flat, empty tummy seemed so lifeless, so barren. I'd wonder how big my bump would have been, or how much the baby would be moving by now. No one else was aware of these dates, but for me Tuesdays were hard for a while, as I was always thinking of what could and should have been.

There are lots of unavoidable appointments, dates and events you have to face after you have lost your baby. My first trip back to the hospital where Miles was delivered was excruciating. Brooke had told me to plan the day carefully and have something comforting locked in after the appointment, to make sure I would be surrounded by people who would take care of me. I booked in lunch after my appointment with my friend Julia, who'd tragically lost her baby at fourteen weeks, as I knew she would be sympathetic and also able to handle whatever topics I threw at her.

Stupidly, and I still don't know why I did this (well I do know why, I'm a people pleaser who hates fuss), I told Josh he didn't need to come with me to this appointment. Big mistake. Huge!

Josh had been insanely busy at work and had asked if I wanted or needed him to come along. I did want his support and the thought of going back to the place where I'd last seen Miles haunted me, but I also didn't want to drag Josh there in the middle of a busy work week. Often the wait time for appointments was unpredictable and we had previously waited about two hours to see our doctor. Knowing this was a possibility and given how flat-out Josh's week was, I decided I'd be okay on my own.

I regretted my decision from the minute I parked the car and started to walk toward the entrance of the hospital, holding back tears. It was definitely not something I should have been doing alone. I sat in the waiting room, trying to calm myself down. Everything was familiar: the plastic sofas, the posters on the wall with advice on maintaining a healthy pregnancy, the flickering fluorescent light in the corner. The dread I had felt when waiting in exactly the same room for news of Miles' condition returned with full force. The flashbacks were so strong, it was like time had stood still and I'd never left, the only difference being that Miles was no longer with us and unlike the other women in the waiting room, I was no longer pregnant.

I decided to call Josh and tell him to come in, but just as I was about to, I was called in by our doctor, after the tiniest wait in hospital history: just ten minutes. The Maternal Fetal Medicine Doctor who had seen us before Miles was delivered, took me into his office and yet again, I knew I really should have brought Josh with me. I hadn't been entirely sure what this appointment was about. I didn't know if it was to check how I was recovering physically after labour and surgery, or to discuss the findings of the autopsy. It was both and more. Our doctor also wanted to know how we were coping emotionally and to find out what we were planning to do in regard to contemplating another pregnancy.

I cried through the entire appointment. The tears would not stop falling, despite my best efforts. Big fat heavy tears, which pooled under my chin. It was gut wrenching to be sitting in exactly the same chair, talking to the same doctor as I had when we found out that we'd lose Miles. Thankfully our doctor was incredibly kind and compassionate; I'm sure he'd seen it all before. He thanked me for coming in, telling me that a lot of parents cannot face returning to the place in which they lost their child and last saw, held or felt them. He assured me that what was revealed in the autopsy confirmed what the ultrasound and MRI prior to delivery had indicated.

The blood clot in Miles' brain had been firmly in place, ultimately causing irreparable damage. We had known we had no choice, that Miles basically had no chance of survival or any quality of life, but to have this confirmed was strangely comforting. We discussed the possibility of more children and whether there was a risk of what happened to Miles reoccurring. There were no definitive answers but it was a chance to ask as many questions as possible. Again, I realised I really needed Josh. I couldn't think straight or absorb information adequately, let alone ask the questions that needed be asked. My emotions were in overdrive and I was expending a lot of energy trying to calm myself down. The entire situation was too much and far too intense for one person to handle alone.

I was supposed to collect Miles' memory box from the hospital social worker after seeing the doctor, but once my appointment was over I had an all-consuming physical need to get out of the hospital. I pulled on the dark glasses and practically ran to the nearest exit. I couldn't bear being in the building for another moment. It wasn't that I cared about people seeing me crying, or my big puffy eyes. I felt haunted by the memories the building held and unprepared for the impact of returning to it. Sometimes you just can't be brave, and you shouldn't always have to be. I have returned since for other appointments and each time has been a bit easier than the first visit, but I still can't say it's something I am able to do without an ache in my chest and a lump in my throat.

One thing from this appointment that has stayed with me was our doctor's understanding of why people feel the need to try again after losing a child. He said, "You had a plan, you may still have that plan. You lost a baby, but that doesn't necessarily mean you have to change your plan." For me, the plan was still to one day see four kids at my kitchen table. If we are lucky enough to have another, I will have fulfilled my dream, with an extra angel watching us from above. What I took from our doctor's sentiment was, *you have lost Miles and he is with you forever. He will not be replaced by another baby but it is completely natural to want to stick to your original dream. Another baby would not be instead of Miles, but because of him.*

When a respected professional, a leader in a specialist field of medicine, shows as much insight and compassion as our doctor did, it does a lot for the soul. His medical expertise was sought globally and over the years, he had seen countless couples endure heartache like ours. It comforted me that he didn't think we were mad for wanting to try for another baby and that he recognised just how devastating losing Miles had been for our family. Not once while in his care did I feel ridiculous or histrionic, even though all I seemed to do in front of him was cry!

After exiting the building as fast as I could, I made a beeline for my car and rang Josh. I didn't bother with the usual pleasantries and jumped straight to, "If you ever, EVER, ask me if you need to come to an important appointment involving a child of ours again and I say no, take it as a yes! You know if you ask I'll always say, *don't worry, I'm okay on my own,* which I absolutely AM NOT." I wasn't cross he hadn't been there, merely cross that I hadn't properly acknowledged to myself just how hard that appointment was going to be. I'd been jittery all week and hadn't been able to put my finger on exactly why, but it was obvious afterwards.

I went to lunch with my beautiful friend. We laughed, cried, shared our stories and I felt a million times lighter than I had that morning. We talked about Miles and she asked me how I had physically been able to leave him behind and how it had felt to deliver a baby I knew I'd never take home. It was so comforting to share my whole story, unedited, being given the chance to speak openly without fear of saying too much or making her feel uncomfortable. I knew she could handle it and wanted to know what it had been like and, in turn, I relished the opportunity to unload, as I didn't get the chance very often. The next few days felt much lighter. That's how my weeks have flowed after losing Miles. I've had days where I've felt almost fine and days where I've felt incapable of functioning and had to wipe away the tears, grit my teeth and do my best to get on with day-to-day life.

I thought grief would be linear. It would start at one point, like a line at the bottom of a chart, and over time move upwards, back towards normal, happy. Oh how wrong I was! It peaks and dips, goes backwards and forwards and loops in full-on figure-eights. There is nothing linear about it and many of the ups and downs can't be predicted. Events I feared would trigger a huge reaction sometimes felt easy and at other times, the smallest of reminders would set me back.

I kept thinking; *I wonder what stage of grief I am in? Am I up to denial? Anger? Is it five stages or seven?* I had expected it to follow a set pattern over time, a logical linear progression. It had never occurred to me that you could feel the emotions of each stage of grief in one single day, in one single hour or even in one single thought. I came to see that these stages were each going to be revisited multiple times, that I didn't tick a box or get a badge for one stage and move onto the next. If only it were that simple. I found out, after a bit of research, that the theory on the five stages of grief has not necessarily always been interpreted as its original creator, Elizabeth Kübler-Ross, intended it to be. "Kübler-Ross originally saw these stages as reflecting how people cope with illness and dying, not as reflections of how people grieve," observed grief researcher Kenneth J. Doka in his book *On Grief & Grieving: finding the meaning of grief through the five stages of loss.*

I was relieved, as I had read through the stages and they didn't mirror my path at all. I had felt the first four stages - denial, anger, bargaining and depression - all in one single breath, not in a nice neat pattern and the final stage – acceptance - didn't resonate with me at all. If I had tried to subscribe to this theory, which was never intended for people who were grieving the loss of a loved one, I would have permanently felt like a square peg in a round hole, as though I was not making progress at all.

I eventually realised there was no end point, no set pattern and no final destination. My love for Miles would be with me forever and there was no rush to get to the 'end' of the grieving process as it simply didn't exist. He was my child, I would miss him forever, love him always and never had to get over his death. Regardless of how long it took, there was no timer being set, and no expectation of how I should approach it. It was my journey with Miles and it was entirely up to me how I chose to make my way through it. At first I thought I would be this sad forever and wouldn't have believed anyone who told me otherwise. But my bursts of happiness were like rays of sunshine on a cloudy day. They stubbornly kept poking through the clouds and even though the clouds kept trying to smother them, they shone on and eventually through.

I spoke with a friend who is a life coach and asked her what advice she would give to someone starting their journey on the rollercoaster ride that is grief. What she wholeheartedly advised was not to resist it, not to push it aside, but to let it go where it needs to in order for the healing process to begin. Here are Laura's words:

Wholly embrace it. Here and now.

Don't focus on getting through it, just move through what you feel today, how the grief feels today.

See it as exactly what you are meant to be feeling right now.

See your grief as perfect just the way it is.

Be with it.

Not raging against it, numbing it, thinking you just need to 'pull your socks up' and get over it.

Let the tears roll.

Then notice the thoughts you are having and grab hold of them for a moment.

Do you want to be thinking and feeling like this right now?

If you do, be with it.

If you are ready, consider more neutral thoughts, or thoughts that look toward meaning, purpose.

Know that in time the tears will lessen. But that those tears are ESSENTIAL for you to be able to move forward in time, when you feel ready, and there is no timeline that is right or wrong.

It will never leave you. It will feel different in a year's time, and maybe different again many years from now, but it will always be part of who you are now. And from that you will reshape your life.

Create meaning and purpose from the loss.

Continue your baby's legacy.

Reconnect with relationships that align with who you have become through that grief.

Release relationships that no longer do.

Reawaken to yourself, a you who you recognise but who is so different; wiser, with scars, but we heal stronger where our scars are our friends.

And know. Evolution requires solitude and loneliness and pain. You are exactly where you are meant to be.

I loved the notion that wherever you are is where you are supposed to be, that there is no set path, no pattern to follow, that you do whatever is necessary to build a new normal. It is easy to feel pressured into feeling better or appearing to feel better, but what is really important is embracing your feelings and doing what is best for you. I found comfort in accepting that there would be bad days, that significant dates would trigger a huge response and that there would be seemingly normal days, that like a wolf in sheep's clothing, would attack me by surprise.

How you feel able to publicly respond to and share your loss can also change. Sometimes you may have a strong desire to talk about your baby and what you experienced, but this does not mean you always have to be so open. Only you can set the pace and dictate the boundaries. There are some aspects of your journey you may feel more comfortable sharing than others and that is also okay. Just because you're comfortable sharing one element, does not mean all aspects of your life become public property. You can open and shut your book as you wish and do so at your own pace.

An analogy that I think perfectly describes moving through grief after the loss of a baby is the game of snakes and ladders. You roll the dice, hope to move forward and are sometimes met with a lucky break, a ladder that gives you a little help upwards. Perhaps it is a message from a beautiful friend or a few days of feeling lighter and less snowed under. You move forward with hope, only to land on a snake after your next roll. Down you spiral, backwards and free-falling. There is no way of predicting whether you will land on a snake or a ladder and everyone else playing the game is also at the mercy of the number they roll. There is no way of controlling it and everyone follows their own path, navigating independently through whatever obstacles come their way. When grieving, there are some obvious triggers we can attempt to prepare ourselves for but equally, there are the unexpected snakes that send us spiraling back into the darkness. We just have to hope that on our next roll of the dice we will find a ladder.

Chapter 23 Losing more than just your baby

I'm a planner. I think many women are, in terms of the big picture. I might forget to return library books or to put toilet paper on the shopping list but when it comes to the year ahead, I like to have a good sense of what is in front of me. In my adult life, I'd spent many years working in catering, most of them as the owner of my own business and a few as an event coordinator. It is a fast-paced, unpredictable industry: you never know what dates you'll be booked out on and which periods of the year will be quieter. Once I had children, this unpredictability frustrated me. I was always juggling last-minute childcare arrangements and missing out on weekends with the kids when I had big functions to cater.

The year we started trying to fall pregnant with Miles, I also decided to have a career change. I'd always dreamed of getting into the creative side of the food industry, in particular styling and photography. Combined with my skills in recipe writing, I felt that would be the perfect niche market for me to forge a new career in. My plan was to get the new business up and running so that by the time the baby arrived, I'd have established a good name for myself, which would enable me to put things on hold for a few months, then build back up to full-time work after my maternity leave.

I loved my plan and I was excited about the year ahead. I adored the creative aspects of food styling and photography and, if anything, wished I had made this move earlier. I was also so excited about welcoming my last baby. I have an affinity for newborns: they're my thing, my drug of choice. I love the smell of them, the feel of them and the absolute wonder and delight a tiny baby brings. I had decided that while on maternity leave I would finally have the opportunity to start writing and testing recipes for my own cookbook, a goal I'd had for many years. From where I was sitting, 2019 was going to be one of those magical years. I had all of my ducks in a row and felt both excited and grateful about what was ahead.

When Miles died, I suddenly had no idea what to do with myself. I was cast into limbo, my beautiful plan destroyed, my confidence shattered and my mind in panic mode. How was I going to face clients and work deadlines? Did I have to return to work? If I didn't, what on earth would I do with myself? At times I could barely get through mundane daily tasks without crying, let alone contemplate putting on a professional work front. Early on I'd also lost my drive. I simply didn't give a rat's arse about my business or personal success. I didn't want to be working, I wanted to be heavily pregnant or at home with a newborn. I didn't want to be kicking career goals, networking, building my portfolio. That all seemed so meaningless.

I'm also one for big statements. I announced to a friend early on that I was still going to take full maternity leave. I was entitled to it, so why not? I soon realised this left me totally at sea, with no work and no baby at home to care for. In the end I decided to throw myself back into work. What really got me back out there was my involvement with a charity called Mum Kind, which I had volunteered to work with on a significant project in the first months of 2019. I was helping organise and coordinate a fundraising event for a campaign that would supply one thousand pantry packs to women and children in crisis in my home state.

It was my task to design the packs, work out what long-life ingredients would work best in them and write recipe cards to show how best to use what the pack contained. The launch event required a great deal of my input, as I was overseeing the menu and the production of lots of the canapés to be served on the night. I couldn't let the charity down at such short notice and the director was a new but very dear friend of mine, so I met with her in early January to assure her I was still on board. I told her that I needed a month to catch my breath but after that I'd focus on the packs and the launch event.

This turned out to be the best thing for me. I still didn't have a clue what the year would hold for me, nor did I want to start making major decisions about my future. With this commitment to fulfil, at least I wasn't in absolute limbo. This volunteer work forced me to practice putting my professional hat back on, producing work and meeting deadlines. I stumbled a lot, held in tears. Many times, it felt odd to be out in the world, talking to people who didn't know about Miles and having to act as though nothing had happened. It also felt good to be out and momentarily distracted. I came to realise that this year might simply have no plan and the best plan was to take it one day at a time.

For those who are not self-employed, the options and expectations around returning to work may be clearer. Your flexibility and ability to adapt your work to suit your mental state may be limited. Returning to the 'real world' of work is not easy. My fear of returning was compounded by my wish not return to work at all. I wanted to be starting maternity leave as planned. Some women are also in part time roles, dividing their week between paid work and unpaid work caring for older children, many women may also be full-time mothers. Whatever your work situation looks like, stepping back into your old role can be very difficult and breathtakingly sad, as the year ahead no longer resembles any of the visions you previously held for it additionally.

At times, I felt I'd taken on too much too soon, but being run off my feet and forced out of bed each morning had huge benefits. I often didn't want to face the day, but overall it was so good for me to be pushed out of my comfort zone and given a purpose. It was a two-month project, so if by the end of it I felt like I needed time off, I would take it. A few people expressed surprise that I was considering taking time off, probably because I have always been such a worker and loved my job, but I think from the outside people couldn't see how debilitating my grief was, or didn't realise how much energy it was taking for me to function 'normally'. Putting on a brave face and getting on with things, can make people underestimate the impact of what you're going through.

Not knowing what is next for you is hard to accept, especially if (like me) you have a burning desire to know - and to an extent control - what the future holds. I desperately wanted another baby, but wasn't sure if this was possible, as we had no idea whether what had happened to Miles could happen again. There were genetics doctors and experts at the WCH investigating our case. We met with the head of the genetics unit, who asked if we were comfortable with Miles being included in a study they were doing in conjunction with Harvard University about unexplained fetal conditions. We were warned that it was like searching for a needle in a haystack and there was about a 5% possibility of the study finding an answer. We were also told that given how rare Miles' hemorrhage was, it was also unlikely to reoccur in future pregnancies. But no definite answer could be given.

This placed us in further limbo. I felt like I had already lost so much, the thought of losing the opportunity to have another child was devastating. When you lose a baby, you lose so much more than the baby itself. We decided to start trying again anyway, as I didn't want to waste time. The Harvard study promised only a slim chance of getting any results and I couldn't stand the idea of waiting, especially since it may never give us an answer. We had had a perfectly healthy baby together before and I had two other healthy children, so what happened to Miles was, I hoped, a one-in-a-million stroke of bad luck.

Trying to fall pregnant brings with it another sense of living in limbo. The waiting, the hoping, the disappointment. I decided it was best for me to go back to work, as an idle mind can be a dangerous thing. This decision brought with it some testing moments though as I felt I couldn't accept certain jobs in case I was lucky enough to be pregnant or have another baby later in the year. Until I had a better idea of what the year(s) ahead might hold I wouldn't be able to formulate a new plan or commit to certain things in the future. This, like everything else, left me feeling completely bewildered.

For the whole year before Miles was born, every decision I made was based upon getting pregnant or being pregnant. The first six months of the year were about getting pregnant, so I avoided booking concerts, trips or anything major in the future in case I did and couldn't go. Similarly, for the second six months of the year everything was planned with our baby in mind. I realised later how much I'd put on hold and sacrificed during this time. It hadn't bothered me then, as the final outcome was exactly what I had dreamed of, but the thought of having to do it all over again left me feeling defeated and deflated. I had put so much into Miles and anticipating his arrival that the thought of another year of uncertainty filled me with dread. I didn't know if I could go through it again, even though I knew I wanted to have another baby. It was a question of whether that desire outweighed the fear and disruption the process entailed.

During all of this, my mind always turned to the stories of women who had endured long, hard years of infertility and/or recurrent miscarriage. I knew I was incredibly fortunate to have children and to have fallen pregnant with relative ease in the past. As difficult as I was finding my own experience I couldn't comprehend the level of distress and uncertainty such women would face. My challenges were experienced over a relatively short space of time. Given how rudderless I felt, I just couldn't imagine the toll it would take on your mental health and wellbeing over an extended period of time. There seems to be a stigma attached to IVF and infertility, which we need to get rid of. It is also often assumed that IVF is a surefire way of falling pregnant, a seamless medical procedure which guarantees success, though in reality it is often anything but.

Many people never reveal that their children were conceived via IVF, (not that they should have to disclose this). I wonder if this is because people are reticent to reveal that they needed help conceiving. Couples I know enduring infertility are often told by insensitive friends and relatives that they just need to relax and by doing so it's sure to happen, rather than being given support and understanding during a difficult time. All this while warding off questions about when they are going to start a family or have another baby. It must be such a long, lonely excruciating period, especially if you don't have considerate or understanding friends or family.

It's hard to plan or get excited about the future when you have no idea of what it holds. I'm not a *what will be* will be kind of person, I wish I was! But until I learn how to approach life like this, I need to accept that sometimes *not having a plan* is going to be my plan. As much as this may not sit well with me, sometimes it is what it is. If like me the loss of your baby brought with it a series of what I call secondary losses, it's okay to feel frustrated. They're constant reminders that your life was abruptly turned on its head. Eventually for me, a new plan took hold. It was different to the one I'd imagined and was missing one precious part, but once I got used to it, I realised it wasn't as bad as I'd initially feared it would be.

Chapter 24 Fear of being perceived as too absorbed in grief

I spent a lot of time worrying that every time I spoke about Miles and how I was feeling people, would think I was dwelling on him for too long or obsessing over what had happened. I suppose in some ways this notion was reinforced when people stopped asking how I was going. I worried people would see me as being self-indulgent or attention-seeking, when I was feeling anything but. I was just so consumed by what had happened that it occupied nearly every thought for a very long time. Not talking about Miles or how he had died felt unnatural. If he had lived, he would have been front and centre, so it felt wrong not to mention him just because he never made it home. We had so many exciting plans and dreams for him and these did not vanish the day he died. They were replaced with a thousand *what if's* and *why's,* which kept him ever present in a very different way to what we had been expecting.

I didn't want to dominate every social situation with my sad story, to be the downer, the dark shadow in the group, but I felt almost disrespectful when I wasn't acknowledging Miles in some way. I had been changed fundamentally and permanently because of him. It took me a while to mention him comfortably, longer still to mention him without dissolving into tears. People find crying so uncomfortable, so confronting and often stop listening to what you are saying and instead focus on trying to get you to stop crying. Responses such as *don't cry* or *have you considered going to see someone to talk about this* are common, though crying is a very natural and necessary part of healing and should not be suppressed.

I wanted to talk about Miles and realised that sometimes, for the conversation to continue with greater ease, it was easier for people to handle when I held back the tears. I found that when I was able to raise the topic and talk about it in a calm, open way, others found it easier too. It's not that I was trying to hide my sadness or pretend that it wasn't there, and in no way am I saying don't cry, but when I did start really sobbing, people would change the subject in an attempt to stop the flow of tears, which robbed me of the chance to say what I needed to say. I also would sometimes change topics myself in an attempt to stop crying, as I could see how much it alarmed some people, or because I started feeling self-conscious or embarrassed by my tears. It took me a very long time to tell my story without crying, and lots of practice runs of saying his name and being honest about my feelings. For at least the first few months, every time I said Miles' name I would well up with tears and be unable to say any more, even though I really wanted to.

I wondered what it was about saying his name that was so confronting and why I was so averse to letting people see me cry. Why do we avoid this natural outpouring of emotion? Why do we feel embarrassed by it? Is it because it's too raw, too vulnerable? Is it because I was worried people would think I was attention-seeking, depressed, overreacting? It confused me. Despite my attempts to put on a brave face, I felt I was sabotaging my own recovery by not being open about what I was going through. Writing helped me to come up with ways to talk about Miles that were measured and meaningful. I felt too much pressure on the spot to answer questions as simple as *How are you going?* and often answered with *fine* or *better than I was at the beginning*. Sometimes I wanted to delve further and talk about how scary and confusing I was finding everything. To explain my desperation for another child, but do so in a way that explained to people that another baby would not be a replacement for Miles. I wanted to say no, I wasn't fine or better and I might not ever be, without sounding dramatic. That potentially this overwhelming sense of loss and the intense sadness could stay with me forever.

People often want to hear that you are okay. They're thrilled if you respond with "much better", as they have most probably moved on from their own initial shock and anguish and really hope, in the kindest of ways, that you have been able to do that too. Time for the bereaved moves so slowly. At about the eleven-week mark, a friend said how happy she was to hear me sounding better and that the months of healing had served me well. She was shocked when I said it was only eleven weeks since we'd lost Miles. To her, it felt like he had died a long time ago, to me it was still so fresh. I needed to process it, talk about it, and I realised that perhaps by avoiding opening up about Miles during the first months for fear of being perceived as being self-indulgent, I may have missed my chance. So I started to weave Miles into everyday conversation. I was ready to talk about him and had built up the courage to mention his name without dissolving into tears. I realised too that if I did, and it made someone else uncomfortable, they probably weren't the right person for me to be around at this time. Most people were not in the slightest bit fazed and were happy to listen.

I had a very active Instagram page for my food business before Miles was born and for me, it was an integral part of my marketing and networking. It gave me a daily opportunity to show what food I'd been cooking, styling and photographing, as well as giving me the opportunity to connect with other foodies and clients. I didn't have a personal page, as most of my friends followed my food page and as a sole operator, my private life often merged with my business life. I struggled with whether or not I should post anything about Miles to my page after the initial post announcing his birth and death. I've always believed in being transparent and dislike the side of social media that only shows a highlight-reel of life, with none of the hard stuff. I didn't want to scare off potential clients who might think that as a bereaved mother, I was not up to the task of producing work to my usual quality, but I also felt that my page gave me a good platform to share my experience.

Each time, (and it was only a handful of times), after Miles died that I posted about anything related to him, my finger hovered over the 'send post' button, indecisive as to whether I should share my feelings so openly. Is this what people following my foodie page wanted to read? Would people think I was trying to get attention or that I was milking my story? I realised that if it wasn't what they wanted to read about, or thought I was posting to get sympathy, they could keep on scrolling or even unfollow me. I worried that people would think, *Oh, here she goes again, banging on about her baby.* But people responded with great warmth and most encouragingly, offered their unwavering support. I received a beautiful card from a friend in New Zealand which strengthened my resolve to keep posting about Miles and eventually give him his own page. She wrote:

To Dear Annabel

I have not stopped thinking of you since the birth announcement of baby Miles.

He really is perfect in every way.

My heart broke for you and the family that day but I have since witnessed the most extraordinary levels of strength and resilience and I am amazed at how well you conduct yourself professionally and being brave enough to grieve, not in silence, but in a way that offers hope and strength to other families living through similar sad times.

When it came down to it, this was one of the main reasons I wanted to share my story – to help others going through the same heartache. I did want to talk about Miles, but I mainly wanted to help people understand what life was like for me after losing a baby. Yes, in the other twenty posts put up that month, I was busy working, cooking, photographing, but alongside this I was mourning the loss of my child. I didn't want a round of applause or a medal, I just wanted to let people know that even though life does go on the grief remains and sits alongside the ordinariness of everyday life. They are not independent of one another.

You can have career success and be proud of this while still feeling incredibly sad. You can miss your child with every ounce of your being and still have a ball at a fun event. Life may still be full of friends, family and fun but within the ups and downs, the sadness remains. Sometimes the pain seemed stronger and at other times, it kindly hid itself away to let me make some new happy memories.

The most beautifully sad and inspiring stories often came from me opening up about Miles. One friend told me about the pain and sorrow of a miscarriage that left her husband so heartbroken he couldn't bring himself to try again. But at the wife's insistence they did and they were overjoyed by the arrival of their rainbow baby a little while after. Stories of medical staff, who went above and beyond to care for women in the hardest of circumstances. People who had never spoken of their loss before for fear of being judged, opening up and feeling a million times better after finding someone to share their story with. So even though I initially feared people would think I was over-egging the pudding if I continued to talk about Miles, I knew this was far from the truth. I wanted to find ways to weave my child into the narrative of my life, not hide him away. Talking about him was one of the best ways I could think of doing that.

As time went on I felt a burning desire to open up the conversation surrounding baby loss and infertility. I wanted people to know that we need to talk about it openly to help those going through it. Once my focus shifted from telling my own story to sharing it with the hope of normalising the wider conversation around baby loss, my confidence grew, as did my voice. I knew I had to keep talking, for others who were yet to find their voice.

This book began as a journal and very quickly 10,000 words became 40,000. Before I knew it the word count had reached 90,000 and beyond. Writing allowed me to share all that I was thinking without the fear of others judging me. I didn't tell Josh until I had reached the fifty thousand mark. Many times when he arrived home from work he'd ask, "What have you been up to today?" I'd mumble something about client work, running around after the kids or doing housework, really I'd spent at least half the day writing and then madly scrambling to catch up on all the jobs I'd neglected.

Writing gave the time and energy that would have gone into caring for Miles as a newborn somewhere to blossom. It also forced me to look at the topic of grief very closely. I realised my fear of being perceived as self-indulgent wasn't irrational. If a woman has a miscarriage, people may give her platitudes like, "Well it was very early, silly to get your hopes up" rather than ask how she is recovering physically or emotionally and acknowledge the loss. The expectation that people can move on or find closure also makes it hard for the bereaved to authentically share how they are feeling because as time goes on, the expectation for them to be better is strong. I feared people might think, *Gosh, she's still going on about it, that was months ago.* It's a slow journey and once the initial support dries up, a lonely one too. That is why for me it feels right to keep sharing, to keep talking and to keep honouring Miles. No one who has lost a baby shares their story for notoriety: we'd all give anything not to be in the position we are in. Trust me, there are far easier and less heartbreaking ways to seek attention. So talk away, post on social media as often as you feel the need to. It is not attention-seeking or self-indulgent to acknowledge the loss of your baby, but a natural and necessary way for many people to parent their baby and keep their memory alive.

Chapter 25 Guilt and anger

For a while it felt wrong to smile or laugh after Miles died. I worried that it was disrespectful to him and that in some way any happiness would minimise our loss. I worried that if people saw me cracking a joke or roaring with laughter they'd think, *Great, look how happy she is! She's over it, let's all move on now, nothing more to worry about there!* I was almost protective of my sorrow, as it connected me to Miles. When you suffer the loss of a baby, you don't have many tangible items to honour them with or memories to look back on, so in some ways your grief becomes a talisman of their existence. In the early days, I felt closer to Miles when I was purely focused on him and the pain I was feeling. I felt guilty enjoying life and taking pleasure in my children's lives, as it seemed so unfair that they were here, whereas Miles had never had the chance to start living his life with us.

Two weeks after Miles' birth, we went away to Kangaroo Island, off the coast of South Australia. We have a family beach house there and Josh and I agreed it was the perfect place to escape to with Alfie, Ted and Bonnie until school went back at the end of January. The midsummer weather was glorious, the water as warm as a bath and the kids were in heaven. Day-long trips on the boat, ocean swims, jet-ski rides, followed by toasted marshmallows by the fire at night. Pure summer holiday bliss. But I felt disconnected the entire time we were there. My mind was awash with notions of how unfair it was that Miles would never get to do this with the others, how Josh wouldn't get to teach his youngest child how to drive the boat, how Miles would never get to spot dolphins with us or dive into the clear blue sea with his siblings. The contrast between life and death felt ever-present. Why hadn't he made it? Why couldn't Miles have been spared? He would have loved this and we would have loved having him here with us.

Usually I'm filled with delight to see my children having the time of their lives, soaking up summer, adventuring, swimming and having endless fun. But I wasn't feeling it and could only focus on the one who was missing. I wanted to shut out all their playful squeals and innocent happiness, as life seemed too cruel, too unfair. But I came to realise that although I was mourning Miles, I was allowed to enjoy life. I had lost one child; I couldn't let my grief absorb me to the point where I couldn't enjoy my other children. Josh is always positive, the kind of person who sees the bright side of life. He, too, was sad but for him, losing Miles highlighted the beauty of what we did have. I knew I needed to pull myself out of my melancholy and focus on this too. When I allowed myself to relax, have fun and soak up the kids' happiness, I came to realise that grief and joy can sit side by side, that it was okay to smile, to laugh, to have fun. That wouldn't take anything away from Miles, in fact: it would be in honour of him.

I knew I was going to be sad for a very long time but I was also allowed to be happy. It didn't mean I was over him or okay with what had happened. The ever-present feelings of grief are exhausting, they sit heavily on your heart. Feeling like this all the time is unsustainable long-term. I felt it could lead me spiraling into clinical depression, or worse. I had to take whatever joy was thrown at me and embrace it as best I could. I would still have bad days, (and I can assure you lots of them were very ugly), but if I could give myself a tiny break from the melancholy, then I knew I'd survive this.

To be honest, I also got to a stage where I craved some fun. I wanted to let loose, be my old carefree self and enjoy the freedom of feeling unburdened by grief. I missed my old self and I really missed life being simple. Often the grief held me back, but so did my own expectations of how I should behave. At times I was bored of the self-imposed restrictions I'd placed upon myself as a bereaved mother. I needed to give myself permission to switch off and just have fun: be silly and superficial and at times not focus on what was ahead of me or behind me.

At first, my brave front was incredibly fragile. It took me a while to realise that it didn't really matter what other people thought. If they thought I was fine and over the whole sad story, then that was okay. People close to me understood there were good days and bad and that ultimately we would miss Miles forever.

In addition to feeling guilty for moving forward, I felt guilty about Miles' death in general. Perhaps I had done something to cause his brain hemorrhage? I worried that perhaps I hadn't taken enough folate in early pregnancy. Despite highly intelligent and experienced medical professionals telling me that it was a rare occurrence with no obvious cause, I still couldn't help but feel that perhaps I'd had something to do with it. I was the one who was supposed to keep him safe as he grew and developed inside me.

I felt guilty that perhaps we'd made the wrong decision, that possibly Miles would have had a chance of surviving. But at the eight-week appointment with the hospital's geneticist, these fears were shown to be ungrounded. The clot was well and truly in place and the damage clear and obvious. Genetic termination or interruption of pregnancy for medical reasons is traumatic, confusing and bewildering, regardless of all the facts presented. As a mother, you can't help but hope that they are wrong, and feel so guilty that ultimately you were forced to make the call, to flick the switch. I feared telling people about Miles' condition, in case they didn't grasp just how serious it was. I suppose in many ways this was exacerbated by the treatment we received from our private obstetrician whose stance on not helping to deliver Miles and other babies in similar situations made me feel judged. His personal views added the burden of guilt at an already hellish time.

The backing we had from the specialist team at the Women's and Children's Hospital and Josh's steadfast belief that we had absolutely, without question, made the best decision for Miles, a decision made out of love, did ultimately help to assuage the guilt. For parents who are told their baby no longer has a heartbeat, I can imagine that sometimes the endless question of *why did this happen?* could lead to a deep sense of guilt, and if no answer can be given, logically or otherwise, they could assume that it must be because of something they have done.

I think medical professionals need to be especially mindful of this and always try to reassure parents that they are not at fault. Guilt is the kind of emotion that festers inside you and fills your mind with shame and self-condemnation. This is the last thing you need as a grieving mother. You need to be told by someone else, someone who is an expert in this field, that you are not to blame. Any guilt you feel is a reflection of the love you have for your baby, and a natural need to give their death a reason. Feeling guilty in no way translates to *being* guilty: it just means that you are using your imagination to fill in any blanks in your baby's story.

Just like guilt, anger can be easily sparked after losing a baby. If fed enough oxygen, it can spread like wildfire burning through all aspects of your life. It is completely natural to feel angry that your baby has died. It is natural to feel anger towards people with living children, unwanted pregnancies, wanted pregnancies and everything in between. It is also completely normal to feel anger towards people who you feel are not responding to your loss with the support or sympathy you hoped for, or angry with God, your doctor, the hospital. You may even be overcome with anger in the most unlikely scenarios - angered by the rudeness of someone you encounter after your loss when you're just trying your hardest to leave the house, get jobs done or book an appointment.

Anger, especially in the past, has not been considered an appropriate response for women in our society. We are supposed to cry and talk it out, but it is frowned upon for women to punch a wall or shout in anger. It's often considered an ugly, unfeminine emotion and people don't always know how to respond to it. We see it as a male response, a testosterone-fuelled reaction to a bad situation. Women acting out of anger are sometimes deemed hysterical and their responses are dismissed as being over the top. Personally, being told that I'm overreacting usually just adds fuel to the fire! If I'm angry about something its usually best I talk it through and unpack the root of the anger. Bottling it up just exacerbates the problem.

It is completely understandable to feel angry that this has happened at all, that it happened to you and your baby. Hearing people complain about their children, not having the birth they planned for, or talking about how easily they fall pregnant may fill you with pure, red-hot rage. I've always found that it's much easier to feel really angry about something than it is to delve deep into dealing with why a particular topic or event has upset me so much. It feels good to release some built-up tension by flying off the handle, but rarely does it actually get to the root of the problem or begin to change it. When you're grieving, it's no surprise that anger bubbles over, as it diverts you from the pain you are in.

Working through anger takes incredible strength and self-awareness. I can fester on things for weeks before letting them go, which I'm not sure is healthy, but it is what I need to do to move forward. Physical activity, music and writing can help distract me.

Often explaining out loud to someone who is not the object of my anger helps me process my feelings and work through them. Sometimes it is a simple as getting something off my chest: halfway through my story I realise that I'm already starting to get over my issue (depending on how big or small it is!) but needed to address it out loud to begin the healing process.

Anger towards specific people and events I think is therefore easier to work through, anger towards the bigger picture, (i.e. 'why did my baby have to die') is a lot harder, as there is nothing tangible you can direct your hurt towards. Many people find that this is a topic they work on with a trained professional, as it's too big an emotion to work through unassisted. Being freed from anger can be liberating, as you come to realise that so much of your energy is wasted on it. It's a scary process, but such an important one.

Chapter 26 Stillbirth, Elke and Emma's story

Elke's story
By Emma Bowes
Instagram: @honestly.emma

How do you carry on after the loss of your baby? How do you continue to live? It's a question I asked myself many times after Elke died. I wasn't sure how I would ever function normally again.

When your baby dies, it feels like your world is smashed into a million pieces. Nothing feels the same. Everything that felt true before, no longer does. It is so hard to see the way forward. You don't actually want to move forward. You want to rewind time, you want to go back to before, when your baby was healthy and alive, and replay all of the moments that led to their death. You want to work out a way to change the outcome.

I replayed every scenario in my head and tried to work out how I could have saved Elke. But I realised these thoughts were fruitless. She had died, and I couldn't change that.

Elke is our 4th child. She was born still on 7th November 2019.

The week beginning the 1st November, I noticed that I had felt less movements. I told myself it was nothing and not to worry. I had never had any reason to be concerned in all of my other pregnancies, so I think I just pushed the concern away. I woke up the next morning and again was worried I hadn't felt any movement, but a few hours later I felt a lot of movement and thought everything was ok.

I now understand that ANY change in movement, either a decrease OR increase of movement, is reason to be concerned. But at the time I wasn't aware of this, and so after I felt movement again, I went back to doing life and put all concern out of my mind.

However, on the morning of Thursday 7th November, I woke up and I just knew I needed to go to hospital to have my baby checked. I was concerned I couldn't remember the last time I had felt movement.

The midwife used a doppler and spent a few minutes trying to locate baby's heartbeat. She wasn't having any luck and went to grab another midwife. At this stage, I was still telling myself that everything would be ok.

The second midwife also couldn't locate a heartbeat and advised that I would need to go up to Tweed Hospital (40 mins away), to have an ultrasound to see what was going on. I would later find out, that the midwives were quite sure that my baby had died, however they are not permitted to give me that news in the absence of an Obstetrician.

So I called my husband, Leon, who was in Brisbane and he jumped straight in the car to meet me at Tweed. I called a girlfriend in Byron to drive me up to the hospital.

Once I arrived at Tweed hospital I was taken into a room and was met by an Obstetrician and a midwife. There was a bedside ultrasound machine in the room. I asked if I could wait until Leon got there, he was about 15 minutes away. The Obstetrician advised that it was best to do the scan straight away because if the baby was in distress, we would need to go to surgery straight away.

I agreed for the scan to happen. Almost immediately I could see the heart chamber on the screen. I had been to enough scans to know what the screen was supposed to look like. A hive of activity, blood flowing in and out, valves opening and closing. But on the screen, there was nothing.

An empty chamber.

I already knew what was happening before she said those words. "I'm sorry, there is no heartbeat. Your baby has died".

No tears came. I was in shock. I looked at the doctor as she spoke to me, not believing that this was happening. Yet some part of me *had* known. My subconscious/intuition, whatever you want to call it, had been tuning into this for a week. But my conscious mind pushed these thoughts so deep, it didn't allow me to entertain it.

I became aware of the midwife's hand on my leg, and I just stared at it. Such an intimate gesture from someone I had just met. I put my hand on top of hers, and finally the tears came. I fell into her arms and sobbed.

About 15 minutes later Leon arrived, and we were told what the next few days might look like. We were presented with all of the options, but the main recommendation being that I give birth to my baby naturally. I knew that was the case, as I had a good friend whose firstborn, Charlie, was stillborn 17 years before. I also knew that we would be encouraged to spend as much time with our baby as we needed, and that it was ok for other people to come and meet and hold our baby.

We were given the option to go home and come back the next day, but I chose to stay at hospital and be induced as soon as possible. I didn't see any point in going home and delaying the inevitable. Before they could induce me, I had to have a formal Ultrasound with a qualified Sonographer. It was during this scan that we found out that we were having a girl. We had always kept the sex a surprise until birth, but I needed to know who our baby

was, so I had the most amount of time knowing her before we had
to say goodbye.

Shortly after, I was given the first lot of drugs to stimulate
contractions. I was told it could take anywhere from a few hours up
to a few days for our baby to be delivered. Thankfully a long labour
was not my experience. 8 hours after the first dose, and only a few
hours of intense contractions, our beautiful girl was silently born
into the world at 11.56pm on 7th November.

Elke Pixie Bowes.

She was simply perfect. She looked exactly like her brothers and
sister, the same little nose as all of them. It was hard to comprehend
that she wasn't alive. Every part of her was completely perfect,
except her heart had stopped beating.

The next 20 hours were spent with Elke in hospital trying to
create as many memories as we could. She didn't leave our arms
in all of that time. Our kids came up to meet their baby sister and
give her cuddles, both sets of grandparents and one of my close
girlfriends also came to meet Elke.

We were told that we could stay as long as we needed, but by
7pm the next day, both Leon and I were completely exhausted. We
hadn't slept for 36 hours, and with the added heaviness of acute
grief, we knew we had to go home to our own bed.

Saying goodbye to Elke, and leaving her at the hospital, was the
hardest thing I have ever had to do. It was an impossible ask to walk
away from our baby. But we knew we had to do it. We walked out
of the hospital with empty arms and broken hearts.

In those initial weeks and months, I made my world as small
as I could. I couldn't speak to anyone on the phone, it just seemed
like such an enormous task to answer phone calls. So I limited my
communication with people to text messages. That was all that I
could manage. I ventured out when I felt like I could, but I spent a

lot of time in the safety of our home. I did the Lighthouse walk in Byron often, that has been a huge part of my healing.

I sought out any books I could find on grief, loss and specifically baby loss. I found myself searching hashtags on Instagram and discovered a whole new world of baby loss that I didn't know existed. This community was actually my lifeline. I was able to read other women's stories, read their heartache, and how they continued to live after the loss of their baby. I reached out to women thanking them for sharing their stories and formed incredible connections that helped me through those early days. Even now, every day via Instagram, I am connected with women who have lost their babies. It is such a supportive community, and a place where I feel completely understood.

I allowed myself to fall fully into my grief. I had already finished all of my work ready for maternity leave, and we were fortunate that Leon was able to take 4 months away from his business. This was so helpful for my healing journey, and for the healing of our family. For the first 6 weeks, I didn't leave the house much. I couldn't do anything, I found it hard to even put a load of washing on.

Slowly over the months, I started to step back into life, and I felt like I could do basic daily routines, like dropping kids to school, cooking dinner, and grocery shopping. It felt like a huge step to be able to function as an adult and a mother again.

But inside I felt like I was dying. The pain and heaviness of the loss of Elke was huge. I thought about her every minute of every day. There were reminders everywhere of what we were supposed to be doing. Mums pushing prams, families of 6 on the beach, ads on my social media feed of newborn clothes. It was excruciating, yet somehow I had to find a way to carry on.

I turned to writing very early on. It has been a huge part of my grief journey. I started journaling about 4 days after Elke died, and it felt so good to get words onto the page to express how I was feeling. After a few weeks I realised that I was often just writing the same thing over and over, and I didn't feel like it was helping me. It was like I was just rehashing the same thoughts over and over and I was stuck in a holding pattern.

I had this burning desire to share Elke's story. I felt she deserved to have her story told, but I knew that I was in the depths of grief and I didn't want to share it publicly at such an early stage. So I asked a small group of people to bear witness to her story, and I started writing *Elke's Entries*. I knew writing the Entries for myself wasn't enough, I needed them to be witnessed.

Each entry was about a different area of my grief, and sent via Mailchimp, with photos and quotes. Each entry took me about 5 or 6 hours to write, edit and proof-read, so by the time I pressed send and it went out to my intimate support network, I felt like I had completely processed that part of my grief. It was so healing to share my grief this way.

Living in Byron Bay, I had access to a range of healers, and I accessed them all. From psychologist to psychic, acupuncturist to womb healer, NLP practitioner to intuitive bodyworker, kinesiologist to Integrative Doctor, I used all of these people to help me work through the pain that I was feeling. I sought help to try to make sense of the feelings I had inside of me. There were days where I felt like I was going to explode.

On a few occasions I did explode. I had just dropped my son at a birthday party and was driving away, and I felt an urge to scream. Gripping onto the steering wheel I just started screaming and screaming. I had to pull over because I couldn't see where I was going. I screamed the most primal scream over and over, until my voice was hoarse. I didn't recognise the person sitting there in the car making that noise. I realised there was a lot of anger within me that I needed to try to work through.

A few weeks later I stayed with my friend Rachel, and we decided to release some anger in a pumpkin smashing ceremony. It was incredibly cathartic.

4 pumpkins, a rolling pin and a shit tonne of anger. Rachel and I found a semi-secluded space in the bush. I went first and Rach held space for me.

I whacked and screamed and yelled and I beat the crap out of those pumpkins. It was hard going smashing a pumpkin with a rolling pin, so it took a lot of strength to break them up. I focused all of my attention on the pumpkin and channelled all of my anger. Incredibly my mind was blank as a smashed the pumpkin. It was almost meditative. The anger was moving through me, without any thoughts attached to it.

I had so much anger inside me, and so much of the emotion moved through my body and released. I felt lighter afterwards. I had a horse throat and blistered, bloody hands, but it was worth it. It helped move the anger, and I think it helped to move me through that phase of my grief.

Phase probably isn't the right word, because grief is messy and inconsistent. It often feels like you're in the ocean and you're being tossed around by huge waves. Just as you come up for air, you get pushed under again. The pumpkin smashing helped me move through the emotions that were stuck, and that helped my grief in that moment.

As I write this, I am only 10 months into my journey. I feel like I have come so far, yet I feel like I haven't moved at all. I'm slowly learning to embrace my grief, rather than try to fix it. I spent the first 9 months, desperately trying to make myself feel better. I've realised now that maybe there is no *better*. Instead, I just need to learn to grow around my grief. Each day I feel a little stronger. Instead of feeling better, maybe I just need to aim for stronger.

I'll leave you with my last few words. If you have lost your baby, walk gently with yourself. Allow yourself the time to feel all of the emotions. Try not to run away from them. It doesn't matter how fast or how far you run, they will be waiting for you. So let yourself feel them.

Write, walk, run, scream, cry, box, meditate, pray, move, create. Find your way of allowing your emotions to move through your body. And know you are not alone. There are a tribe of women who have walked this path. Find them, reach out to them, share your heart with them. I have found this community so incredibly supportive. We are all in this together.

Chapter 27 Deciding to have another baby

Parents who've lost a baby tend to fall in to two camps: those who want to go again straight away and those who cannot contemplate it, at this point in time, or ever. Trying to conceive and pregnancy after loss are such momentous topics that they need their own separate book. It's a whole new entity in the story of life after baby loss.

I wanted to try for another baby immediately, but we were waiting for the autopsy report and for some blood work to come back from a highly specialised lab in Brisbane, to give us an answer on the possible diagnosis of F-NAIT, the disorder which was initially thought to be a factor in Miles' condition.

If we did have F-NAIT and wanted another baby, it would be an incredibly high-risk pregnancy and I would need to have weekly, six-hour platelet transfusions from twelve weeks gestation until delivery at thirty-six weeks. Delivery would need to be via caesarean to ensure the baby was not put under any distress and to reduce the risk of internal bleeding. After birth, the baby's platelet count would need to be brought up to a safe level by multiple transfusions in order for the baby to survive.

Understandably, this would be a huge undertaking, not without side-effects and significant risks. The platelet treatment can cause various problems for the mother and fetus and it would be a very stressful pregnancy which, on top of the anxiety of a pregnancy after loss, would have been a minefield. Josh felt he couldn't cope with this scenario. We didn't need to take such a huge risk, given the beautiful children we already had in our arms.

I felt so differently. I would have given away a kidney to be pregnant again. If I could have walked out of the hospital after having Miles already pregnant again, that wouldn't have been soon enough. I was willing to go through whatever medical treatments were necessary, despite the obvious risks involved. My hormones overrode all logic. I felt like this couldn't be the end to our story. It's not what I'd imagined our final chapter to be. I felt guilty for not being content with the number of children we had and Josh continually reminded me that we were lucky: incredibly fortunate. Many people would dream of having two gorgeous boys and a beautiful little girl. I knew this, but could not ignore the insuppressible desire to have another baby. It couldn't be explained, but I desperately wanted to hold a baby of my own in my arms again.

I read a medical study published in Ireland about the responses of mothers and fathers to wanting to try again after stillbirth. Fathers predominantly did not want to, for fear of the tragedy reoccurring. They felt that the risks far outweighed the benefit. The mothers overwhelmingly expressed an urge to be pregnant again, as early as one or two days post-delivery. For them, the desire to be pregnant was immediate. They also felt that if for any reason they were unable to have another child, this would be another scenario to grieve, on top of grieving for their lost baby. Most of the mothers in this study knew they were not done having children.

I've talked to lots of women about this - the notion of knowing when you're done. One friend who has two little boys says without hesitation that she is done: all desires to be pregnant again have evaporated. For another, like me, the craving to go again is ever-present and something she fears she will regret forever if she doesn't try to make it happen. These two examples are of women who have not lost babies, so their situations are not further complicated by the experience of a loss. I had always wanted a fourth child, and after losing Miles that want became an absolute must. I thought quite possibly I would never, ever, get over it if I couldn't have another baby. I was determined to rewrite the final chapter.

We found out about eight weeks after Miles died that we did not have F-NAIT, but tests did indicate some kind of reaction between our platelets. The basic test had been positive and the advanced test negative. It was very confusing. I didn't really understand what any of this meant. The doctor explained that we might need to be treated for F-NAIT in future pregnancies, but in his opinion it was more likely that we wouldn't. We were told that it was highly unlikely that what happened would recur, but they really couldn't be sure. Answers may never be found and at best, we wouldn't have these for at least twelve months. We decided to take a leap of faith and try again. My fortieth birthday was approaching and I decided to take matters into my own hands, as the uncertainty of trying month after month, combined with my grief, was a recipe for disaster. I was constantly on edge and wanted to gain some control over the situation we were in. With this in mind, I booked in to see a fertility specialist.

Having had a D&C to remove my placenta after I delivered Miles, I wanted to make sure there were no issues with the recovery of my uterus. I hated the idea of trying for a year or more and finding out later that post-operative scar tissue was the reason we weren't falling pregnant. I made Josh get checked out too: men account for 50% of your likelihood to successfully conceive.

Having a plan calmed me somewhat. Even though I still couldn't control the outcome, I felt as though I was doing everything in my power to get us to where we wanted to be. The rollercoaster ride of trying to conceive was not something I felt I could deal with emotionally without some reassurance that all was in order. Josh wanted to have another child too, but he didn't possess my single-minded urgency. He was happy to go with the flow and was more than content with our family as it was.

The monthly cycle of having your period (the cruelest reminder that YOU ARE NOT PREGNANT!), the following week of meticulously timing when you should try, then the dreaded two-week wait before you can do a pregnancy test is a draining scenario, full of intense emotions. When you're trying to conceive, it's not uncommon to put many other parts of your life on hold. I didn't book trips away or commit to things like concerts or ticketed events. I tried not to drink alcohol, cut back on coffee and tried "to relax!"

Before baby loss getting pregnant can be difficult to be calm and casual about. After loss, feelings of fear, hopelessness, frustration are amplified to an almost deafening pitch. You were already pregnant and you should either still be pregnant or have a baby in your arms. My state of confusion and sadness made it harder. I would oscillate between trying really hard to do everything right in terms of my health, to thinking, *sod this, I did everything right last time and look how that turned out.*

It is natural to feel anxious that you won't be able to get pregnant again. This terrified me and played constantly on my mind. I was older, I felt like we'd lost time and there were no guarantees that we would be able to get pregnant again just because we'd been lucky enough to conceive before. There is no joy in knowing you can get pregnant, as it has no impact whatsoever on the final outcome. Yes, we can choose to try again, but we cannot control how our story ends and that is terrifying. As baby-loss mothers, we are also well aware of the trauma baby loss brings and have understandable doubts as to whether we could endure this level of pain again.

Like me, you might find it hard to talk to people about your desire to be pregnant again. Generally it's not something people broadcast. I think when people are having trouble falling pregnant, they keep it quiet. It feels like a personal failing, an inability to do something which should be so simple, so natural. I felt ashamed that my body wasn't doing what it ought to. Like the silence surrounding baby loss, I feel that the silence surrounding trying to get pregnant isolates couples and robs people of vital support. I started thinking *What's wrong with telling people we're trying for another baby? Why does it have to be kept secret, in case we fail? In case we have success only to endure another loss?* But overwhelmingly, I preferred to keep it private. I also knew that if we were fortunate enough to fall pregnant again, we would be unlikely to tell people until we got past twenty weeks at least.

It was hard to anticipate how people would react and I wanted to avoid negative opinions. I didn't want to hear anything that wasn't supportive, as our decision to try again was full of fear and anxiety. We knew it wasn't going to be easy, and the last thing we needed was an outsider's critical opinion. Since it was our family, our private decision, I didn't want to invite the reactions of others unless they were going to be positive and caring.

I only told a few close friends that we were trying again: who I knew would encourage us and understand what motivated us. I suppose people don't want to see you go through pain again, but what they may not have realised was that for me, the pain of not having another child overrode the fear of rolling the dice and trying again. I knew if I didn't, I would look back in thirty or forty years and think, *Why didn't I just go for it?* I knew firsthand that not everything in life goes to plan and that sometimes really bad things do happen. But I also knew there was nothing that could be done to control or avoid this. What would be, would be: and the only thing I was utterly certain of was that I wanted to have another baby.

Chapter 28 Deciding not to have another baby or not being able to

For many people, the idea of having another child after the devastation of losing a baby is too much to bear. This is understandable: you have been through the absolute worst, the fear of it happening again is very real. The trauma associated with miscarriage, stillbirth and loss in infancy can have a lifelong impact, so any subsequent pregnancies could easily trigger these overwhelming, at times debilitating, feelings. Conversely, some people may wish to, but are advised not to by medical professionals. Some may want to try and be unable to conceive a much-wanted child. I used to look at families of only children and assume that they only ever wanted one. Naively, I thought having one child was usually by choice. Now, I understand that in many cases, parents had hoped for more children. I now see families and think, *What sadness have they possibly had to endure? What tragedies may have changed the course of their dreams and taken away their opportunity to have another child?*

My father who grew up in a very Catholic family in the 1950s, was an only child. I never gave much thought to why he didn't have any siblings. I knew it was unusual for his era and thought that perhaps because his parents were older and waited until after the war to marry and have children, they decided to only have one. He said it was never spoken of. He thinks that there may have been other pregnancies and miscarriages, but he was not told anything about them. The classic Catholic family in the '50s was one of countless children, so topics of infertility and baby loss may have been delegated to the realm of the *Lord's will* or *God's plan*. Baby loss was shrouded in even more secrecy than it is today.

Nowadays people are quick to comment *Just the one!*, implying that it was a conscious decision, when it may have been far from that. I can't imagine having to cheerfully fend off these observations time and time again, with well-practiced responses like *yes, we are very happy with our one* when in fact there may have been several losses, or years spent trying for another living child. Uninvited observations such as *he/she needs a sibling* or *your child is so good with babies, you should have another for him/her* must also sting. We really need to stop saying this kind of thing altogether. We are quick to comment and pass judgement, but I don't think many people would expect a truly honest answer or a warts-and-all recount of what a person has actually been through.

Large age gaps can also attract unwanted comments. People have assumed that Bonnie was an accident, an afterthought, as she is five and seven years younger than her brothers. When I let people know that this is because she is from my second marriage, they seem happy with the explanation. By contrast I think some people would not be as comfortable hearing about an age gap as the result of loss. I find it frustrating that people clam up and become instantly embarrassed if an answer is given which is not what they were expecting. If people are curious enough to ask personal questions, they need to be prepared to respond to whatever answer is given with the respect it deserves, not to quickly change the topic entirely.

Not being able to have another baby, or deciding not to, would, I imagine, bring with it a new wave of grief. The grief you have for your lost baby could be compounded by the additional grief associated with letting go of your dreams of having another child. Your initial plan before losing your baby is no longer achievable.

Growing up, I think many girls and boys have beautifully innocent dreams of what their family may one day look like. Some may picture themselves with two children, a pigeon pair; others, a tribe of four trailing behind them. We are told to be careful, not to get pregnant too young or by accident. At school it was almost implied that getting pregnant would be simple and effortless. Not getting pregnant seemed to be the focus of all sex education. Apart from the risk of contracting STDs, this was the most important message. It led me to believe that getting pregnant was easy. I assumed that you just stopped using contraception and *bingo, after nine months of bingeing on ice cream and pickles here comes a baby!* We weren't told that factors such as infertility, divorce, parental health, mental health, and baby loss could alter your life so ferociously and permanently. These risks are generally not spoken of until they are encountered head-on. Life doesn't always turn out like you planned, which can be incredibly hard to accept and adapt to.

I kept comparing myself to people whose stories I felt were far worse than mine. Couples who had struggled with infertility for years and were only able to have one baby (or none at all), or girlfriends who missed the chance to ever have a baby, as they had not met the right guy or girl by the right time. These women weren't over-focused on their careers and nor were they too fussy: they just hadn't met the person with which they wanted to start a family. Nama, whose story comes next, was robbed of the chance to have another child after her divorce. She had frozen embryos, siblings to her son which she was ultimately unable to use. The many assumptions people make about why women don't have children (or more children) rarely address the struggles these women have faced, or the reasons why they had to abandon their dreams.

Sadly there is little room for women to talk about this pain, this loss of their dreams. People tend not to understand that it is justifiable to mourn an idea, to mourn a dream. I have friends who have not had children and I have always been scared to raise the topic for fear of upsetting them, but some women may welcome the opportunity to talk about their experience. Many may not, but the topic should not be universally silenced. At many girls' catch-ups I go to, fifty percent of the conversation is about our children: what they are up to, what we're proud of and what they've done to drive us nuts that week. I often feel guilty and try to steer the conversation back to other topics like work, travel and current affairs, so as not to exclude friends without children. Our conversations never seem to invite the opportunity for these women to open up about their experiences.

Asking people outright why they don't have children seems rude and invasive, especially if you don't know them well, but I would love to find a middle ground, a way of opening up the conversation. We shy away from topics deemed personal - the loss of a job, financial hardship, divorce - but these are distressing life events for which people need support and the opportunity to talk through their experience. Advice and solutions are not always necessary, but gentle company and a listening ear can ease a sense of isolation and heartache. Grieving the absence of a child who lived entirely in your heart alongside your hopes for the future is valid. It is mourning an intention, a monumental, life-changing experience. As abstract as a child who was never conceived may seem to others, you are entitled to yearn for this person, this child you longed to create.

You never really know what someone has been through trying to create a family. Throwaway comments like *one and done* may be painful to hear, just as asking someone when they are going to start trying for a baby might seem harmless. But if the person you are asking has lost a baby or is struggling with infertility, they should not have to be put on the spot and made to justify their situation. We need to give people the space and confidence to share if they feel up to it, not shut them down the second a conversation lands on an uncomfortable topic. Not all families are what people wished for and pictured. We need to be mindful of this and proceed with adequate sensitivity. In the next chapter, I share the story of journalist and mother Nama Winston.

Chapter 29 Embryo Loss, by Nama Winston

When something is missing on Mother's Day
By Nama Winston

This is my story, which I'm sharing in solidarity with the mums out there who, because of miscarriage, stillbirth, illness, accident, death, or struggles with fertility, have a part of them missing on Mother's Day.

You're not alone, my friends.

I had my first and only child through IVF. It was relatively easy for me in comparison to so many of the stories of others I know. Yes, there were three rounds, and all the injections, fasting blood tests and appointments that entailed. Looking back, it was horrible, but also, it mercifully went by in a blur.

I was very lucky. I never had a miscarriage.

My friend had seven miscarriages and stopped going to the birthday parties of her friends' children. People really judged her for that.

But I knew a little of her fear, and anguish. I understood she had to protect herself.

Too many people don't appreciate what infertility can do to a woman's soul.

What's wrong with me, what's wrong with my body, why don't I deserve this, why does she deserve a baby?

You ask yourself these things every month you don't fall pregnant when that's all you want; which, for me, was 24 months.

I recall my first failed IVF attempt and a friend, who was already a mother, wouldn't acknowledge I saw it as a loss. It was a lost chance for my husband's sperm and my egg – our embryo – to become a much-wanted child.

She didn't understand how a woman can feel that vanished hope, that disappointment, in her heart.

"You haven't lost a baby," was her response as a 'friend', as a woman who had fallen naturally and easily pregnant three times.

Oh, I thought. Thanks for that.

Yes, I knew it was nothing like having a miscarriage, or losing a baby. Obviously. But as an alleged friend, one would have thought she'd have the capacity to throw a little empathy my way. Apparently not.

But I soon got my happy ending.

After three rounds of IVF, I gave birth to a beautiful, healthy son, twelve wonderful years ago. From the moment he was conceived, I knew he'd be my greatest achievement, the best thing I've ever done, and the best thing that's happened to me.

This child was my entire purpose for being, which is why, when I decided to leave my husband just two years later, I honestly felt that as long as I had my son with me, I would always be the richest woman in the world.

That remains true – with a small complication.

My ex and I never discussed what to do with our son's four 'siblings', who were chilling - literally - in the embryo freezer of the IVF clinic where he had been conceived.

I'd read that some couples argue about what to do with embryos after a divorce, but apart from it not even occurring to my ex, it was never an issue to me; I figured there was no point in bringing a child into a family when there was barely a relationship between the father and the existing child.

That was my rational approach; but I'd soon discover, my heart felt very differently.

At age 32, I believed I had so much time ahead of me, and hoped that that one day I would be able to fill my massive seven-seat SUV with car seats, as I had intended to when I bought it, albeit with a different partner.

The potential of this dream was confirmed by my reproductive doctor, who assured me I would not have any conception issues with a new man.

The doctor also informed me that the clinic's policy was to not permit a separated or divorced couple to use their embryos – meaning that had I wanted to, I would have had to fight them in court about it. I was fine with that. Given our situation, I didn't think it was the right thing to do, anyway.

So, after that appointment, I got into that seven-seat SUV with its one Turn-a-Tot car seat installed in the middle, and drove home, still feeling like the richest woman in the world, with one miracle baby and hope for more in the future.

And then, an unexpected event changed my calm acceptance of the situation.

A few months later, I got a letter from the IVF clinic informing me that I had four options; continue to pay a yearly $1200 storage fee to keep the embryos (no, since I wasn't planning to use them anyway), donate the embryos to a couple who can't have their own babies (no, for deeply personal reasons due to my own experience of adopted children), donate the embryos to science, or have the embryos destroyed.

The third option, donating the embryos to medical research, to help other people needing IVF, seemed like the best choice. That is, until I read the caveat; the clinic could keep the embryos for years, and I could one day out of the blue be contacted to ask if they could be used on a project, or whether I had changed my mind.

Did I want that emotional disruption at some point in my future? Could I handle it?

Needing to further examine the options, I turned to a close friend, whose first response was, "Don't you want to give your son a full biological sibling?"

It was a guilt I wasn't expecting to be projected on to me.

I had not even thought about it that way. To me, a sibling is a sibling, whether they are technically full or half. I told my friend that I firmly believed that family is not always dictated by blood, and it is what you make it.

But, the concept had now been planted in my mind, and it was a torment I could have done without.

I felt sure at the time, but what if I felt differently later? What if I didn't go on to have more children with another partner? Was I selfishly denying my son the chance to have brothers or sisters when the opportunity was there now? Wasn't it a natural feeling for many people to want more than one child so that the kids have someone to grow up with? Was I wasting the chance to give him that?

The deciding factor for me was the growing fear that, one day, if I was contacted by the clinic about the embryos being used for a project, and if things had not turned out as I hoped in terms of more kids with another partner...would I be tempted to fight for those embryos?

Eventually, I decided that the uncertainty that came with the possibility of being randomly contacted one day was too much of a risk for everyone involved; it was a potential minefield.

And so, the embryos were 'destroyed'.

Signing the form to select that option broke my heart. I know there are much, much worse things to endure; I didn't have a miscarriage, or a stillbirth, and I didn't lose a child from illness or accident.

They were embryos, not living human beings. There had been no guarantee they would even be viable and result in successful pregnancies.

But the word 'destroyed' destroyed me for a while. It was so final. And fate didn't make the decision - I did.

I recalled how excited I was when we were told after years of treatment that I finally had five embryos ready to go whenever I was - and here I was, a few years later, making a conscious decision to destroy four of them.

It's not how I thought things would be. But life never is, is it?

Ten years later, on a rational level, I stand by my decision. And yet, despite having a wonderful, rich and peaceful life with my gorgeous son, fantasy still occasionally creeps in.

When I eventually traded the seven-seat SUV for something half its size, I did look at the unused back seats and wonder what could have been.

And I think of my maybe babies every Mother's Day, too.

Chapter 30 Ectopic pregnancy and Endometriosis - Keira's story

In the last 4 years Keira Rumble has endured endless heartache, physical pain and emotional trauma. Yet somehow, she remains optimistic and shares her story of love and loss to help others facing similar heartache. Next she's embarking on an IVF journey which she hopes will bring her the baby she has dreamed of.

Keira has endured 6 pregnancy losses, one of which almost cost Keira her life, and led to a diagnosis of severe endometriosis. Her faith in the medical world was rocked after she was turned away from a hospital emergency department on multiple occasions when presenting in acute pain. Despite there being many unique diagnostic symptoms on each occasion, she was told to go home, take painkillers and see a psychologist. It turned out she had an ectopic pregnancy and it was only when her tube ruptured, and her belly began filling with blood that it was finally diagnosed.

"It was a heterotopic pregnancy, which was a dual pregnancy – one in the uterus which miscarried, and one ectopic. While they were all heartbreaking, my most recent losses really shook me to the core, partly because there were a lot of unknowns from the medical staff and how they handled my diagnosis, and partly because I was much more aware of the statistics of having multiple miscarriage and infertility challenges."

"Due to the hospital waiting so long to take action, my fallopian tube ruptured, causing me to have emergency surgery and my left tube removed. As a result of surgery, I was faced with chronic pelvic pain on my left side, and now my ovary is stuck to my uterus causing significant discomfort." Understandably this experience has had a significant and ongoing effect on Keira emotionally. "Having the medical system tell me that there is nothing wrong with me when I knew there was, was incredibly traumatic and demoralising."

The day I rang Keira to chat to her about her chapter of the book she let me know me she'd just been through another early miscarriage. She knew that something wasn't right from the moment she fell pregnant so had an early blood test done which confirmed that her HCG levels were very low. Not wanting to have to wait and see how this would play out over the weekend she went to her GP and requested a scan as the anguish of not knowing what was happening after so many previous losses was understandably too much to cope with. Sadly, the scan confirmed what Keira had feared and the pregnancy wasn't viable.

I asked her if with each loss the grief changed. For Keira, the emotional pain has always been immense but the shock of what's happening has never changed, the 'why me' question naturally remains. What has differed is how she handles the physical side. Rather than being blindsided by the cramps and bleeding she now goes into pilot mode, preparing for what is inevitably ahead physically; making sure she has pain medication, pads and heat packs.

On a spiritual level Keira has found some small comfort in believing that this is possibly all part of something bigger in the context of her life purpose. "I keep on bringing it back to there being a reason why this is happening, and I honestly believe that it is in some way, my journey to help women by talking about my experience. Maybe my experience needs to be IVF and maybe I do need to go fully in depth and show my raw emotion of going through all of these fertility struggles."

Another spiritual element of Keira's life which has helped is Vedic meditation. She started because she "knew [she] was so stressed about not being able to conceive or not being able to keep a baby." She knew for her own sake she needed something which would help her remain calm, give her energy and avoid feeling as though she was constantly in fight or flight mode. It also gave her some respite from the constant and all-consuming thought patterns trying to conceive and life after loss can bring.

One special meditation Keira did was a visualisation of cutting cords. She visualised her loss and her babies and symbolically cut the cords which joined them to her. This helped her begin to move forward as she felt the weight of her grief was holding her back. Keira also has a crystal broken into 2 which symbolises the 2 babies she lost when she experienced a dual pregnancy loss.

Keira runs an incredibly busy business as well as connecting with and fostering an honest and supportive community of women on Instagram and her wellness blog. Despite all of these external factors she admits that at times, all she can think about is falling pregnant, which is why tapping into the power of meditation is so important. Despite being diagnosed with PTSD in response to a childhood experience, as well as living with a diagnosis of clinical depression, it's hugely important to Keira that she maintains her optimism for life and a positive mindset as they are both an integral part of her healing journey.

I asked Keira what she advice she'd give to a mother going thorough baby loss. She believes it's incredibly important to talk about it, especially with women who have also been through it. That women need to be gentle on themselves, and that it's crucial to find support from within your own circle as well as beyond it. "There are Facebook groups you can join dedicated to your specific type of baby loss and these are wonderful to find others to lean on who've been there and a safe place to ask questions."

Even though you can feel utterly alone, there are so many women out there facing similar challenges. "It's honestly shocking to find out some of the statistics that are associated with endo and miscarriage. It's far more common than I ever could have imagined, and we are still a long way off from where the dialogue needs to be to help those that experience them. I felt so alone during each and every one of my losses and felt deeply ashamed with myself for what was going on with my body. I had no answers and was embarrassed to ask for help. It wasn't until after my pregnancy losses that I started to seek answers and find a community to help me get through what I was going through."

For Keira there were significant ongoing complications after her rare heterotopic pregnancy and the emergency surgery she went through to remove her left fallopian tube. The constant pain she contended with afterwards was intense, and to add insult to injury she also had to cope with being asked repeatedly if she was pregnant due to extreme bloating. This was especially challenging given that the cause of her bloating stemmed from her devastating loss.

Keira bravely documented the severe pain and bloating she was dealing with on her Instagram account and ended up deciding to have it looked into. A surgical investigation revealed significant endometriosis around her bladder, bowel, ovary, nerves and remaining right sided tube. It was considered to be aggressive and fast-growing endometriosis. This focused Keira's mind on falling pregnant again as soon as possible. There is always a risk the endometriosis will return and regrow so she felt there was a small window after surgery in which her chances of conceiving would be greater. Keira tragically endured another pregnancy loss after surgery which is why she believes that IVF is the journey she will now need to undertake.

Keira continues to openly share her devastating experiences of baby loss and endometriosis with the hope of making other women feel less alone. The honest way in which she tells her story and details the really hard parts will bring comfort to so many facing similar challenges. She has inspired many to take action and seek answers for the debilitating pain endo brings. Her openness will raise awareness and give women the confidence and tools with which to seek answers and treatment. It can take a long time to be diagnosed with endometriosis, which for many, means years of crippling pain, bloating and bleeding. It's not normal to endure severe period pain month after month so by telling her story, Keira will give validation to so many women who are also enduring the many painful challenges endometriosis brings.

Chapter 31 Dealing with other people's pregnancies and babies after baby loss

I think for anyone who has lost a baby, the thought of seeing or hearing about other people's pregnancies can, for some time feel like another blow to your heart. Most of my friends had finished having babies, so in my immediate circle there was not a high risk of this happening. I knew a few girls who were pregnant and I was bracing myself for when I ran into them and had no idea how I would cope. A friend who lost her baby during what she describes as a baby boom said every pregnancy and birth announcement sent her into an instant state of despair, anger and anguish.

If you are struggling with infertility or have just lost a baby, it is totally understandable if you don't want to be around pregnant women, babies, or even older children. Putting your feelings above those of others for a period and protecting your broken heart in whatever way works best for you is hugely important. Some people may not understand or respect your decision and this can be both hurtful and difficult to accept, but what matters most is your state of mind. Others may not realise just how painful it is for you to be around a newborn or to attend a baby shower, but it really isn't up to them to decide what you are and are not capable of when you're grieving the loss of your own baby.

People who are in a bubble of excitement about the impending arrival of their own child, or the beautiful bundle of joy they have in their arms, may not be able to see how their happy news could impact you. They may see the two events as being unrelated and not understand why you don't want to see them, meet their newborn or attend a christening. But don't feel pressured to go somewhere or be forced into a situation that you know will be too much or too painful for you to bear. Many people don't realise the pain of seeing something close-up that you want so desperately is brutal. The unfairness of your loss is highlighted in comparison to the abundance of joy others are experiencing.

Not being able to share in your friends' excitement can feel horrible, like you are the worst version of yourself, but it is totally okay if you don't feel up to joining in or being a part of it. Having to put yourself alongside what you have just lost ,or what you have been dreaming of and striving for, can be deeply upsetting and may feel impossible. If people don't understand this, you're not required to justify your actions. If you feel it will help, let your friend(s) know that right now you are unable to visit and celebrate with them, but are very much looking forward to doing so at some point in the future. That as happy as you are for them, you don't yet feel strong enough to be a part of any celebrations.

There are so many baby related events that come up, especially if your social group is in the baby-making stage of life. Gender reveals, baby showers, sip-and-see parties, christenings, and first birthdays, to name a few. And there will be pregnant people everywhere! At the shops, work, school, in doctors' rooms or just walking along the street, so chances are you will encounter a pregnant woman or a baby. Whether you run for the hills, instantly burst into tears, feel angry or even feel absolutely neutral, just be assured that your reaction is absolutely natural and part of the process. If all you want to do is curl up on the sofa and eat ice-cream, then do it. If it leaves you feeling like life is completely unfair, let yourself feel like this. Life *is* unfair at times, so don't put pressure on yourself to react in any way other than how your heart is responding.

During the first month after losing Miles, when we were away on Kangaroo Island, I ran into a bunch of girls, some of whom I only knew vaguely and others I knew well, at the local beach. We were all there for an Australia Day drink and a bit of beach cricket with the kids. One of the girls was obviously pregnant and I was overwhelmed by feelings of intense jealousy. I was also feeling awkward, as I was unsure who else in that group knew about Miles. I'd been for a walk along the beach earlier with the girl I knew best in the group and we had talked about Miles, but upon returning, no one else said anything, though I'm sure some of them had heard the news.

I went over to chat to a pregnant girl who I'd met once before. She looked gorgeous, positively glowing, and I knew through others that it had taken her longer than anticipated to fall pregnant with a much-wanted second child. In the past I would have gushed over her bump, asked questions about the due date and how she was feeling, but I just couldn't find the words. I was too scared to mention her pregnancy or my loss for fear of dissolving into unstoppable tears, or incase my uncharacteristic jealousy seethed out of me. So instead, I stood there for about half an hour making basic chit-chat with the rest of the group, in the back on my mind thinking, *I gave birth and said goodbye to my baby exactly one month ago, that is fucking major. Why can't I bring myself to talk about it?* I realised that no one else was going to bring it up, so felt it best to act like nothing had happened, which did not sit well with me.

I suppose I didn't want to kill the vibe. It was a glorious day, everyone was relaxed and happy. I didn't want my sad story to alter this. No one asked and I didn't volunteer any information. I felt so empty compared to the pregnant girl in the group and so guilty for feeling this way, given that she was so excited. It was overwhelming to be standing so close to a pregnant belly, I couldn't even look at it.

I knew this would be the first of many times I would encounter someone who was pregnant and that I would have to come up with a healthy way of dealing with it. Pouring myself another glass of champagne wasn't going to cut it, or be an option in most situations. I hoped that each time it would get easier, less brutal, but knew I had a long way to go. I wasn't resentful of the pregnant girl and her baby, I was sad for myself and angry about what had happened to Miles. I was so jealous of her beautiful belly and baby kicking away inside: by contrast mine seemed ugly, disfigured and barren. I was happy she had been spared my heartache, but I wished I had been too. I wished I still had my hope, my innocence, my baby.

The other aspect of being around a pregnant person that upset me in the early days was the pregnancy chatter. *How are you feeling? When are you due? Where are you having the baby?* I wanted to block my ears or *scream shut up! Do you not realise how hard it is for me to hear all this and not burst into tears! You should be asking me this too but it's no longer relevant as my baby has already been born and he died.* It got easier with time, but was incredibly difficult at first. Very soon after returning from Kangaroo Island I had work commitments to fulfil: the charity I was helping was to be featured in a magazine and it was my role to cook and style the food elements for a photo shoot. I knew one or two of the other girls involved personally, so contacted one to tell her about Miles. I knew she would be expecting to see a big round belly by this stage, so wanted to give her the heads up via text message before we were in a work setting with other people I didn't know as well.

She replied with shock, disbelief and sympathy and then let me know that she was pregnant. I was immediately worried with how I would cope with returning to work with this added factor. Returning to work, school and reality in general one month after Miles died felt enough in itself. I figured I could put on my big-girl pants and a professional face and just make myself cope. She is a very caring and kind-hearted girl, so I knew she would be very understanding if I seemed a little distant.

We had two shoot days together and inevitably her pregnancy was excitedly spoken about, with the usual questions asked. None of this was easy for me to hear -it was too soon - and at the very mention of anything pregnancy-related, my chest tightened, the tears started to well and I had to turn away and block it out. Despite this, I could not begrudge her the sheer joy that a first pregnancy brings. I remember being pregnant for the first time with Alfie: you feel so special and it is probably one of the only times in your adult life during which people are magically drawn to you. I didn't think that my private sorrow and tragedy should prevent others from basking in this rite of passage, or deny them their opportunity to share with others this truly special time, but simultaneously I found it hard to cope with.

I felt rude and mean spirited not joining in, so avoided the conversation altogether. I really wanted to say something about Miles or hoped that perhaps he would be mentioned by someone else, but knew that in this situation, the people who knew me were probably not bringing him up out of respect for me, given that we were in a work environment. They probably felt that I would prefer to keep my recent experience to myself or were waiting for me to make the first move.

I was scared of raising the topic for fear of being labeled depressing or unprofessional in a work setting. So the end result was uncomfortable silence. If people can talk about good pregnancy outcomes and being pregnant at work, perhaps we need to make it easier for people to talk about the experiences of those who have not been able to enjoy such happiness. For as long as women are falling pregnant, women will also lose pregnancies. Their paths will inevitably cross in all aspects and areas of people's lives, and especially so in many workplaces.

A girl I'd known for over twenty years was a week or so ahead of me in my pregnancy with Miles. It was to be her third baby and my fourth. We bonded over our mutual dreams of having big families, the realities of being pregnant with children underfoot and the chaos that would ensue once these babies arrived. We were booked into the same hospital and swapped notes on how we were feeling when we crossed paths weekly at the nursery school drop-off for our two daughters. It was exciting to have someone else due at almost the same time. When I lost Miles, I contacted her to tell her what had happened and to tell her not to feel awkward. Yes, it was going to be incredibly hard for me when her baby arrived safely in three months' time, but there was no need for her to feel uncomfortable.

Initially I did avoid bumping into this friend. I didn't feel strong enough to see someone at the exact stage of pregnancy I should have been at. When I lost Miles, I was about to get to the point in pregnancy where your belly just explodes. To see this in person was a lot to handle in the context of getting kids to school and coping with daily life. I hid in my car quite a few times, or on other mornings, circled the block to avoid bumping into her. When I did finally feel up to it and put myself in a position where I knew we would run into each other, I was surprised by how much of a relief it was to have this encounter over and done with. Talking to her and seeing her gorgeous pregnant belly up close was nowhere near as hard as I had imagined it would be. We cried and talked about just how cruel life can be, and agreed that we all need to be more open and honest about struggles with infertility, miscarriage and stillbirth.

I still felt so sad for my own situation, especially when comparing my loss and her expectant happiness, but I realised that feeling resentful or jealous *long term* would not change anything for me. It would not bring Miles back, nor would it guarantee I would have another baby myself one day. It would achieve nothing. I was initially ashamed of my envious feelings and thought of myself as being a horrible and bitter person. Later I could see I was neither of these things: I was just hurting and wishing things could be different.

When her beautiful little boy arrived, my grief escalated. The little baby was to be Miles' hospital buddy, but Miles had already been born and not had survived. It was a stark reminder of what we had lost. I hated the way I was feeling, but knew it was a reaction produced from a grief-filled mind. I didn't resent their happiness, I just wished I was in the same position.

Pregnancy announcements had a similar effect. When I'd hear of a new pregnancy I'd immediately think, *why not me? How long will it be until it is my turn again?* These felt like bratty, childish, it's not fair thoughts. They were not thoughts easily expressed without sounding petulant. Sadness can often manifest as bitterness and anger: it is easier to feel mad than hurt. I also felt fearful for my pregnant friends, knowing that not everything goes to plan. It was hard for me to be excited for them, as I was genuinely worried.

Initially, I found talking about the usual pregnancy milestones - scans and so on – painful, as these memories were still so fresh. Having to fake happiness for a friend feels dreadful. You feel like the worst version of yourself. It got easier for me, but initially it was too much too soon. I didn't have the capacity or emotional strength to process it. Two of my closest friends (we had been bridesmaids for each other) announced pregnancies in the weeks after we lost Miles. Given that most of my friends had completed their families, these were somewhat unexpected. Due to how close I was to both women, I was able to feel happy for them far sooner that I may have been for someone else. I needed to allow myself to feel sad and not feel guilty for being unable to fully embrace and celebrate their news when I first heard it. I knew these feelings would pass and it would have been unrealistic to expect myself to respond in any other way.

One of these friends struggled to share her news with me. I think she tried to get the words out during about two or three phone calls, but wasn't able to, each time. In the end, she texted me her news to allow me to respond in my own time. I was so grateful for her sensitivity. I was also touched by how aware she was that her news might be really hard for me to digest. I felt a heavy weight in my heart that my friend's happy news had to be delivered to me with such caution and trepidation. That my reaction was not what it previously would have been. I responded quickly with words of congratulations, but it took weeks for me to genuinely feel what I had said. It's a huge relief to now say that I am genuinely over the moon about her baby's impending arrival.

I found it helpful to try really hard not to connect or compare other people's pregnancy or birth announcements to our quest to have another baby. There is not a finite number of babies left to be born: one person's conception success did not mean imminent failure for us. At first it was easy to imagine us as all part of some gigantic baby lottery, like bingo perhaps. When your number is called out, it's your turn. I worried that my number would never be called out again, that all the numbers would be used up. But logically, (and thankfully), that's not how it works.

That said, it can still hurt like hell. I was surprised by how hard I found the arrival of a friend's baby seven months after Miles. I was feeling really strong and genuinely believed that it would have little effect. What I hadn't predicted was that the flurry of congratulatory texts that erupted from a group text announcement afterwards would upset me. I was overwhelmed with renewed sadness that Miles' birth (and death) announcement had, for such obvious reasons, not been met with such joy. No one says *congratulations*, or *can I see a picture of your baby* when they have died. I did want him to be celebrated as I thought he was magnificent, but the situation as a whole was no cause for celebration. I felt so sad that we never had that chance with Miles. Again, I realised the feelings were not actually directed at others, but were a response to my own sadness.

I had one relatively new friend who was pregnant at the same time as me. We'd chatted at a party in November as the only two sober ones and hatched plans to hang out with our babies once they were both born: hers in December, mine in April. In the end our babies were born only two days apart: Matilda arrived on the 27th and Miles on the 29th of December. As my labour was being induced, I read her ecstatic birth announcement on Instagram. Naturally, I was immediately jealous, as this compounded the inevitable fact that my baby would never come home with me. I messaged her directly about a week after Miles arrived - in another circumstances, I wouldn't have hesitated to send her a congratulatory message. She replied expressing her utter anguish at my situation and especially given the obvious contrast between what we had both just experienced at the same time.

We met for lunch when Matilda was ten weeks old and there was no awkwardness whatsoever. I thought I wasn't going to cope with holding a newborn. I had a horrible irrational fear that the minute the baby was placed in my arms, I would drop it in disgust, or do something completely out of character, but much to my own surprise, I was fine. It made me realise that other babies did not replace my baby.

My baby, a little boy called Miles, had died. As beautiful as the little baby I was holding was, she was not mine, so I shouldn't be envious of her. The baby I lost was unique, one of a kind and mine entirely, so while I was sad for myself, I was happy for my friend and in many ways proud of myself for facing my fears and picking up this precious newborn. What I was missing was Miles: not just any baby, but my unique baby. Adopting this way of looking at other pregnancies and babies helped me move forward. Miles' place on earth hadn't been given away to anyone else, he just sadly didn't get to stay here with us.

Chapter 32 Significant dates and anniversaries

As I hit the month Miles would have been born in, I fell in an absolute heap. I hadn't realised just how much significance I'd placed on this month, April 2019. I had planned so much for it and around it and as I was doing some of those things, I kept thinking, *I should be about to give birth* or *I should have a newborn in my arms.* To make matters worse, the media was in overdrive with constant coverage of Baby Sussex, and reports on all things pregnancy and birth were on high rotation. Every time I turned on the TV or flicked through my phone, there was an article on the impending arrival of the royal baby or the Duchess's baby bump. Everything screamed BABIES! BIRTH!

I had hoped I would be pregnant by the time the due date rolled around, and was devastated to get my period exactly three months to the day Miles had been delivered. In hindsight, I can see how naive my optimism was, but I wanted the comfort of knowing I would have another baby. During February and March, I had been distracted by coordinating the launch event and food hampers for the charity I was assisting. I was running around, cooking and planning and being able to do all my tasks for the event with ease, as I was neither pregnant nor had a newborn in my care.

The pain I felt during what I called my due date month was as strong and debilitating as the pain I felt when Miles was born. My mind was in overdrive, thinking of the endless should-have-beens. I had been so busy that I think I pushed a lot of my grief down, but once the launch event was over, it all overflowed and I was overwhelmed by a new wave. Why did other babies make it and not mine? I knew Miles' hemorrhage had not been caused by anything I had done and we still had no idea what had caused him to bleed as he did. Not knowing made him not being with us seem even more cruel and random.

My third appointment with Brooke, my psychologist, was in the first week of April. I told her about how I had sunk back into a very low state and felt like I was going backwards in my recovery. She said that this was, completely normal and to be expected, especially since my loss was still so recent. Just hearing this lifted some of the heaviness. To hear from a mental health professional that my reaction was completely normal helped immensely. I was putting far too much pressure on myself to be okay in a very short time-frame when what I needed to do was accept the fact that I would never really be normal again. I would always live with this pain, and though it may lose its sharpness over time, it would always be there. There was no expectation that I should ever have to feel completely better or get closure, nor should I be striving to reach this point, as it didn't exist.

Mother's Day can also be especially triggering for many. I found my first Mother's Day without Miles to be nowhere near as hard as I had anticipated. Perhaps after the intensity of Miles' due date passing, I had worked through a lot of issues by the time Mother's Day arrived. I was in a stronger place emotionally, having let it all out and allowed myself to feel really low on the bad days. I felt ready to enjoy some weeks, or hopefully months, of calm and happiness. If the month before Mother's Day hadn't been so significant, it would probably have been very different for me.

Everyone is different, and each of us attach different feelings and expectations to days like Mother's Day. I feel it is especially important to honour and respect all kinds of mothers, and not to forget those whose children are not here with them physically. A mother is no less of a mother because her baby could not stay with her; she always has been and always will be a mother. In my opinion, it's one of the toughest of roles a mother can be dealt: to mother and love a child that you cannot nurture, cannot hold and cannot see grow. To be the mother of a child whose existence and presence on this earth sometimes has to be explained to others, as its significance is not always understood. A mother's love does not stop when a child dies: it continues to grow and no amount of time will change or stop this.

In Australia and in many places around the world, Bereaved Mother's Day is held the week before Mother's Day. I initially felt offended by this, as I misunderstood the intention of it. I thought that it was a day created for bereaved mothers in lieu of the traditional Mother's Day. Then I realised that it was intended to be recognised in addition to the official Mother's Day. It was created to acknowledge the pain of mothers who have lost children, not to exclude them from celebrating the following week. We are entitled to be a part of both and are a part of both.

For me, the significance of Miles' due date was that our journey together in terms of dates dedicated to him was coming to an end. He was to be my April 2019 baby and once this month passed, in a whole new way he too had passed forever. Those dates connected to him would, from now on, be in the past tense. The shock of what had happened was wearing off and reality was sinking in. I could see now that my feelings were grief, not depression. Grief mimics depression in many ways, but it is a reaction to a traumatic event rather than a chemical imbalance.

I was hypervigilant about monitoring my mood and keeping my doctor and psychologist informed of how I was feeling, especially in the lead-up to significant dates. The line between grief and depression felt very thin and I was conscious of the fact that it would not take much for one to tip into the other. It helped to know I had someone keeping an eye on me, that someone would step in and help me should things spiral out of control. Services such as SANDS, PANDA and The Pink Elephant Network offer free counselling services over the phone and also via video link. These services are run by trained volunteers, the majority of who have also experienced baby loss first-hand. As much as friends and family love and care, having a trained professional keep an eye on you in this incredibly difficult time can make a huge difference.

In the first week of April when I was really struggling, Josh suggested that I take a few days off to just cry, have a couple of really shit days and be kind to myself. I would never have thought to do this if he hadn't suggested it. My psychologist backed this up, saying treat yourself during due date month as you did straight after Miles was born. Cry, sleep, escape, grieve, wail. Sometimes other people have to give you permission to do this, even though is it totally justified. I'm sure if you saw a friend struggling with the same thing, you would tell them to do whatever it is that would help them survive. Giving yourself that same permission is vital. If the grief is not let out, it will build up and one day explode in a dangerous and debilitating way.

Saying that you're struggling is not something which rolls off the tongue easily for most. It's so hard to admit that you're not okay, especially as time passes. As others move on, often you are the only one left remembering your baby, which can feel very lonely. In the lead-up to significant anniversaries like Miles' due date and first birthday, I felt distracted, angry, irritable and out of sorts. I couldn't work out why these dates felt harder than any other day of the year. We missed him all the time, so why did these specific dates feel so much harder? Perhaps it was the confronting fact that losing Miles still hurt so much, that time had not changed that pain. Significant dates are such definite marks of time passing.

The really sharp edges of my pain have been smoothed over with time and, the days are no longer predominantly dark, but the pain can still re-emerge and feel as intense as it initially did. So many tough feelings are brought up by anniversaries and you can feel like you are in a time warp, sucked straight back to the early weeks and months. It still shocks me, regardless of how much time goes by, that this really did happen. It can still feel surreal. I'm not sure that this will ever change.

I've come to accept that there will always be dates that trigger me: the anniversary of his birth and death, the year he should have started school, or graduated from school. The list is endless, as is the tendency to wonder what your child would have been like at that age and stage. It has felt overwhelming to me that I would always have these dates on my calendar to anticipate with a mixture of wistfulness, sadness and love. Like grief itself, there is no way of avoiding what is ahead. My greatest hope is that over time - and I'm sure this will take a very long time - we will look forward to doing something special on these dates in Miles' memory and that they will become happy celebrations, not sad reminders of what we have lost.

Chapter 33 Ways of remembering and honouring your baby

For a long time, I felt like my grief for Miles kept me closer to him. When I was sad I was honouring him, and not disrespecting his memory. That mindset made being happy, joyful or hopeful really difficult at first, as I felt like I was betraying him and his memory. How can I be happy when my child has died?

You don't need to stay in mourning forever to honour your loss. By living your life with love and hope, you are honouring your loved one by moving forward and making the most of the life you have. It's not easy and some days it seems impossible, but enjoying life again doesn't mean that you don't miss your baby and wish that they were here with you.

At first, not wanting to move on was driven by my wish this had never happened in the first place. I wanted to stop time, press rewind and make everything go away. I wanted to have a baby, not just any baby, but Miles specifically. Once the initial shock wore off and I began to deal with the pain of loss, I found that I did want to enjoy life again and I wanted Miles to be by my side in some way.

I found little ways to remember him with an emotion that wasn't anguish or sorrow. Whenever I saw horses, I thought of Miles. There is a set of beautiful drawings by English artist Charlie Mackesy that depict a little boy going on adventures with his friends the horse, the mole and the fox. They all have beautiful quotes and the image of a little boy riding high on his magnificent horse made me feel calm and happy. I liked to picture Miles like the little boy, riding high on his noble steed, galloping through the fields, being kept company and looked after by his friends.

Some of the quotes touch on grief and loss and the fragility of the human spirit. One reads:

'We have a long way to go,' sighed the boy. 'Yes but look how far we have come,' said the horse.' This made so much sense to me. Although I felt carrying the burden of grief was a long journey, much of it was still ahead, when I allowed myself to look back, even I could see how far I had come. Other favourites are:

'Tears fall for a reason, they are your strength not weakness',

'Never be ashamed of the way you feel'.

And lastly, for all the lost babies,

'You have been loved, you are loved. You always will be loved.'

The moon was another sign I looked for. Three weeks after Miles was born, a spectacular full moon dominated the night sky right in front of our house. We were away on Kangaroo Island and still in the hardest, most brutal initial stage of grief. Josh said he could see a little face in the moon and perhaps it was Miles. Josh is not one to look for signs, so hearing him say this made me incredibly happy. I liked that he was in some way also looking for his little boy. Josh had said that for him, Miles lived on in our hearts, he had not gone to a higher place but lived on within us. I wished I could have found as much comfort in this as Josh did. I needed to see Miles in things and I think this was because of my screaming physical need to mother my child. If I couldn't hold him, I wanted to feel him and see him in some other way. It's very hard to explain, but I could not take comfort alone from the idea of Miles' spirit living on within us. I don't see any harm in finding tangible ways of remembering your baby. It may be that you remember them when you see a toy rabbit, or certain type of flower. Whatever feels right to you.

The blue wren, a bird that holds great meaning to Josh and I, became my favourite symbol for Miles. We have several wrens living in the garden of our house on Kangaroo Island. I love the cheeky way they hop around and their inquisitive nature. They are tiny, beautiful and are always seen in pairs. I chose the blue wren as the image to accompany 'Miles Apart' as when we were on Kangaroo Island shortly after Miles died, one thing I found great solace in was sitting outside, looking out to sea and watching the blue wrens dance around in the garden. I saw Miles in them and felt that they were a very fitting and meaningful way for us to remember him.

Butterflies are often used to symbolise babies who are no longer with us. They are beautiful, delicate creatures and one charity, Still Aware, has created an annual event Birthday for Babies, which is a 'birthday celebration for all babies chasing butterflies in the sky'. At this event, held on February 12, families can release a butterfly, stay for a picnic, and meet other families who have walked a similar path. This is a beautiful community event that brings people together to remember and celebrate their babies. There is an official twilight market event organised each year in Adelaide and Still Aware encourages families in other states to contact them if they would like to organise a celebration in their own home town or state.

Similarly, during Baby Loss Awareness Week, held annually in October, and Baby Loss Awareness Day, which is on October 15, there are many services and rituals families can take part in all over the world. SANDS holds 'A Walk to Remember' and many cemeteries hold services dedicated to babies who died in the womb or as newborns. All of these events give parents the opportunity to physically do something to honour their baby, be it lighting a candle, releasing a balloon or a butterfly, or talking about them with other loss parents.

After Miles died I received some beautiful gifts. From my sister-in-law, a bracelet with four silver charms, each of which had the first initial of all four of my children: A for Alfie, T for Ted, B for Bonnie and M for Miles. I have worn it every day and cannot imagine ever not wearing it. All my children are there together, equally acknowledged. It was such an overwhelmingly beautiful gift. It said to me: *I see him too, he is part of our family, your fourth child and with us forever.* Another group of friends bought me a silver heart with Miles' initials engraved on one side. My Mum also gave me a necklace with an 'M' engraved on the pendant. If Miles cannot physically be by my side as I go through life with his brothers and sister, his initials are with me every day and stay close to me wherever I go.

I have seen other beautiful ways to remember babies. Stars can be named in their honour. A map of the night sky the day they were conceived, born or died can be ordered and hung proudly in your home. Trees can be planted or a special bench placed in a garden, which friends and family can visit. I was content to wait until the right thing came to me. The way in which I feel I honoured Miles most was through writing about him. If what I wrote never saw the light of day, I knew that perhaps, when they were older, my children might find what I had written interesting and they might like to read about the little brother they never had the chance to know. I hoped that by growing up in a family that had gone through baby loss and spoken of it openly, as adults they would be better equipped to support their own friends and family. I truly hoped they would never need to do this, but given how common it is, I know that it will touch their lives again in some way in the future.

Many families find comfort in writing their baby's name in the sand whenever they are at the beach. Some choose to run a marathon for charity or knit socks and beanies for other stillborn babies. I feel that any action you undertake in memory of your baby is a way of parenting them. The energy you would have put into caring for your child is directed into another activity done in their honour. To me it was a huge comfort to find something to do for Miles. My writing has always been done with him in mind and for me, it gives him a tangible legacy. It may be hidden deep inside, but I'm sure in all of us there is an energy we can harness. It may be tending a beautiful garden planted for your baby, it may be helping people in a field related or completely unrelated to baby loss, or it may be as simple as creating a small shrine in your home dedicated to your baby.

I have also created a memory box, in which I have kept everything I have that is related in some way to Miles. The pregnancy test I took, the ultrasound pictures, medical records and the beautiful cards and letters people sent us after he died. The tiny teddy that lay with him in the hospital cot is there, as is the top I was wearing the day I said goodbye to him, and the outfit he wore.

The day before the first ultrasound that indicated he was so unwell, I took my older children to see Father Christmas and have their annual photo taken with him. At the time, I thought the composition of the photo was a little odd. Alfie and Bonnie are squashed up together and Ted is sitting on the other side of Santa, leaving a large empty spot on the other side of him. One friend commented, *Ted's left room for one more* and I believe that he unwittingly had. There is a clear spot for Miles and I have placed a copy of this picture in the memory box, along with the pictures that were taken of him in hospital.

In time, I will create some rituals within our immediate family to remember Miles. In the initial stages of grief, I was too fragile and I couldn't think of how I wanted to remember him meaningfully going forward. As time went on, I felt strong enough to give this some thought and come up with ways of including Miles. I decided I would have a cake for him each year to mark the day he arrived and became a part of our family. On his first birthday I made gnocchi Bolognese for dinner, a dish I craved endlessly when pregnant with him. I also decided to buy a special Christmas ornament with his name on it to hang on our tree each year and to buy a similar-aged child in need a gift in his honour.

To the best of my ability, I include Miles when people ask how many children I have. What had always been such a simple, straightforward question has become difficult to answer. Yes, it can be confronting, awkward, and yes, at times it was a conversation stopper, but it is important to me that he isn't forgotten or ignored just because he's not physically here with us. Sometimes it feels safer and easier to gloss over the details: it really depends who I'm talking to. I've come to realise that you don't always have to elaborate or expand on the answer you give, but overall I do feel better when I include Miles in the headcount as otherwise it feels wrong and disrespectful.

I hope, too, that if I can find the courage to say Miles' name and include him in the family headcount, hopefully others might be inspired to also say his name, and the names of so many other babies who were taken too soon.

Chapter 34 What not to say

I'd say that ninety-five percent of people who have the courage to say something to acknowledge your loss manage to come up with something kind and thoughtful. Sadly, it's the comments of the remaining five percent, who say something completely insensitive or inappropriate, that stick with you the longest. When your defences are down, it can be incredibly hard to process such remarks. I certainly didn't have my usual resilience after Miles died. Everything hurt, especially ill-thought-out comments, people who tried to give me a reason for my loss or offer unsolicited advice – particularly those who hadn't been through this themselves. Many other loss parents I spoke to suffered additional pain from comments they received. This is in many ways an additional loss: the loss of understanding from those you turn to for comfort and support. While you're in the thick of it, it can be really hard to articulate why something was hurtful or to stand up for yourself. So perhaps share this chapter with those around you who you think might benefit from it. People often have no idea what to say, so they may be grateful for some guidance.

This chapter was really hard to write, as many of the hurtful comments here were said by people I am highly likely to see again. (In many cases, by people I see often.) However, I felt that the comments were too important to ignore. Even though they were not intended to cause any hurt whatsoever, they did, and I'm sure my emotional responses were not unusual for baby loss parents. People don't need to walk on eggshells around the bereaved forever, but in the first months I would encourage people to really think before they speak. The impact of ill-thought-out comments and actions can be enormous, even if they're coming from a good place.

A bad comment would set me back for days. Any unsupportive statements and actions I encountered early on shaped my perception of how I believed other people viewed our loss. This perception was warped at best and based on the comments of the minority, not the majority. I would feel outraged by anyone who'd upset me further: I was already dealing with so much chaos in my mind, I didn't need the added burden of talking myself down from their comments and trying to get them off my mind. Below are some comments I encountered that caused me further anguish.

'It's really common'

Lots of people said to me, 'it's really common'. Sadly, baby loss as a whole *is* common. Around 1 in 4 pregnancies end in miscarriage, 1 in 125 pregnancies are stillbirths and approximately 1 in 10 couples struggle with infertility. If someone hasn't been through it themselves, all I hear when they say this is: *get over it, it happens all the time*. The fact that miscarriage is relatively common does not make it any less heart-breaking for each individual who encounters it.

Anecdotes that don't involve first-hand experience

Please don't tell me about your cousin's hairdresser's friend who lost a baby. Stories without a genuine heartfelt connection to a baby did little to help me and I felt like they were there to fill a gap in the conversation. The stories shared directly by other grieving parents *did* bring comfort, as they made me feel like I could talk to someone who really understood what I was going through. It opened up meaningful conversation between parties who know first-hand how painful this kind of loss is.

'Are you feeling better?'

This is a hard one. It made me feel like I ought to be better, like I was wallowing in my grief and that it was self-indulgent to still feel so sad. I knew I would never feel better about losing Miles, that I will probably go to my grave missing him. In time, I'm sure it will become less intense, but I can't imagine it will ever disappear completely. Nor do I want it to. It took time for the good days to begin to outweigh the bad. Feeling pressure to expedite the process didn't help.

I am aware that my sadness will rear its head at times both expected and unexpected. When I see another child who would have been Miles's age start walking or talking, and when his contemporaries start school, turn eighteen, or get married, I will feel my loss and wonder what might have been. My lifetime will be full of 'what if's and 'if only's. Would Miles have been as tall as Josh, or taller? Would he have loved food like I do, and fishing like his dad? Would he have been sporty? Funny? Kind? I will never know these things, just as I will never 'feel better' about losing my baby. I've lost more than a baby: I've lost a life, a person I should have known, a child I should have nurtured. I know that will never go away.

'Time heals all wounds'

This glib cliché is not at all appropriate after the loss of a child, for reasons very similar to those surrounding asking a bereaved parent if they are feeling better. Time may ease or alter the intensity of the pain, but I can't imagine it will ever completely erase it.

Grief will not necessarily decrease in an orderly fashion. I think comments like this are offered from a lack of anything better to say. It's a generic line, trotted out in many different scenarios. However well-meant, it's not a helpful response (and this applies to people grieving many different losses) and is probably best left unsaid. You should never feel like you need to 'find closure' or 'come to terms' with the loss of a baby or any loved one. Perhaps people witnessing your sadness hope that you will feel better at some point in the future. I'm sure it is said innocently, with hope that you will one day have healed completely from this trauma

Complaining about newborns

I felt really uncomfortable listening to mothers complain about their newborns in the first few months after losing Miles. At a lunch one day the girl next to me was talking about how little sleep she was getting because of her six-week-old baby. I allowed the conversation to flow and sat there politely imparting my knowledge of sleep, telling her about how different each of my babies had been. I desperately wanted to escape the conversation as soon as possible. In her defence, I had allowed the conversation to flow and let it continue by offering advice. I had felt rude removing myself from it. My behavior probably indicated that I was totally okay with the topic, though it was actually really painful for me to talk about, knowing that I should have been dealing with newborn sleep deprivation then, too. These kinds of conversations became less difficult with time, but initially, they are confronting triggers.

Other people's birth and pregnancy stories

Quite a few people told me their birth and pregnancy stories after I lost Miles. Hearing about a threatened miscarriage and how stressful it was during a pregnancy that went on to be successful didn't help me at all. I didn't want to seem bitter, but I just thought, *lucky you, I wish I'd also had that happy outcome.* If a story ends with a live birth and a living child, it brings no sympathy to the bereaved, just a reminder of what she is missing: a living baby. It is not similar in any way to what a loss mother has endured. Sometimes someone would preface a story about their pregnancy experience with something like: "I have no idea how you must be feeling, XYZ happened to me and I could barely cope with that, so I can't imagine what you're going through." This showed empathy and an awareness that even though they had also faced adversity, it was in no way similar to my experience. Any story involving a living, breathing baby on the premise that it was comparable to my experience usually made me more upset.

Stories of complicated deliveries

Hearing a long-winded story of a complicated delivery is also really hard to process. When listening to a story like this, I might think, *oh god, was the baby okay, did it live? Are they telling me their story because they too have had to endure this tragedy?* If the story ends in a live birth and a living baby, it's just not helpful to someone who has lost their baby. Yes, birth can be traumatic and pregnancy extremely stressful and anxiety-ridden, but perhaps these stories are best shared with mothers who have encountered similar experiences, rather than a stillbirth. A difficult birth is incredibly confronting and deserves attention: it can be a valid trauma with an ongoing psychological impact. But it should not be told as a comparison to the birth story of a baby who has died. Someone who has had a miscarriage or stillbirth ended up with death and devastation, and such a story may only remind them of this, while potentially also bringing up traumatic flashbacks of what they went through during delivery.

Inferring blame for your baby's death

It's hard to believe, but many bereaved mothers have had things said to them that in some way suggested they might be to blame for their baby's death. This happened to me once when I was having girls' drinks at a friend's place, around the date I would have been due. I was a bit drunk, to be honest. It had been a really emotional week in the lead-up to the due date and rather than adopting some mature coping strategies, I thought that too many glasses of bubbly would take the edge off. One woman I was talking to said something along the lines of, "You were pushing your luck with a fourth". She went on to explain her theory, telling me she knew lots of 'older' women who had lost a fourth baby. She then told me that my body must have known it wasn't up to a fourth pregnancy and that it would be wise of me to give up any hope of another baby, and be happy with the three I already have.

Shocked, I put it down to her having had too many wines, and didn't respond. I was so offended I think I just walked off, but her comments really stayed with me. I felt like she was saying *serves you right*. I had worried that what happened to Miles was because of something I had done and was trying to process that privately, even though I knew logically that no cause could be found for the hemorrhage and blood clot that caused his condition. The doctors were still searching for some clues as to why it happened, but one thing I knew to be true was that my age had nothing to do with it. If I hadn't been reassured by doctors that I was not to blame, these comments could have done a huge amount of damage.

Loss mothers have shared other experiences with me in which it was insinuated that perhaps the thoughts and feelings they had towards their pregnancy had an impact on its outcome. One woman who fell pregnant unexpectedly with her fourth child and felt apprehensive about the unplanned pregnancy was told by her mother-in-law that perhaps the baby sensed her ambivalence and that was why she miscarried. I have also heard of people being told they were too stressed out, were working too hard or were not excited enough - all cruel, unnecessary and unfounded comments. I think many women feel guilty enough after baby loss and wrongly blame themselves. Thoughts and feelings alone cannot end a pregnancy.

Stories that mean to empathise, but have no relation to your experience

Nearly everyone has a person in their life who always manages to tell a story about a completely unrelated situation they've been in as a response to what you're going through, seemingly in an attempt to empathise. A bit like birth stories from mothers whose baby has survived, these types of stories left me feeling frustrated, not comforted. About two weeks after losing Miles, we ran into some people we know while away on Kangaroo Island. I wasn't up for socialising or spending time with other people, but our kids desperately wanted to have dinner with theirs. The woman we were with started talking in great detail about her experience with grief after her son lost an eye in a backyard accident, a decade before.

She likened the trauma of our experiences to hers, and the mourning period she experienced after her son lost an eye to how we were feeling after Miles' death. I felt sorry for her and her son and agreed that it was a horrific life event, but I couldn't help but feel that our stories had very little in common. All could think was: at least your son is alive, mine is dead.

Some people tend to bring everything back to themselves. I don't think this is done consciously; it's almost a knee-jerk reaction to tell a story of their own, no matter how tenuous the link. This kind of story rarely helped me, unless there were significant similarities. Stories about when the cherished family pet died, or a scary medical episode, felt really strange and awkward. I was too frail to offer genuine sympathy in the first months after losing Miles. Most often, I walked away from this kind of conversation full of anger and frustration.

Suggesting it was 'God's will' or somehow destined to happen

I hated being told that my baby was not meant for this earth, or that he was too precious for this world. Nothing in the universe can explain or justify to me why he is not here. If as a bereaved parent, I feel that my baby's loss was somehow destined, then I can say it: if I have found a higher meaning or spiritual purpose that brings me comfort, it's up to me to share this. But I have never taken any comfort from other people imposing their theories or beliefs upon me. When I hear someone say, *it's for the best*, or *perhaps there's a silver lining*, all I hear is that my grief is not valid: that my baby's death was a good outcome. Sometimes truly devastating, horrible things happen and there is absolutely no reason for them, and no silver lining. So when people suggested I look for one, pointed one out to me, or told me my baby was in a better place, I felt like his worth and place in the world were being diminished.

I also find it really inappropriate when people put the loss of a baby down to 'God's will' or anything similar, probably because I'm not particularly religious myself. I imagine that even people with absolute faith in God can have it rocked when they encounter a tragedy of this magnitude. From my childhood in Catholic schools, I have some fairly upsetting memories of being told that unbaptised babies remain in limbo for all of eternity. It's a horrible, haunting thought. Even though I am not a practising Catholic, I believe Miles is in a good place, like heaven: not lost in no-man's land with all of the other babies who were not baptised.

'Count your blessings'

I really resented being told to count my blessings and focus on the children I have. I have always done that: they, along with Miles, will continue to be my purpose in life. I felt like some people thought that because I had living children, I should be less upset by the loss of Miles. For me, having children did not minimise or alter my heartache for Miles. He was his own person, held his own place in our family. It's like saying to someone who had just lost their father, *don't be sad, you've still got a mother, surely that's enough.* You've got one left so don't be sad about losing the other one!

I had vivid memories of the newborn process etched in my brain and did feel especially grateful that I had been able to experience it. There are so many rituals surrounding babies: the feeding, the wrapping, the settling. I physically felt this absence in my home and in my heart when we had to leave Miles behind at the hospital. I had continual flashbacks about my other babies and what I had done with them in the days after we left hospital. These memories constantly reminded me of what I was missing out on with Miles. I would never get to nurse him, hold him, or watch him sleep. The indescribably beautiful newborn scent was missing, as was the sheer joy of new life. So telling me to count my blessings felt especially cruel. I had counted them a billion times over, but this didn't make losing Miles any easier to cope with. I was being pretty hard on myself and feeling extremely guilty about my living children being potentially affected by my grief, so I didn't need any reminders as to what a blessing they were. I was so grateful for what I did have, but simultaneously felt so sad for what I had lost. The first feeling did not erase the latter: they were separate.

'At least you know you can get pregnant'

I felt really misunderstood when people said this to me. I know I can get pregnant, but I also know that this is not a guarantee of carrying to term a healthy baby who I will bring home. Many bereaved mothers are terrified of getting pregnant and being pregnant again, despite a strong desire to have another child. From talking to those who have gone on to have another baby the experience of pregnancy after loss is riddled with fear, anxiety and often guilt. Guilt that this baby may live when the other(s) didn't. Fear that disaster will strike again. Constant worry that something will go wrong, which is understandable, given that you have experienced first-hand what it is like when things do go terribly wrong. (However, one friend of mine *was* comforted by this statement, as it gave her hope that it was likely she would be able to have another baby. This just goes to show how personal grief is.)

'It could have been worse'

One woman told me that after an early loss, a few people told her stories of others who had lost babies later on in their pregnancies, telling her that she was lucky to lose hers early on. The implication being it could have been worse, that a later loss would have been more painful. Gestation is irrelevant and the age at which a baby dies does not in any way dictate the depth of your grief. There is no 'easier' time to endure loss. To say, 'at least it was early' or preface any comment with 'at least', belittles someone's grief and their baby's life.

Using medical terms to refer to your baby

Medical terms that are used to diagnose and determine procedures required after the death of a baby can also seem cruel and uncaring, they tend to dehumanise your loss. If your doctor or midwife refers to your baby as the product of conception, the fetus or a blighted ovum, it implies that your baby is merely a medical incident, not a much-wanted child. In other areas of medicine, we do not refer to people in such cold clinical terms. For example, if speaking to a family about their father's cancer diagnosis, he is not referred to as 'the elderly male cancer patient', but as a father, husband, or brother. We need to start universally applying the same kind of language to babies lost in the womb as to their parents, they are not a medical term or an unfortunate pregnancy outcome, but a much-loved baby.

Random strange comments

Sometimes I encountered comments which were so strange that I couldn't work how to process them. At a family lunch one day, Bonnie, aged two, was carrying on. A relative kept remarking upon how spoilt she was and what a pain she was being before saying to my mum (within earshot of Josh and me), "You know, that's why it's such a shame about Miles. Another baby would have taken the focus off Bonnie. She's totally ruined, they focus on her way too much."

The two things were completely unrelated! A two-year-old behaving badly had absolutely nothing to do with the fact that her baby brother had died. We were dealing with a two-year-old who had missed her nap and been thrown into a noisy group. I was horrified at the idea that someone thought the greatest shame of Miles dying was that his presence would have helped take the focus from our two-year-old.

I dwelled on the comment for weeks, even arguing with Josh over it. He agreed that it was horrible, but was able to put it aside and move on. I couldn't: it played over and over in my mind. This was such a huge waste of my energy.

Josh managed to convince me that it was not said with any intention to hurt me. It was just one person's opinion and simply didn't matter. We knew what kind of parents we were. We knew that our children were lovely, polite and all-round good kids, and we were doing the best we could. I resented that my parenting was questioned a mere seven weeks after I had given birth to a stillborn baby. I wish I had been able to laugh the comment off. In the end, people will say things that hurt you. It's okay to feel like crap afterwards, but it's also important not to let it really get you down. Sadly, there are much bigger hurdles to jump after losing a baby.

People avoiding conversation with you, or mention of your baby

When talking to people who hadn't experienced baby loss, I needed to feel that people weren't afraid of talking to me because they couldn't handle what had happened to me.

I can appreciate that for many people, these conversations can be daunting and feel uncomfortable to begin. But for the person living with loss, this discomfort is now a part of their daily existence. I often worried that people would feel disheartened if they were met with little response, or if a series of texts went unanswered. I was always incredibly grateful for people who made contact and said something about Miles to me, even though I sometimes didn't have the energy to respond.

I was very conscious of never brushing off someone who acknowledged my situation. Even if I didn't want to enter into a long conversation about Miles at that exact moment, I always thanked them for saying something. Hand on heart, I appreciated every kind word that was spoken. Many messages and emails did go unanswered as I didn't always have the bandwidth to reply to everyone, but many wonderful friends were not discouraged by this. They kept on making contact and specifically asking how I was going, regardless of whether I replied or not. To me, that showed true friendship and understanding.

Common hurtful comments (a loss mothers' list)

One loss mother I spoke to who lost her fourth baby almost forty years ago can still vividly recall some of the things people said to her after her baby was stillborn. Faith was her fourth child and fourth daughter. Some people said to her, "Just as well it was another girl. It would have been terrible if it had been a boy." I can't imagine how hurtful that would have been. Another person asked, "What are you going to do with it?" as though Faith was something to be dealt with, not a precious child to be laid to rest and farewelled. Jano, Faith's mother, sent me a list of comments she'd compiled with a support group back in the eighties and they still ring true today, forty years on. I found comfort in the fact that attitudes had started to shift, but as a society, we still have a long way to go.

Cheer up! You'll soon get over it.

Don't cry, you'll only upset yourself.

It's bad luck.

It's meant to be. / It wasn't meant to be.

It's just as well. There might have been something wrong with it.

It's nature's way.

I understand (from someone who had never experienced baby loss).

At least you've got other children.

What you need is another baby.

You're young enough to have another.

It won't happen again.

It will be okay the next time.

Pull yourself together, you've got other responsibilities.

Time heals.

Forget it and don't talk about it.

Keep busy.

At least you didn't get to know it.

It was God's will.

Just as well it never lived.

Better now than later.

You've had a pretty good innings.

Count your blessings.

Try not to think about it too much.

Life goes on.

Perhaps you tested too early, in the old days you wouldn't have even known you were pregnant. (After an early pregnancy loss)

Talking to someone who had lost a baby almost forty years ago and still felt this loss so deeply brought me comfort. It helped me to validate my grief and embrace it as a lifelong journey.

Chapter 35 What to say and do for the bereaved

During the really gritty, hard stage of grief just after losing Miles, there was very little that anyone could say to make me feel better or take away my pain. At this stage, I just needed people to call on if I felt like talking, crying, walking, screaming or anything else that might help.

Sometimes there are no words, but it's important that those closest to us dig deep and say something.

Comments I found comforting and or supportive were:

I am so sorry.

I don't know what to say but I am here to listen.

There are no words.

I have been thinking of you.

You've been in my heart.

This is shit.

We will remember your beautiful (Miles) forever.

He will not be forgotten.

Life can be so unfair. This is so unfair.

I can't imagine how hard this must be.

I can't imagine how you are feeling.

Did you name your baby?

Would you like to talk about Miles?

How are you recovering physically?

I would love to see a picture of your baby if you are happy to share one.

People often ask *How can I help? What do you need?* When you are in the throes of grief, you don't know which way is up, let alone what you need. Your world has been tipped upside down and nothing makes sense. There is absolutely no way you can direct traffic and allocate well-meaning friends jobs or tasks to help you with. I had an intense need for privacy when I first lost Miles. I didn't want to see anyone and could barely talk. Company was not something I sought. I couldn't respond to messages and texts, let alone make suggestions or give instructions as to how people could help. Helping someone who is feeling like this is hard. Working out what to do (or not do) is like walking through a minefield. Here are some helpful things which you may be able to suggest to people who are offering to help.

Report your sad news on your behalf

People can, on your behalf contact your immediate and wider community, workmates, people you may know through school, gym, sporting clubs to let them know the news. In my case, this extended to letting people know not to send flowers. I loved the bunches we'd been so lucky to receive, and especially cherished the notes which accompanied them, but we were about to go away, so I didn't want to receive any more.

Organise outings for or respite from older children

It might be helpful if others were to organise outings or activities for older children within your family. Not everyone will be comfortable with this, as some parents have a strong need to keep their children close and are incredibly fearful of letting them out of their sight. The worst imaginable thing has just happened to one child, so letting go of others may be hard. On the other hand, you may be feeling so exhausted that the idea of caring for children at this point may be impossible. You could suggest someone helps with the kids for an hour, a day, a weekend, whatever works. Perhaps a school run once a week or someone to take children to their swimming lessons would be a good start and give you a small moment of respite.

Everyday errands

If people offer to drop off food or groceries, you could ask them to help run errands or pick up extra things for you on their way over. Normal day-to-day activities can become arduous tasks as grief takes over every aspect of normal daily routines. You are completely entitled to let people know that you will not necessarily be up to seeing them when they come to your house. It may be too much to get out of bed or off the sofa so it's okay to ask for things to be left on the front doorstep. You may feel reluctant to accept help in case it entails expectations of a visit or a catch-up, but it's perfectly understandable to let people know you're not ready for this.

Help with funeral or memorial

If you are having a funeral or memorial, perhaps you can ask people to help with one aspect of this. Cards, flowers, food: whatever is needed. Be specific about what it is exactly that you'd like done. You could ask someone to make finger sandwiches for the wake, to drive you to and from the ceremony, buy ice for the drinks, stand by the entrance and greet people. You may need help with the care of any living children on the day if they are attending the funeral or they may need to be looked after at home if they are not. There may be an annoying guest or relative who you'd like to be kept away from, as the likelihood of them offending you (accidentally or otherwise) is high. You may ask someone to stay with you once the funeral is over, or to keep you company the next day. A funeral can be an exhausting and overwhelming experience, but in no way does it mark the end of the grieving process. It is merely one small step along an ongoing path.

Advice for loss parents: accept help

I find accepting help really hard. I'm sure I'm not the only one who is wired like this. Perhaps we feel self conscious that we need this help, or are very private, so the idea of an outsider seeing the inner workings of our household feels a little uncomfortable. Regardless, I urge you to accept any offers that are helpful. Say *yes, please* to a casserole to on your doorstep, or the offer of someone watering your garden or organising for a cleaner to get your house in order before you come home from hospital. While a surface clean would be a godsend, don't feel shy about letting friends know whether you would prefer it if any items related to your baby are kept in place. Some people may assume you'd prefer cots and onesies hidden from sight, however this may not be the case. One friend offered to help me with the school run and let me know her offer had no time limit, I could take her up on it anytime.

Make a meal

One incredibly kind girl who I worked with over a decade ago made contact with me and said that she would love to make me a meal and drop it off. I wanted to say no, the offer seemed too generous and I was conscious of her busy life with children and a full time job. In the end I said yes and she replied, "good, I was worried with you being so self sufficient that you'd say no!" It was such a treat to be cooked for, something which I rarely get. I think being a foodie, most people assume I have this area of my life covered. It was so nice for both Josh and I to have one night off and what it really did was fill my heart with warmth and gratitude that someone had gone to that effort for us. And she made the most insanely delicious cookies for the kids. I ate most of them and each bite made me smile.

Messages and gifts

I received some other lovely messages and items which made me feel supported and loved. A fellow foodie I met via Instagram sent me an incredible box of dried fruits from her family orchard. That someone I have never met in the flesh took the time to do this for me was incredibly touching. Another friend gave me a beautiful candle, which I lit for Miles during the international wave of light for baby loss awareness week, months later. I was also given a baby book specifically designed for babies who die: a place to record moments and memories which might otherwise be kept only in your mind. When a baby passes away, the reactions of others are often the exact opposite to what they would have been if your baby had lived. People shy away as there is no baby to celebrate. Yet in the eyes of their parents, every baby – even one born still – is a precious and beautiful being who deserves to be celebrated. The gifts I received created for me this sense of communal celebration and tangible items to associate with Miles.

Message that explicitly say 'no pressure to respond'

Some of the best messages I received were those that took the pressure off me to respond, reply, or interact. Messages that began, *Please don't reply, I just want you to know I'm thinking of you.*

Invitations to events preceded with, *I understand if you can't make it but I want you to know you are invited and we are ready to see you when you're ready, no pressure.* One friend invited me to a lunch a month or so after Miles died. I said I'd try to make it and even though I was two hours late, she kept a spare seat for me the whole time, just in case. When I did get there, after a hug and a *how are you?*, she said, "We are here to listen or here to distract. If you'd like to talk about Miles, we would love to hear all about him. If you don't, that's okay too. Whatever is best for you." This gave me permission to talk, to cry and to also chat about banal things such as the weather or my washing pile, and not feel guilty.

Share your own experiences with baby loss, if you have them

If you have been through something genuinely similar, open up. I found the greatest comfort in talking to people who had been through it too. Lots of women said, *I can sort of imagine how you're feeling as I had a miscarriage during the first trimester which was horrible, but nowhere near as bad as what happened to you and Miles.* Initially I agreed with them as I felt I should have been home safe, I had reached the point in pregnancy where a baby even if delivered incredibly premature could survive. I soon realised that while the timeframes and physical repercussions of respective gestation were different, the feelings were incredibly similar. We had begun making plans around our due dates, we had started thinking of names, dreaming of the changes to our family dynamic, planning changes to our home, our work, our life as a whole. Regardless of the specific circumstances, the loss is similar. A child had been lost, a child who cannot be replaced.

Ask to see pictures of the baby who has been lost

This isn't for everyone or applicable to all types of baby loss, but some friends asked if I could show or send them a picture or two of Miles. This meant the world to me as I did want to share him with people but was generally too scared. I didn't think anyone would want to see a picture of a baby who had been stillborn, that it would be too confronting for anyone apart from Josh and me. By asking to see him, I felt like they were saying, *he existed, he matters and I want to create my own memories of him.* I often felt that to many people, he didn't exist. That he was simply an unfortunate pregnancy outcome, not a child. Sharing his picture helped him become real to other people. It allowed me to share what I knew, that he was real. It's perhaps best captured in this quote from the children's book *The Velveteen Rabbit*: "Once you are real you can't become unreal again. It lasts for always." This is how I see babies lost in the womb: they were real and will forever remain so.

Acknowledge significant milestones

Another really lovely way that friends and family can show their support is to acknowledge significant dates and milestones (i.e. your baby's first month or one-year anniversary). I found these hugely triggering dates. Even though I felt shy to talk about them and unsure of how to mention their approach, I was glad when I did. From the people I reached out to, I received the support I needed. Receiving a simple message of love or an offer of company on my baby's sixth-month anniversary, due date or first birthday was exactly what I needed. On Miles's approximate due date, I organised a lunch with a small group of girlfriends. It felt good to be with people and to celebrate Miles with others. Understandably, I assume people may not understand the significance of the original due date. But for loss mothers, it seems be universally difficult. For me, it was almost like the end of a chapter, one big scary hurdle to get over. People asking when it was or remembering the date really helped, as did people who acknowledged Miles's birthday/anniversary. It was so nice to know he was remembered and loved by others. I wanted him to be remembered and celebrated as our much-loved fourth child: not an unfortunate event that occurred, but a beloved family member.

Offer to come to appointments as moral support

One friend offered to come to appointments with me. I felt too silly to ask people to keep me company. It felt like too big an ask. But a few times, I did wish I'd brought someone along with me, even if it was just to take notes, or to drive me there and back. We're all so conscious of not imposing on others these days, but in many situations, you really do need someone to hold your hand – or at the very least, drive you to and from difficult appointments.

Donate to baby loss charities or similar

Some close friends, in lieu of flowers, made a donation to a charity that was either directly connected to baby loss, or (in one case) associated with the hospital where Miles was delivered. I had said very clearly that I didn't want my house to resemble a florist, and this was a great option for people who really wanted to do something to let me know how much they cared. Most of the charities dedicated to baby loss are small and are in desperate need of funds to help them continue the incredible and important work that they do. It was always a gesture of kindness that warmed my heart. I loved the idea that a donation made in Miles' memory would help others.

Use the lost baby's name

I loved it when people weren't shy to use my baby's name or ask what it was. Calling a child 'the baby' may feel easier but if 'the baby' has been named it is so nice to hear his name spoken. I regularly contribute recipes and photographs to a child and family focused magazine called *KIDDO*. The night before the edition after we lost Miles was going off to print, the editor messaged me to ask if I would be comfortable with her dedicating the issue to Miles. I was so touched that she had thought to do this and said yes immediately. Seeing his name in print was beautiful and gave his life a tangible record for all to see. Similarly, when people wrote his name in a card or a letter it really moved me, he wasn't just 'the baby', he was his own beautiful little soul called Miles. He had a name, he had an identity and I wanted people to know this.

Share baby loss reading

I loved it when people forwarded articles onto me which were related to baby loss or grief in general. It made me feel like they were trying really really hard to see things from my perspective and gain an understanding into what it was like for me. I felt like I wasn't going through this alone, that someone was thinking of me and finding a way to tell me this. I knew lots of people were thinking of me but unless they said so, it had no impact. Similarly, if someone shared with me something they'd seen or done which had made them think of Miles, I really loved hearing their stories. Alfie, my eldest, pointed out a baby to me one day and asked if Miles would have been a similar size by now if he had lived. It was so sweet – and yes, in actual fact, the baby looked to be exactly the same age Miles would have been. Pointing this out gave us the opportunity to talk about Miles together.

Acknowledge the loss

In everyone's life there are many people that you will come into contact with on a daily basis who are not within your immediate circle of close friends or family, but regardless they are a regular presence in your life through work, sport, hobbies or mutual friends. It's often hard for these people to know if they should say anything at all. I think the rule of thumb should be if you knew about the pregnancy and had acknowledged it in some way previously, it is important and above all kind to mention the loss of the baby you knew they were expecting. People may feel intrusive or like its none of their business but a simple, "I heard that you lost your baby and I just wanted to let you know I have been thinking of you" or "I am so sorry for your loss" will go a long way. The comfort it may give to a bereaved mother who is dreading returning to work, or rejoining their favourite yoga class may be immeasurable.

This also creates a safe place within an environment which you may be feeling hesitant to return to. When someone acknowledges your loss they are giving you permission to speak of your child in this area of your life. I think this is especially important in the workplace. Grief is not something you can simply pack up and leave at the door or in your car when you head into work, for some time it may follow you everywhere and affect your ability to concentrate, interact and function on many basic levels. If you have no one to turn to, to discuss these fears with, any anxiety surrounding returning to work is magnified. If a colleague were to return to work after sustaining an obvious physical injury the conversations upon returning to work may flow with greater ease, "how did the accident happen?", "what is the next step of your recovery process?", "is there anything we can do to make you more comfortable while your injury heals?" I would love to think we could adapt these questions to support people retuning to work after baby loss.

I think often that when someone sees you for the first time after you've lost your baby they wait for an appropriate moment to say something, but sometimes if they wait too long the moment passes and the opportunity is missed altogether which is really awkward. Sometimes there is absolutely no chance to say something, so a hug or a squeeze of the hand can instead convey what they're feeling and at least you walk away feeling as though they care.

Show your own emotions about the loss

One of my 'favourite' things friends did after Miles died was cry, and cry unashamedly with me. I know that might seem strange but it made me feel like people really truly felt my pain and to an extent understood it. Most of my friends would immediately start apologising for crying, saying 'I'm so sorry I'm crying, you're the one going through this' but it never upset me to see them cry, if fact it did the opposite and gave me immense comfort. One friend called me about two months after Miles died in absolute floods of tears, she could barely speak, and finally said, "I've just been watching Grey's Anatomy and two of the main characters found out that like Miles their baby was incredibly unwell and they knew they had to make the choice to have him early knowing he wouldn't survive." She told me that she could barely cope with watching these imaginary characters on a TV show go through such an ordeal and couldn't believe that it had happened to me and I had been through something so similar in real life.

She said that she'd tried to imagine what it had been like for us and after watching the show, felt closer to understanding and utterly shell-shocked by just how horrific it must have been. Her candid, honest response made me cry too but it also made me feel

validated, heartened and recognised in my grief. Her outpouring of
unchecked sorrow gave me great solace. It was so nice to have a
really frank conversation with a trusted friend who had the courage
to say *what happened to you was dreadful, you poor, poor thing*, without
it feeling like a one-woman pity party.

Invite conversations about the baby who has been lost

I was so grateful to anyone who gave me the chance to open up and
talk about Miles. The friends who were brave enough to ask about
his diagnosis, his delivery, his ashes, his place in my heart. Once I
started sharing, it often felt like a dam had been unplugged and all
of the memories inside me were finally given the chance to flow
freely and without reservation, which I really needed.

Chapter 36 Grieving differently to those close to you

Men and women often respond to things very differently, and especially in grief. Josh was able to make phone calls, go to the shops, look after a few things at work, in the days straight after we lost Miles. Action gave him purpose. I could barely eat, think, shower or function. To me, it seemed he moved on far more quickly than I did or could. At the three month mark, I remember clearly feeling like I was still in the absolute depths of my grief, whereas Josh appeared to have moved on. I knew he hadn't, I knew he was still so sad, but he was able, somehow, to just keep on going and carry on with life. At this time I clearly remember him asking me if everything was okay between us as he hadn't been feeling much love lately. I remember being stunned. I don't think he realised how all-consuming the grief still was for me and it occurred to me then that we were moving along this path at very different speeds.

After the first month passed, I was able to get back into work, in addition to caring for children and seeing some friends, but it was all clouded with heaviness. I would have a few good days in a row, then fall in a heap of tears and despair. I felt like it must have been a nightmare, a nasty trick of the mind, that Miles was still due to be born, but I would remember that he was gone and would never come back. How we coped was so different at times and I felt really frustrated that Josh seemed okay, but he may have been that way because he felt that was what was expected of him. People didn't generally ask how he was as much as they asked after me, so I think society as a whole doesn't always give the other partner the support they need. I think it is also often assumed that the non-birth partner will be a pillar of strength for the other, as they have not also had to endure the physical trauma of the loss.

I had to be very careful not to feel angry with Josh for handling it so differently. He was incredibly supportive, kind and caring, but sometimes I wished I would see him cry so that I didn't feel so hopeless about my own reaction. I wished I could be as strong as he was. I didn't offer him any support in his grief: instead, I felt like I became his focus. He directed all of his energy into caring for me and making sure I was okay. I didn't have the capacity to do the same for him in return. I can see how easily relationships could be derailed by the loss of a baby, as individuals can react with different intensity and focus, which can dramatically change the dynamic of a relationship.

It is often said that men like to fix problems, women like to talk about them. I found this to be true in my situation. Josh used to say in response to something I was mulling over, *don't worry about that*, or *don't think like that*, and I'd reply, *but I can't just stop thinking about it or change how I feel about it.* If I had my mind firmly focused on something very little could distract me. I am a catastrophic thinker and I can overthink the simplest of situations. Being told not to worry about something usually makes it worse: I want my worries acknowledged and validated, not dismissed as silly or irrational. Having had anxiety, I am familiar with how out of control pervasive worries and thoughts can become, but I always find it better to address them rather than park them. Ignoring them has never worked for me, as the volcano will eventually erupt!

Ultimately, Josh's positivity helped me immensely. His optimism rubbed off on me and over time, as I felt less weighed down, the differences in our response to Miles' death lessened. This took a while and we had to not see the differences in our feelings as an indictment of our own reactions. All along, Josh felt that we were incredibly lucky. I thought he was crazy, what was lucky about our situation? He said we were so lucky to have three beautiful children, that compared to someone who lost a young child or a teenager, we were incredibly fortunate.

I didn't want my grief compared, evaluated and scaled according to the challenges others faced. To me, it was huge, it was 'the worst thing' and the comparisons made me feel like I had no right to be feeling how I did. Josh wasn't being cruel or in any way saying that what we had gone through wasn't dreadful, he could just see other scenarios which in his mind would be far worse. Over a considerable amount of time, I could start to see his point. Some people face adversity of such devastation that you wonder how they are ever able to get up again and continue to live their lives. Someone might look at us and think, "I could never cope with that", just as I look at some people and think that what they have been faced with would destroy me.

There is a saying that comparison is the thief of joy and I think comparison is also the thief of grief. There is no benefit to comparison: how you feel is valid and just as important as another, even if your stories are different. There is no quantitive scale upon which tragedy is measured. Put ever so eloquently, it's not a pissing contest and should never be allowed to become one. There is no hierarchy of loss.

Grief altered our relationship in many ways. I become more dependent on Josh and needed his support far more than I ever had. I struggled when he didn't see things from my perspective or didn't feel as angry about something as I did. Josh had to cope with me being hypersensitive for a long time with my very low tolerance for humour or sarcasm.

At times, I had to remind myself of just how much Josh cared about me. He was doing so much and cared about me endlessly, but I think in the fog of grief I was so caught up in my own feelings I couldn't see what was right in front of me. I also had to be mindful of the fact that my way of coping was not Josh's. I could sense early on that while he was more than happy to listen to me talk about Miles as often and as much as I needed, I could not expect him to mimic that desire or feel that need as keenly as I did. You can't expect one person in your life to meet all your needs. After such a terrible loss, it is only natural to turn to the person who shared that loss with you, but that puts enormous pressure on both of you. Josh was my greatest confidant, but I also leaned on friends and my psychologist. I didn't think that it was fair to always burden him with my worries, even though I know he never felt that I was burdening him.

Sometimes one small moment can completely transform how you perceive another person's reaction. Sitting down for dinner with Josh, the day I had met up with the volunteer who had photographed Miles, (six months after we had first met in hospital), I was recounting what she and I had spoken about, and just how emotional I had found seeing her again. She was one of the few people who met Miles and her presence in the hospital room that day had a huge impact on both of us. Mid-sentence, I looked over and realised that Josh had tears rolling down his cheeks. I started crying too. It was so rare to see him cry that I welled up instantly, both relieved and heartbroken to see it. I asked him what was it that had moved him and he replied, "The memories, hearing about Elizabeth brings it all back so vividly. The hospital room, Miles, the whole thing." As horrible as it sounds, seeing him cry brought me great comfort. It made me feel less alone and reminded me that we both wished we'd never had to say goodbye to our precious little boy. We both missed him dreadfully, we just had very different ways of outwardly expressing it.

My children reacted differently to how I had anticipated. Ted, who was seven at the time, likes to tell everyone about Miles. He became quite obsessed by the notion of having a "dead brother" as he often referred to Miles. He asked lots of innocent questions, which were quite sweet, even if they were a little confronting. He wanted to know if Miles had come out crying, if his brother had looked like him, and most importantly, when were we getting another one? Ted felt angry about the whole thing. Angry with me that I had 'lost' the baby, especially as it was a boy and that was what he had wished for, and angry that he never got to meet him. As confronting as some of these questions sound, they were actually great, as they allowed me to talk about Miles and opened up conversations that helped his siblings remember him.

I could show them pictures and from the start, they saw him as their little brother who had never come home, not just a baby who was lost and would therefore be forgotten. Ted told all of his friends and teachers as soon as he went back to school and on a few very naughty occasions, he told his older brother, Alfie, that Miles was his favourite brother and that he wished Miles was here instead. I had been dreading telling the boys and Bonnie, because I thought it would break their little hearts. Alfie, who is very sensitive, asked if Miles had been in any pain. He asked if he had been delivered in the same way as the rest of my children and wanted to know how big he had been. Bonnie was oblivious to the whole thing. It will be up to us to tell her about her brother as she gets older, as it is unlikely she will ever have any organic memory of him or this period of our lives.

The boys' uninhibited comments actually made it easier to include Miles in our family. It doesn't occur to most kids, not to ask questions for fear of being inappropriate. Everything is on the table; no topic is a taboo. They didn't seem to feel his absence like I did, as to them he had never been completely real: he had always been an abstract. Kids also appear to get over things super-fast! I reckon about half an hour after telling the boys about Miles, one of them asked what was for dinner, the other if would they be getting a special treat that night after dinner, and what were we doing to do tomorrow.

I think that as they get older they will realise the significance of losing a sibling and recognise how much it has shaped our family. When a classmate of Alfie's announced that his family was expecting a baby brother, Alfie delivered this news to me hesitantly and with what I saw as a sensitivity far beyond that of a nine-year-old. I think he was worried the news would upset me. I told him that I was very happy for his friend and thought it was lovely, exciting news for his family.

Ted often spoke about Miles in relation to household items, such as the high-chair and a step we have on our kitchen which props little ones up to bench height. He'd tell people, "that was Alfie's, then mine and Bonnie's and it would have been Miles' next, but he died." So even though at times I thought that the older boys didn't give Miles a great deal of thought, these little comments made me realise that he was also on their minds and in their hearts.

To weave Miles into conversations, I would sometimes comment on a baby and say, "Miles would have been the same age as that baby." I did this with Archie, the Duke and Duchess of Sussex's baby, when he was on the news. Alfie found this interesting, but Ted was less impressed. He said, "What's so special about that baby? It's just a baby, there are millions of other babies the same age but they don't make the news." I took that as a little dose of brotherly pride and I agreed there were millions of babies just as special and our Miles was one of them.

Chapter 37 A partner's perspective

After we lost Miles someone told me that fifty per cent of relationships do not survive the loss of a child. This shocked me, but thankfully I felt that despite Josh and my differences, we seemed to be handling this trauma as a team. Yes, the team's resources were mostly tilted in my direction, but we both seemed comfortable with that.

Grief after losing a baby puts enormous strain on a relationship, so it's not surprising that many suffer. You have two broken hearts trying to make sense of what has happened, while also attempting to hold the other up. Without open, honest communication, it would be easy to assume that one person does not care as much as the other or that perhaps the spark or connection you once felt has also died. There are also very obvious physical differences between the partner who carried the child and the other, who plays a support role. Sadly, this sometimes dictates the rest of the script: one partner feels they need to remain stoic for the other and in doing so, hides their own pain. This can create a vicious cycle with the person being supported wrongly assuming that their partner didn't care about the baby.

I spoke with some partners and asked them how they coped after losing their baby, what they saw their role as being and whether they felt they were adequately supported. When I put the call out on Instagram inviting people to share their story, I was stunned by the speed in which so many people, fathers in particular, contacted me. I felt they were bursting to share and thrilled to finally have an opportunity to do so.

Everyone who responded spoke of the utter joy of finding out that they were going to have a child. Michael, 'The Infertility Bloke' on Instagram recalled, "It was like every Christmas had come at once. I couldn't believe that I was going to be a dad and my wife was going to be a mum! It was an incredible feeling that I'll never forget. We were in a bubble, a happy, dream bubble me, my wife and our little baby." He remembers going to a party a few days after he and his wife saw their first positive pregnancy test. "A lot of my friends were there with their children and babies. This usually made it hard to go to parties like this but not this time. This time I was looking at them all and thinking about my baby, my little poppy seed my wife was carrying and thinking, in nine months time my little one will be here and I'll be a dad like my friends."

This elation turned to dread a week later, when his wife said she was no longer feeling pregnant and did another pregnancy test, only to see a negative result. The couple had conceived via a frozen embryo transfer and decided they would go to the hospital to have bloods taken. Their greatest fears were confirmed by the hospital later that day; the transfer had not been successful. Michael has vivid memories of this moment. "I could see my wife's face, I could hear it in her voice but I still had a glimmer of hope. It wasn't until she hung up the phone and looked at me that I knew. Our baby was gone. We held each other and sobbed. Every emotion flowed through me. Sadness, anger, worry, jealousy. Every single one. Our bubble had burst and all of the pain of the world could get to us again.

"The days passed and the grief got worse as it began to sink in. It literally felt like someone had reached into my chest and was squeezing my heart and they wouldn't let go. The pain now felt real, it felt physical and it was amplified each time I looked at my wife. We leaned on each other though, we confided in each other and needed each other and formed a new bubble. A bubble that was filled with sadness but also love, love for each other, love for our family and love for our baby.

"Neither of us are over this loss. The truth is I don't think I ever will be. With time the hurt may lessen, the pain may subside and the sadness may get easier to deal with but I'll never get over it. I find myself daydreaming of who my baby would have been, what they would have achieved, how they would have looked. Daydreaming about this as an escape from the mundane reality of life, as a way of escaping people talking to me, people getting on with their lives as though nothing has happened. But life does go on. It has too. My relationship with my wife has become stronger after this and I believe it is because we can talk to each other and we're honest with each other on our bad days."

Another partner who shared his story was Thomas. He and his wife Alex lost their baby at eleven weeks. "All I could keep thinking is that our baby, our child that we'd dreamed about for years, was now gone." After leaving the scan that confirmed their baby had no heartbeat, Thomas recalls, "Alex broke down and slid to the floor. All I could do was wrap my arms around her and let her cry. I felt awful too, but I can't imagine how Alex felt, feeling so broken at the fact that the baby she was carrying was no longer alive. Women will always have a closer connection to their unborn child as they will hopefully go on to carry it to full term. They go through all the changes in their bodies and emotions and will experience the pain of childbirth. It is a unique experience that I, as a male, will never be able to fully understand. All I can do is be there for her, every step of the way.

"While I know that focus is going to be on the woman, after all, she carried the baby and felt the loss the most, I do think men tend to be forgotten about too. But I didn't want any focus on me. My job was to support my partner through those terrible weeks, and I'd feel a little selfish if I wanted a moment to myself. They say that most men don't feel like a father until they hold the baby in their hands, but I respectfully disagree. I felt like a father the moment Alex told me she was pregnant. I felt the loss hard, even if I didn't overtly show it. I largely threw myself back into the daily grind to try and get through it. Beyond telling my boss at work, I barely spoke about it to anyone other than Alex."

In a blog post he wrote that "getting this out is such a big help, as keeping it all inside has been harmful to my mental stability. I've felt quite down recently, even though I try not to show it, especially as Alex still goes through her moments and I want to seem strong and stable for her. But I'll sit there sometimes and listen to people around me moan about such little insignificant things. You just feel like screaming 'IT DOESN'T FUCKING MATTER!'. Of course, no matter how small the problem sounds, it may seem like a big deal to that person so I can't just dismiss it all. But following the miscarriage, especially the couple of months after it, I came to realise how fragile life is and how a lot of things simply don't matter in the grand scheme of things. At the same time, I never expected the world to stop just because we'd lost a child. It's our issue, everyone else has their own things going on. But maybe I should have talked about it more instead of largely keeping it to myself.

"When you learn that you're going to have a child you start thinking about all the things you'll do to bring up your child as a happy, healthy and intelligent human being. You go through all the hopes and dreams you have for them, and everything you'll do together as a family. To have all those torn away in one moment is painful. To know you're never going to see that child live their own life and make their mark on the world. To be proud of what they've achieved, to say to people that 'this is my son/daughter'. To see their joy when you arrive home from work. To watch them wobble as they learn to ride a bike. To shed a little tear when they toddle off to their first day at school. To eye their first girlfriend/boyfriend suspiciously. All of it gone, gone in one horrible moment. It's hard to get past that and tell yourself you're going to try again. But we have to get past that. We have to move on if we ever want to create the family we always dream about.

"We'll never forget the baby that came first. We'll never forget an experience that caused so much heartache but brought us closer together. You can never just 'have another child' as some people say, as well-meaning as they might mean to sound. It will be thrilling, exciting, and nerve-racking when we get pregnant again. But nothing will ever replace the memory of the child that came before. It may not have been a fully formed person who had hopes and dreams for their life, but it was your child. You'll never forget that. I'll never forget that."

One father who bravely shared his story was Chris. He and his wife Meagan lost their beautiful daughter Violet at twenty-three weeks after a fatal diagnosis in-utero. They had been through many medical investigations and procedures in the lead-up to Violet's birth and knew her condition was irreversible and tragically incompatible with life. "I'd like to consider myself as an optimistic person. When each scan gave us information that we weren't expecting I remained positive and hoped for the best. After having our final medical consultations, in which we were told there was no hope left, I was a broken man. There was seven days between that meeting with the genetics team at Monash and our entry into the Frankston Hospital's birthing suite.

"For those seven days we did everything; we read to our baby bump, listened to all the music, ate all the foods, watched all the kids' movies, and sang all the nursery rhymes. We felt every bump, kick, poke and prod together and smiled, as bittersweet tears rolled down our cheeks. For those remaining seven days we had together, we wanted to have no regrets and live our best lives together as a family. We did our first real act as parents to take away all of her pain, so that all she knew was love.

"Leading up to the birth, I thought I had come to terms with my soon-to-be loss, I was steadfast in ensuring that my wife had all that she needed during the birth; water when she needed it, blankets when she needed them, food if she could stomach it, head rubs, the list goes on. During the birth, there was literally nothing (else) I could do. My wife was in so much pain. I tried my best to make her as comfortable as possible, but it was rather futile. I wished that I was able to take away her suffering, I've never felt so helpless.

"The moment Violet was born, with no sound, I realised that I was in no control of my emotions. My wife had endured a long day, and the drugs made her fall asleep, whilst I stayed up all hours of the night and early morning crying constant tears. Looking back, it's hard to label what the tears were, but I'd suggest that half of them were from soul-crushing sadness, and the other half were coming from a loving place that I never knew existed.

"Since we said goodbye to Violet my grief has taken various different routes. When I see a random Dad with his little girls at the shops my heart sinks, but I don't get jealous or angry, bitter or twisted, I feel the same love I felt when I held Violet for the first time, and take myself back to that place. I find myself happy for that man that he also gets to experience that love. Violet has changed how I think about the world. She's challenged me to be the best version of myself that I can be."

I asked Chris if he felt he grieved differently to his wife and if he felt that he had to remain strong in order support her. "This one is hard to answer, in that grief is impossible to define and can change in an instant. I tend to do a lot of personal reflection and shed tears in solitude, whereas my wife was almost more trapped by her emotions due to still recovering from giving birth. I was able to occupy my grief with simple, mundane tasks and keep busy. My wife was confined to the bed or the couch. As time moves on, we become more and more aware of our love for each other and for Violet. We're coming to terms with what our new 'normal' is, for us life won't be the same, it will just be a new definition of 'okay'.

"There's a pretty common social stereotype that the male in the relationship needs to be the rock, the solid constant that hides their emotions so that they can be a pillar of strength for others to bounce off. Initially, I hid my emotions from my wife so that she too could have that strength to hold on to, however, as the days progressed this strategy was harming us both more and more. Her seeing me like that made her think that Violet wasn't important to me, or that I'd moved on, which wasn't the case. It's vitally important that we keep our communication happening so that we were able to express how we are feeling, as at any given moment our thoughts and feelings can flip and change."

I was curious to know if he had felt supported by his mates and in general after Violet died. "Losing a child is confronting, people don't know what to say, how to act, or how to be. When it comes to males, and displaying, discussing or becoming aware of any form of emotion (good or bad) we also don't know what to say, how to act, or how to be. As part of my role in the education field, I've done a lot of work in the wellbeing space, and am rather comfortable discussing, unpacking and understanding emotions, both my own and of the students under my care.

"When it came to telling my mates through the group chat we have, they replied with nice messages stating how they were sorry for us, whilst some just chose not to say anything. Most of the communication on that topic seemed to stop there. The following days, our house was overflowing with flowers, cards and well wishes... Ninety-five-percent from my wife's friends and contacts.

"The few of my mates that have partners made a bit more of an effort, whether it was flowers or an Uber Eats voucher to make life a little bit easier, but that was few and far between. There is nothing worse than feeling alone, on the outer, or like 'the other'. After two to three weeks of feeling trapped in the confines of our house, I put out a message to our group to see if anything was happening on the weekend coming up. I needed to get out for a little bit, and have the opportunity to not sit and stew in the grieving process. Unfortunately, nothing eventuated, and my suggestive plea was left on that awkward 'seen' status until it just fizzled out...I've learnt a lot about what makes a quality friend through this experience, and gained some insights into the head spaces of those whom I mistakenly thought were good friends. Similarly, I've learnt a lot about myself, and what I need to do better as a friend."

A familiar theme which I saw reappearing when I spoke to many couples was that one person had a greater need than the other to busy themselves, to return to work, to seek distraction and renter the wider world. It may be a stereotype, but men primarily felt this need far more than women. Perhaps a sense of purpose brings with it a sense of control. Despite this desire to resume normal activities and get back to routine, it is not always easy and the adjustment can be harsh. Chris recalls his return to work and the impact it had on him.

"I returned to work last week after taking three weeks off. I didn't necessarily want to go back, but felt more obliged that it's probably the right thing to do by my employer. Working in a school, it's hard for me to go into full depth and detail about our story with them; that Violet's body had failed her and ultimately at twenty-three weeks she was terminated for medical reasons. People at work offer me their sympathies, but they don't know the real truth. They say that something similar happened to a friend, a family member, etc., so that magically should make me feel better and make me diminish any emotional thought that I'm having. It doesn't. It's the same as what I said earlier; no one likes to be on the outer, be alone or feel as if they are 'the other'... People don't know how to act or what to say, some gave me hugs, kisses, kind words, some shared their own stories, some I could see out of the corner of my eyes just blankly staring at me..."

When he first returned to work Chris said he felt "like a total fraud. I'm letting my students down as I'm definitely not present in the moment when I'm in the classroom. I'm in the room, I'm giving instructions, but the quality and the care factor is at an all-time low. I've tried to begin reading the class text twelve times, and have now given up. The words just mash themselves up into a rambling mess that means nothing to me.

"Truth be told, I don't want to be here. A fellow employee is pregnant, and at the same stage of development as my wife and I were. Whenever I see her, I lose my head. I feel different every time. It's probably all in my head, but I feel like my identity at work has shifted to 'that guy that lost his kid'.

"I've caught myself looking up new jobs on Seek as a way to get away and start fresh, go to a new school where people don't know. I'm not embarrassed or ashamed of my situation, quite the opposite. I love Violet more than anything in this world, I just feel like maybe a clean start might help me with my ability to cope."

Many of the responses broke my heart and made me reflect on the differences between how Josh and I grieved after Miles died. It is inevitable that something as confronting as baby loss will have a significant impact on a couple. The foundations of your life have been shaken, your shared hopes and dreams shattered. Your healing may progress at different rates and in many different ways. I suppose what's really important is to try to rebuild together, as hard as this may be, given everything else that you are facing. If you can somehow remain open and honest with each other, through grit and determination your foundations can be rebuilt to support both of you moving forward.

Chapter 38 Miles apart, forever in your heart

I wish I had a magic potion to take away the pain, I wish I had the answer to why losing a baby hurts so much, but I don't and I don't think anyone ever will. It is something which cannot be explained. There is no one thing that can make it feel any better. It is simply just so sad and so unfair.

The pain does change, and soften but it also can reappear and re-intensify, depending on the day, the week, the year, often without warning or for no obvious reason. The love will always be with you, as your child will always be with you, forever in your heart. My advice is not to fight the grief, not to try to rush through it, and not to be ashamed of it. Just allow yourself to feel all of the feels, and to feel them deeply for as long as you need to.

This is a huge tragedy, an enormous loss and it is your loss. Other than your partner, no one else will mourn this loss as deeply as you. Others will be sad for you, but they didn't know your baby, hold your baby, or love your baby like you did. This death is so different to the death of a relative or friend who was also known to and will be missed by others. This loss is deeply personal to you, it is raw and primal. Scream, cry, run, sleep, hide, talk, celebrate, mourn. Do whatever gets you through.

Other people will seem to move on so quickly, but that doesn't mean you have to. Never feel there's any expectation that you bounce back from this quickly or completely. It is not an event that remains in the past, it is something that becomes a part of you on a lifelong journey. Don't compare your loss to another's. Your baby's age or gestation has no bearing on the depth of your grief. Whether you choose to mourn publicly or privately is also not a measure of your love.

Whether you choose to share openly or quietly if someone cannot handle what you are saying, let them move on or park that friendship for a while. It is okay to be super-sensitive and those around you need to be gentle and not expect you to have your usual resilience. Surround yourself with people who either get it, or try their hardest to get it.

Be patient, and accept the fact that you have been forever changed. This is natural and to be expected. After going through something as life-altering and earth-shattering as the loss of a baby, you cannot ever expect to return to who you were before. The loss of a baby is not simply a moment in or a chapter of your story, but the beginning of a lifelong journey of love, wishfulness and healing.

Be kind to yourself. There will be periods of time in which you feel as broken as the day your baby died and days when you feel like your old self. Days where happiness, joy and hope return and the heaviness lifts. Enjoy these, and don't feel guilty for basking in these days and truly enjoying life. They give you the strength and energy to cope with the darker days that may follow. They do not take away from your baby's memory or your love for your baby. Instead, think of them as a way to honour your baby and their huge impact on your life. Be proud of your strength. You had no say in this and no choice but to be brave and survive, and even if you don't believe me just yet, I can assure you, you will get through this and one day begin to laugh and smile again.

Where to turn next: A checklist

Thank you for reading my story, and Miles' story. To stay in touch you can find us on Instagram @miles__apart I will continue to post and keep sharing our story. We can also be found at www.milesapart.online and Miles Apart by Annabel Bower on Facebook.

If you feel that this book has given you support and comfort and would like to pay this forward to another grieving family, copies of Miles Apart can be donated through the Miles Apart website shop. These books will then be distributed by the Miles Apart Foundation (a not-for-profit organisation) to hospitals around Australia. Some families have purchased books in memory of their baby and asked friends and family to do the same as a way to mark anniversaries and or birthdays.

There is a lot of professional and peer support out there for bereaved parents, but sometimes it's hard to know who to turn to. Rather than simply listing support services, I contacted each organisation to find out more about what they do and also to hear the stories of the people who work so tirelessly behind the scenes to keep these incredible charities running. Nearly all the founders and volunteers have been affected directly or indirectly by the loss of a child, or work in areas of medicine and research associated with pregnancy loss. They are here to help, they understand your situation and most importantly, they want you to know you are not alone and do not have to endure your loss in isolation.

Red Nose

www.rednose.org.au

24 hours support line: 1300 308 307

Email support@rednose.com.au

Every year 3,200 families experience the sudden and unexpected death of a baby or child. This has to stop. Through world-class research, advocacy and education we passionately believe we can put an end to this. Red Nose acknowledges the support we receive from our partners in helping us to fund our education, support services and research programs.

Red Nose has an additional arm Guiding Light, which provides online and telephone services to assist parents and their families after the death of a child.

Red Nose Australia was founded in 1977 by bereaved parents who wanted to save others from the devastating impact of the death of a child, by finding out why their babies died suddenly and unexpectedly, then educating parents and health professionals about how to prevent it. Red Nose supports parents who have lost a baby during a pregnancy, in infancy and in early childhood.

SIDS and KIDS South Australia, Tasmania and Northern Territory

SIDS and Kids South Australia

- 24/7 Emergency Crisis 1300 799 656
- Email administration@sidssa.org

SIDS and Kids Tasmania

- Helpline 1800 625 675, or 24-hr bereavement line 0417 560 981
- Email tasmania@sidsandkids.org

SIDS and Kids Northern Territory

- FreeCall 1300 308 307, or 24-hr bereavement line 0448 849 234
- Email darwin@sidsandkids.org

Supporting bereaved families and providing Safe Sleeping education to the local community,

SIDS and Kids provides bereavement support for individuals and families who experience or are affected by the sudden unexpected death of a baby or child, from conception to six years of age. This includes miscarriage, stillbirth, neonatal deaths, SIDS and any other accidental deaths. SIDS and Kids has been providing support to families for 40 years.

SIDS and Kids also educate the community on safe sleep practices through brochures, information seminars and support education for hospitals, parents, childcare centres and the local community. Their education programs have reduced the incidence of deaths in infancy by more than 80%.

The SIDS and Kids qualified bereavement counsellor is advised of the sudden death of an infant or child by paramedics, local police, GPs, hospitals or through self-referral. Where possible, the counsellor will attend the scene, providing crisis support, acting as an advocate for the family.

SANDS miscarriage, stillbirth and newborn death support

www.sands.org.au

Sands National Support Line: 1300 072 637

Email support: support@sands.org.au

SANDS and Red Nose will merge in November 2020

Sands provides support, information and education to anyone affected by the death of a baby before, during or shortly after birth. *Whether your baby has died as a result of a miscarriage, ectopic pregnancy, medical termination, stillbirth or newborn death, we are here to listen and support you through this devastating time.*

Sands run local support groups in most states of Australia, as well as providing telephone, live online chat and email support services. Sands also provides information about baby loss and grief.

The organisation holds several events throughout the year which helps bring parents together in a relaxed environment. There are friendship afternoon teas, craft and cooking nights, SANDS also coordinate remembrance walks in most capital cities during Baby Loss Awareness Week.

Its confidential telephone helpline provides a safe place for anyone affected by the death of a baby to talk about their feelings. When you call, you will be put in direct contact with a trained volunteer parent supporter. SANDS' compassionate volunteers understand the grief and confusion you may be experiencing, as they too have had a baby who has died.

"I didn't know why I dialed the number, I don't normally like to talk about it ... when they answered, I didn't know what to say, but finding this gentle voice who allowed me to take my time and really listened to me was exactly what I needed. I really felt they understood."The helpline is available 24 hours a day, 365 days a year (including Christmas Day) by dialing 1300 072 637. If you have been unable to reach a Volunteer Parent Supporter on the phone, please email your name and number to services@sands.org.au and a volunteer will ring you back

In addition to the support line, SANDS has numerous downloadable brochures on its website to help support bereaved parents and those around them. Topics include but are not limited to:

- Early Pregnancy Loss
- Creating Memories
- Life, Loss, Hope: Surviving the death of your baby
- For Fathers

- Caring for your other children
- For Grandparents
- For Family and Friends
- For Healthcare Professionals

SANDS also provides training to healthcare professionals as stated on its website:

One of our core aims is to improve the quality of care and support offered in the event of a baby dying. We work in partnership with health professionals and others to ensure the families of those babies who do die receive the best possible care.

The death of a baby during pregnancy, at birth, or after birth is a major bereavement. The care that parents receive around this time has a huge impact on their long-term wellbeing. Good care cannot remove the pain and devastation that bereaved parents experience, but poor or insensitive care makes things worse, both immediately and in the months and years that follow.

Heartfelt - Photographic service for bereaved parents

www.heartfelt.org.au

1800 583 768 (Aust) 0800 583 768 (NZ)

Heartfelt is a volunteer organisation of professional photographers from all over Australia and New Zealand dedicated to giving the gift of photographic memories to families that have experienced stillbirths, premature births or have children with serious and terminal illnesses. Heartfelt is dedicated to providing this gift to families in a caring, compassionate manner. All services are provided free of charge.

Heartfelt also offers a retouching and editing service to families who didn't have the opportunity to have Heartfelt photograph their child, but have some of their own images which they would like enhanced. Throughout Australia and New Zealand, there are printing businesses who offer Heartfelt a discount when printing these precious images, however all printing costs are incurred by the charity alone, with expenses relating to presentation boxes and USB storage devices.

Heartfelt relies solely on donations and the generosity of its photographers to continue to give families these precious memories.

On a personal level, my experience with Heartfelt, in particular Elizabeth, the photographer who came to the hospital the morning after Miles was born to photograph him, had a profound effect on Josh and me. It was such an intimate, extraordinary encounter and apart from the doctors and midwives in the hospital, Elizabeth is one of the only people who ever met Miles.

The minute she entered the room, I was comforted by her calm, gentle nature. She instantly put me at ease and her ability to read the room was exceptional. She was very respectful of Josh's reticence to be photographed holding Miles, but encouraged him to sit next to me while I held him for at least one photo, so we would have one recorded visual memory of us all together.

After about ten minutes, I asked her how she came to be a Heartfelt photographer. Her story did and still does fill me with utter admiration. In very similar circumstances to ours, Elizabeth and her husband lost their son, their first child After he was born still, she knew she needed to do something to not only honour him throughout her life but help others navigating a similar path.

Once the initial, harrowing stage passed, Elizabeth began to study photography for the sole purpose of providing this incredible service. She was initially going to start her own foundation, however upon discovering Heartfelt, shesaw that they were a perfect fit and held the same values and passion that she did. Her parents purchased the extensive (and expensive) camera equipment she needed and her husband encouraged her studies every step of the way.

Like all loss mothers, Elizabeth knew that nothing would or could erase the pain of her son's death or ever make it okay, but at the very least, doing something to give it both a purpose and a legacy might make it easier to endure. Hearing Elizabeth talk about her son and her role volunteering with Heartfelt gave me enormous inspiration and a deep sense of comfort.

The Pink Elephants Support Network - Miscarriage Support
www.pinkelephantssupport.com
Instagram @pinkelephantssupport

The Pink Elephants Support Network are a not-for-profit charity, formed to support women through miscarriage, infertility, pregnancy loss and beyond. The group 'support women through their grief, nurture them as they heal and empower them as they move into the future'. There are a number of resources available on their website including useful information about miscarriage stages, support brochures and downloadable resources. Our downloadable resources will make a world of difference in helping women's key support networks (partners, family, friends) understand how to best support their loved one as they travel the road of miscarriage and early pregnancy loss.

I rang Sam, co-founder of Pink Elephants (alongside Gabbi), to learn about her story and what had inspired her to start a charity dedicated to helping women navigate early pregnancy loss and infertility. Sam and Gabbi believe that "miscarriage may be an individual journey, but no woman should have to walk it alone." Put into action, this sentiment has inspired many of the charity's initiatives, in particular the peer-support counselling service. As outlined on their website: "Our Peer Support Programme is a connection with another woman who has also experienced miscarriage. Our Ambassadors have been trained by a bereavement counsellor in how to best support emotional wellbeing after a miscarriage. We offer six free sessions with the same Ambassador, allowing the continuity of care that is so important at this time. We also want to put women in touch with relevant healthcare professionals who will be able to support and nurture their mental and physical wellbeing. We run regular Facebook Live events in our private support group, providing relevant and trusted wellbeing information."

Creating meaningful connections is an initiative very close to Sam's heart, by bringing women with shared experiences together, she hopes to reduce the sense of isolation many women feel after miscarriage by acknowledging and validating their feelings and offering the kind of support that those who have walked a similar path can offer. Online groups and social media also afford women in all areas equal access to such connections.

Bears of Hope

www.bearsofhope.org.au
Enquiries: 1300 11 BEAR / 1300 11 2327
Email: contact@bearsofhope.org.au
Grief Support: 1300 11 HOPE / 1300 11 4673
Email: support@bearsofhope.org.au

Bears of Hope Pregnancy and Infant Loss Support provides leading support and exceptional care for families who experience the loss of their baby. We seek to provide crucial information and embrace families during their difficult time of loss, and beyond. There are two key elements to our

program that guide families through their choices when saying Hello and
Goodbye to their much loved baby.

I was handed a Bears of Hope remembrance bear after Miles was born. This toy soon became an item very dear to my heart. He is now in my daughter's toy box, she dresses him up and wheels him around in her doll's pram and he will always remain a very special reminder of Miles. It is such a beautiful way of remembering him and knowing that the bears are donated by another family in honour of their lost baby makes it even more personal.

A few months later, I came across the Bears of Hope Parent Support Group on Facebook. It is a closed group for bereaved parents in which you can freely talk about your baby, and your grief, and ask for advice about how to cope with the many challenges you face after baby loss. It is an incredibly supportive community and a very active and accessible one. I highly recommend joining it.

Below are the two main components of the Bears of Hope support structure:

"Families receive a Bear of Hope donated by another bereaved family. This allows the donating family to give their child's brief life a purpose and lasting legacy, whilst filling the empty arms of another family as they walk out of the hospital without their baby. It reinforces the understanding that they are not alone, and that there is an existing community of support. Families also receive extensive information, either in printed or online format, to help them make decisions and memories in hospital, during the memorial and beyond.

"Our Beyond the Bear support is unequalled by any other organisation. We provide exclusive and invaluable support packages that include: a credible foundation of parent led and psychologist facilitated support groups, private online groups, phone and email counselling and annual community events that remember individual baby's and recognise their parents love. Additionally we have a Hope and Healing Resource Library."

Still Aware

www.stillaware.org

Australia's first Stillbirth Awareness Charity, supporting a Safe Pregnancy through Stillbirth Awareness + Education = Action = Prevention.

Still Aware was founded by Claire Foord after her first child, a daughter called Alfie, was born still. Her mission is to decrease the rate of stillbirth by raising awareness and educate expectant mothers and health care professionals about simple actions such as monitoring a baby's movements and sleeping in the correct position while pregnant.

"In Australia more than thousands of babies are born still every year. The definition of Stillbirth in Australia is defined as the death of a baby beyond 20 weeks gestation. It is far more than that. Stillbirth has far more meaning than that. To birth a baby stillborn is a gut wrenching devastation that no family should ever have to endure, particularly in this day and age. The loss of a child at any age is unthinkable and is too often unspoken. Thankfully there are support organisations that can help families to live with their loss and others that are conducting crucial research into the causes of stillbirth. Unfortunately there is minimal financial support for the cause. At Still Aware we strongly believe that awareness brings change." - Claire Foord

Claire campaigns tirelessly and passionately for greater public awareness of both the high rate of stillbirth and the need to lift the taboo and speak of this tragedy openly, to help prevent it continuing at the current rate. The Still Aware website contains important resources for pregnant women about how best to monitor their baby's movements, as well as providing a collection of stories from parents who have experienced stillbirth.

When I spoke to Claire, I asked her what inspired her to start Still Aware and if she did it to honour her daughter Alfie. Naturally, like all Claire's children, Alfie plays a huge part in what she does, but overwhelmingly, it was the gaping need for women to be educated about stillbirth and the simple ways it can sometimes be prevented that motivated Claire. She is also determined to lift the taboo in our society which shuts down conversation surrounding stillbirth and ensure that members of the public and healthcare providers do not shy away from this topic. The fact that the rate of stillbirth has not dropped at all in the last twenty years horrifies Claire and she is determined to do something to help prevent others from going through what she did when her daughter died.

On a video on the Still Aware website, Claire and her husband Brad speak lovingly of their daughter Alfie and the charity. Claire says, "Alfie was our healthy daughter who should be here and had I known that my movements, her movements, mattered so much she would be here. I couldn't sit back and let this happen to another family." Claire and the team at Still Aware work tirelessly to educate women and empower them to be aware of the risks of stillbirth and also to help train those caring for mothers and their babies during pregnancy to help monitor movement and report any changes.

Stillbirth Foundation Australia

www.stillbirthfoundation.org.au

The Stillbirth Foundation Australia is the only Australian charity dedicated to stillbirth research and we are 100 percent community funded. The Stillbirth Foundation Australia is the only Australian charity dedicated to stillbirth research and we are 100 percent community funded.

Every day six babies will die in their mother's womb and be stillborn – a little-known and tragic health issue. A huge amount of investment is needed in vital research to understand why such large numbers of babies are dying; particularly those that are born at or close to term with no known cause of death.

Since 2009, Stillbirth Foundation supporters have funded more than $1,000,000 in research studies. Every year, we continue to dedicate ourselves to raising as much money as we can for the purposes of funding the very best research studies – as determined by the rigorous guidelines set by our Scientific Assessment Committee.

The Stillbirth Foundation Australia is pleased to be able to support much-needed research into the causes of stillbirth. The Stillbirth Foundation works with researchers who are committed to ensuring that the stillbirth rate starts to decline in Australia.

The Stillbirth Foundation Australia believes in acknowledging and remembering beloved babies, and understands that they stay in our hearts always. As a still-parent, we invite you to add your baby's name to our Birth Registry, not only as a tangible way to remember your own precious baby but to help raise awareness that stillbirth still happens. We hope this special section also gives you some comfort that other parents and families all over Australia know what it means to lose a much-loved baby and understand what you have experienced.

Thank you

Firstly, thank you Miles for choosing me to be your Mama. I am so proud and grateful that you came into my life even if you couldn't physically stay; you are forever in my heart.

Josh, words won't cover it but I love you and could not have survived this without you. You have the best and biggest heart I know. I am very lucky to have you by my side.

Anna, I would have sunk without your constant support and understanding. You were the one person who truly got what I was going through. I hope Miles and Henry have found each other up there and are having a WOW of a time!

Sophie, your faith in my ability to do this gave me the confidence to keep writing. Thanks for all of your guidance.

Nama, Eleanor and Sally who bravely shared their deeply personal stories of loss with the hope of bringing comfort to other loss mothers. A true example of the power of female friendship, kindness and solidarity.

Michael, Thomas and Chris who gave a partners perspective of what baby loss feels like for the bereaved parent who didn't physically carry the baby during pregnancy.

To all of the family and friends who kept calling when at first I didn't answer. To those who talk about Miles, remember him, acknowledge his birthday, ask how we are and continue to send their love, thank you.

To the wonderful women who have helped me bring the Miles Apart Foundation to life. Board members and beautiful friends Sally and Catherine. The event committee, especially Kath, Alexis and Jo who have helped raise funds to distribute free copies of Miles Apart to hospitals and early pregnancy loss units. Thanks a million.

To my children, Alfie, Ted, Bonnie, Miles and Tom, (who arrived just before Miles' first birthday). You are all little rays of sunshine who remind me daily of just how precious life is.

To anyone who picked up this book, I hope it has brought you some comfort and at the very least made you feel like you're not alone xox

Milton Keynes UK
Ingram Content Group UK Ltd.
UKHW011048201123
432908UK00006BA/879

9 781922 405067